Organizational Intelligence for Change Adaptability

This book offers a pioneering exploration of how the synergy between knowledge, learning, and collaboration (the KLC approach) drives organizational intelligence and adaptability. Grounded in empirical research and case studies, it examines how the impact of the KLC approach varies based on company culture (adhocracy, clan, market, and hierarchy) and management levels (team, division, and organization).

Readers will discover actionable strategies for fostering collective intelligence and adapting to change, especially in the context of remote work and AI-driven environments. The book highlights the critical role of leaders as architects of company culture and provides practical guidance for aligning culture with business goals. Case studies bring the concepts to life, offering valuable lessons for designing and sustaining a growth-agile mindset.

This research-rich volume is an essential resource for researchers, academics, and students in organizational change, knowledge management, and strategy, as well as business leaders seeking to enhance their company's collective intelligence and adaptability.

Wioleta Kucharska is a professor in the Management Department of the Faculty of Management and Economics at the Gdansk University of Technology, Fahrenheit Universities Union, Poland. Along with scientific passion and achievements, she has 12 years of intensive managerial experience; therefore, her works, in addition to theoretical foundations, always actively refer to management practice.

Routledge Studies in Organizational Change & Development
Series Editor: Bernard Burnes

27. Organizational Behaviour and Change Management
The Impact of Cognitive and Social Bias
Cornell Vernooij, Judith Stuijt, Maarten Hendriks, Wouter ten Have and Steven ten Have

28. Organizational Cognition
The Theory of Social Organizing
Edited by: Davide Secchi, Rasmus Gahrn-Andersen and Stephen John Cowley

29. Organizational Change, Leadership and Ethics
Leading Organizations towards Sustainability, 2E
Edited by Rune By, Bernard Burnes and Mark Hughes

30. Managing the Digital University
Paradigms, Leadership, and Organization
Lukasz Sulkowski

31. Agency, Change and Learning
Accounts of Internal Change Agents
Edited by Julian Randall and Bernard Burnes

32. Edgar H. Schein
The Artistry of a Reflexive Organizational Scholar-Practitioner
David Coghlan

33. Organizational Intelligence for Change Adaptability
The Knowledge, Learning, and Collaboration Cultures Approach
Wioleta Kucharska

For more information about this series, please visit: https://www.routledge.com/Routledge-Studies-in-Organizational-Change-Development/book-series/SE0690

Organizational Intelligence for Change Adaptability

The Knowledge, Learning, and Collaboration Cultures Approach

Wioleta Kucharska

Routledge
Taylor & Francis Group
NEW YORK AND LONDON

First published 2025
by Routledge
605 Third Avenue, New York, NY 10158

and by Routledge
4 Park Square, Milton Park, Abingdon, Oxon, OX14 4RN

Routledge is an imprint of the Taylor & Francis Group, an informa business

ISBN: 978-1-032-77766-5 (hbk)
ISBN: 978-1-032-77884-6 (pbk)
ISBN: 978-1-003-48523-0 (ebk)

DOI: 10.4324/9781003485230

Typeset in Times New Roman
by Apex CoVantage, LLC

Contents

Introduction 1

PART I
Organizational intelligence activation through the KLC approach—scientific evidence 3

1 Company culture matters—study background 5

1.1 Change adaptability challenge 5
1.2 Agility—higher-level adaptability skill 6
1.3 Company culture as superpower 7

2 From company culture to organizational intelligence—conceptual framework 11

2.1 Intelligence-driven organizations. Why are they in focus? 11
2.2 Company culture taxonomy. Why do company cultures differ? 12
2.3 Knowledge, learning, and collaboration approach essence. Why is the KLC approach beneficial? 14
2.4 Collective intelligence (change adaptability) and innovativeness. Why are they in high demand? 16
2.5 Why do culture types differ among managerial levels in the same company? Multilevel analysis: organization, division, team 17

3 Methodology—study method 23

3.1 Sampling method 23
3.2 Sample quality 23
3.3 Sample characteristics 26

4 Empirical evidence—study results 29

4.1 Knowledge, learning, and collaboration cultures' impact on organizational intelligence and innovativeness 29
4.2 Knowledge, learning, and collaboration cultures' impact on organizational intelligence analyzed per culture type 34
4.3 The double bias of mistakes views per culture type 44

5 Meaning of the given findings—discussion 50

5.1 Knowledge, learning, and collaboration cultures significantly affect organizational intelligence 50
5.2 The impact of the different components of the KLC approach on intelligence varies depending on company culture type and management level (team, division, and organization), and culture-type consistency (congruence) 52
5.3 Double bias of mistakes impact on collective intelligence and culture type—discussion 56

6 What else do we need to know?—emerging questions raised from limitations and implications 60

6.1 Knowledge, learning, and collaboration approach, intelligence, and company culture type relations—what else do we need to know? 60
6.2 Future study directions based on research limitations 62
6.3 Practical implications—general ideas 63

PART II
Organizational intelligence activation through the KLC-approach implementation—manual 69

7 Motivation matters—organizational change drivers impact the KLC-approach implementation methods 71

7.1 Motivational powers to sustain organizational openness to change and agility development 71

7.2 Strategy-culture-structure alignment 76
7.3 The KLC implementation framework 78

8 Adhocracy culture 82

8.1 Key challenges in the KLC-approach implementation in adhocracies 82
8.2 KLC implementation plan in adhocracies 84
8.3 Case study 89

9 Market culture 92

9.1 Key challenges in the KLC-approach implementation in market culture organizations 92
9.2 KLC implementation plan in market culture organizations 94
9.3 Case study 96

10 Clan culture 99

10.1 Key challenges in the KLC-approach implementation in clans 99
10.2 KLC implementation plan in clans 101
10.3 Case study 102

11 Hierarchy culture 105

11.1 Key challenges in the KLC-approach implementation in hierarchies 105
11.2 KLC implementation plan in hierarchies 108
11.3 Case study 110

PART III
Organizational intelligence: collective human versus artificial? 115

12 What culture, such algorithms—algorithmic management and company culture type 117

12.1 What culture, such algorithms—because company culture shapes the way work is designed 117
12.2 Adhocracy—KLC and algorithmic management 122
12.3 Markets—KLC and algorithmic management 125
12.4 Clans—KLC and algorithmic management 125

12.5 Hierarchies—KLC and algorithmic management 127
12.6 Case study 130

13 What culture, such virtual workspace standards 133

13.1 What culture experienced, such culture learned 133
13.2 What a leader, such a culture experienced 136
13.3 Case study 141

14 Agile mindset leader's era—new leadership quality to support organizational intelligence in AI-supported workplaces 146

14.1 Agile mindset leader impact on intellectual agility in knowledge-driven organizations today 146
14.2 Is an agile mindset leader made or born? 148
14.3 Collective intellectual agility—how does it happen? 151
14.4 Agility strategies building for adhocracies, markets, clans, and hierarchies 153
14.5 Case study 156

What have we learnt from this book—closing conclusions 161

Appendix 1: Bibliometric analysis *163*
Appendix 2: SPSS PROCESS output *166*
Appendix 2b: The Double Bias of Mistakes (DBM) test per culture type *176*
Appendix 3: Company culture assessment tools *179*
Index *183*

Introduction

In the era of VUCA (volatility, uncertainty, complexity, and ambiguity) and the reality of the knowledge economy, knowledge has become an essential resource for securing organizational survival and growth. Therefore, organizations are interested in collective intelligence building to acquire and implement the relevant knowledge agilely. Organizational agility essence is the collective ability to respond quickly, accurately, and efficiently to business changes. The collective adaptability focus keeps the company competitive and open to new opportunities for growth and development. Apart from management methods that support the smooth identification and implementation of prosperous changes, company culture is the key to creating and sustaining collective intelligence, innovativeness, and agility.

"Company culture eats strategy for breakfast," Peter Drucker says. Indeed, company culture is a powerful, intangible asset worth all efforts to be developed to serve the company's best. For knowledge-driven organizations, the synergy of functional cultures: knowledge, learning, and collaboration (the KLC approach) strongly support the collective intelligence and growth focus. Based on this knowledge, this book presents strategies for implementing the KLC approach to drive adhocracy-, market-, clan-, and hierarchy-dominated cultures to create collective intelligence, sustain openness to changes, and develop agility.

This book focuses on knowledge-driven organizations because collective intelligence is a driven level of those entities that operate on knowledge resources. A company's organizational culture affects information acquisition and its smooth transformation into knowledge, wisdom, and organizational intelligence, which should be understood as the smooth use of apt knowledge, according to the business context.

The whole book is organized around the empirical research which proves that the synergy of knowledge, learning, and collaboration functional cultures (the KLC approach) impacts organizational intelligence, and this impact varies depending on company culture type (adhocracy, clan, bureaucracy, and market) and management level (team, division, and organization). Summing up, according to the given empirical evidence, implementing the KLC approach in each

DOI: 10.4324/9781003485230-1

of the given company culture types requires different methods tailored to the management level to gain the competency of smooth adaptability. This book provides these methods.

Moreover, this book demonstrates that organizational culture type, strength, and consistency (congruence) across managerial levels are critical for gaining the maximum benefits from implementing the KLC approach. However, cultural strength and unity seem to be particularly challenging for organizations that are open to remote work. Virtual teams' efficacy is a major concern of many knowledge-driven organizations today. Therefore, this book also proposes strategies for achieving knowledge, learning, and collaboration culture synergy among workmates interacting remotely.

In summary, a company culture must be experienced, to be learned. Therefore, this book proposes experiential learning through contextual case studies that serve as practical examples. The book delivers a solid base of manuals and case studies that make the given knowledge clear and useful for teaching and business practice.

Researchers, academics, management students, and managers can find this book interesting.

Part I

Organizational intelligence activation through the KLC approach—scientific evidence

Part I presents empirical evidence proving that the synergy of knowledge, learning, and collaboration functional cultures (the KLC approach) impacts organizational intelligence, and this impact varies depending on company culture type (adhocracy, clan, bureaucracy, and market) and management level (team, division, and organization). Conclusions from the research are the basis for formulating strategies for implementing the KLC approach to drive adhocracy-, market-, clan-, and hierarchy-dominated cultures to create collective intelligence, sustain organizational openness to changes, and develop agility. So, research in this section exposes differences and challenges in KLC-approach implementation, which are transformed into strategies, methods, and techniques securing organizational agility skills in the long-run perspective. These strategies, methods, and techniques tailored separately for each culture type are developed in Part II of this book.

DOI: 10.4324/9781003485230-2

1 Company culture matters—study background

1.1 Change adaptability challenge

The highly dynamic business conditions require organizations to adapt to changes smoothly and accurately to survive and grow. Therefore, the organizational ability to respond proactively to unexpected external and internal change matters for its survival and success. Nowadays, everything around us is characterized by constant change. Therefore, companies' ambition today is to agilely adapt to hyper-dynamic business realities to win each opportunity by acquiring new knowledge, developing dynamic capabilities, proactively establishing market innovations, and securing sustainability. However, it is wise for organizations neither to follow each observed change symptom or new trend nor to stay as they are. So, organizational leaders need to identify the best opportunities and see threats that require immediate mitigations, and it is a challenge. In organizations, internal and external sources of change can be equally impactful for organizational long-run success or failure. No one alone can observe and analyze the entire business environment (the internal and external)—the bigger and more complex the organization, the stronger collective acting is needed to be fully aware of all changes that may interfere with the business. So, to recognize these changes and understand their impact (short- or long-run range), organizations need to apply collective intelligence, which is a challenge too.

Change adaptability skill is a proxy for organizational intelligence (Feuerstein et al., 1979). Organizational agile adaptability is a higher-level collective intelligence effect. So, today's companies' challenge regarding change adaptability concerns that their intelligence usually is not collective; it is limited, and these organizations are, in the majority, not agile.

Disruptions connected with organizational resistance, a shortage of flexibility and innovativeness, and, consequently, trouble with sustainability become crucial problems organizations must address if they seek to be agile today. Company culture can support it. It is a precious resource that can serve as a facilitator and even as a driver of change. Adhocracies, clans, markets, and hierarchies determine different conditions for sustainable, timely, knowledge-driven organizational ecosystem creation that support opportunities winning and threats mitigating.

DOI: 10.4324/9781003485230-3

Organizations today must constantly learn to be sustainable (Haapasaari & Kerosuo, 2015). It is best if they learn agilely. It is commonly acknowledged today that organizations cannot rely on a static set of skills or a static base of knowledge at any organizational level, since these quickly become outdated in the reality of hyperdynamic conditions. Therefore, the synergy of knowledge, learning, and collaboration cultures—a functional cultures set proved to strongly support agility and sustainability (Kucharska & Bedford, 2023, 2024) is seen in this book as a driver of agile change adaptability for all types of company cultures: adhocracies, clans, markets, and hierarchies. However, the synergy of knowledge, learning, and collaboration functional cultures (the KLC approach) impact on organizational intelligence varies depending on company culture type (adhocracy, clan, bureaucracy, and market). Therefore, this book exposes how and presents methods on how to implement the KLC approach to drive adhocracy-, market-, clan-, and hierarchy-dominated cultures, to sustain openness to changes do gain best benefits. This book explores this issue more in depth.

1.2 Agility—higher-level adaptability skill

Organizational agility is the collective ability to respond quickly, accurately, and efficiently to business changes. Simplifying, it is an organizational skill that involves the smooth identification and implementation of changes needed. The changes needed are those that secure competitiveness, development, growth, and long-term success of the organization. So, market (client) orientation helps. Identifying changes as opportunities requires intelligence. Since the organization is a collective body, organizational agility relies then on collective intelligence. So, collective intelligence is critical. It is much more than a sum of the individual intelligence of all company members. It is because collective intelligence is not determined by what organization members can achieve alone but by what they can achieve together. So, collectivism is the essence of any organizational competency development. Going back to agility, its essence is smooth collective critical thinking, learning, motivating, making good decisions, and implementing changes—all needed to respond quickly, accurately, and efficiently to changing market contexts. So, company culture and intelligence are altogether vital factors for organizational agility.

Since mindset determines perception and the way of thinking and acting. So, a shared mindset constitutes all desired behaviors into collective habits—the way an organization thinks and acts. Collectively developed habits constitute organizational culture. That is why company culture matters. It is an observable pattern of collecting, thinking, and acting. As Hofstede et al. (2010) say, it is a shared "software of the mind," which power is stronger than organizational rules and procedures in the desired way of collective thinking and acting. Company culture based on values, rules, policies, and procedures can support these values but are not as universal. So, sometimes, we can act quickly in new situations or contexts in which we have not developed rules, policies, or procedures yet. The intuitive way of acting in new territories comes from earlier experiences—all learned behaviors' patterns and the ability to adapt them to new contexts.

Organizational agility has gained immense popularity recently. Agility serves equally efficiently for opportunities seeking as threats mitigating because science, business, and society are interested in creating solutions to minimize the negative consequences of unexpected events that significantly affect organizations, jobs, and the economic condition of societies and nations, as was recently observed during the COVID pandemic (Sahoo & Chaubey, 2024). Moreover, highly dynamic business conditions require organizations to adapt to changes smoothly and accurately to survive and grow. Therefore, the organizational ability to respond proactively to unexpected external and internal change matters for its survival and success. Business leaders have clearly stated that organizational agility does not depend as much on a chosen methodological management approach as it depends on a mindset (Cannon, 2017; Eilers et al., 2020; Moreira, 2013). The recent coronavirus crisis revealed that organizational agility means much more than having agile methodologies-certified teams (Denning, 2020; McIntosh, 2016), which made the agility philosophy of thinking and acting attractive beyond the information technology (IT) world. Agile project management methodologies and agility philosophy have been well developed and explored practically and theoretically in IT for over two decades. However, this philosophy is now attractive in any industry oriented toward fast and accurate reactions to market realities—in practice, for all market players. Agile thinking mobilizes the entire staff across an organization. It is considered the essence of a successful agile enterprise that positions customers and societies at the center, supports employees to reach their full potential, and achieves 20%–40% greater productivity because of gained engagement (Rigby et al., 2020). So, implementing agile methods without developing a shared agile mindset wastes organizational time and effort.

Summing up, a shared agile mindset determines organizational agility (Kucharska et al., 2024a, 2024b). Company culture is precisely defined as a shared mindset (Senge, 1992). This way, company culture is a superpower that drives and facilitates organizational intelligence building.

1.3 Company culture as superpower

In the words of Peter Drucker, company culture eats strategy for breakfast (cited in Kesterson, 2015, p. 56). This statement indicates that no matter how brilliant a strategy is, if the right company culture does not support it, it will have no chance of success. Moreover, Graham et al. (2022) provide evidence that improving corporate culture can leverage firm value. Thus, company culture improvement should be included in long-range organizational planning. Strategy–culture alignment is a necessary condition for the success of any strategy (Kucharska & Bedford, 2023). Long-range planning usually concerns ambitious aims that are complex and require a posh vision and intelligent strategy that is open to constant adaptation to the fast-changing business environment. In light of this idea, any strategic transformation—understood as successful change implementation—is as much about strategizing as it is about company culture. For these reasons, this book focuses on the relationship between company culture type and the functional cultures of knowledge-driven organizations—also known as the knowledge, learning, and collaboration (KLC) approach—in the context of companies' ability to develop collective intelligence and internal innovation. Company culture is a powerful resource that can serve as a change adaptability driver (the KLC approach) and facilitator (adhocracy, market, clan, or hierarchy).

Specifically, we know that adhocracies are considered the most favorable culture type for organizational learning, creativity, and innovation (Chatterjee et al., 2018; Gao et al., 2020; Moonen, 2017; Parikh, 2016; Wiewiora et al., 2019). We also know that clans are in some cases even better than adhocracies for innovation, based on the Italian context (Parolini & Parolini, 2012), and that market cultures perform better in terms of knowledge management than other cultures (Kangas, 2009). Nevertheless, clans and adhocracies are those that generally perform better than hierarchies and markets, as demonstrated by the Netherlands context (Strengers et al., 2022). However, according to Kim and Chang (2019), who represent the Korean context in a longitudinal study, adhocracy, clan, and market cultures have revealed a consistently positive relationship with the majority of the performance variables over the years. At the same time, in many public organizations, hierarchies can often be innovative and intelligent, for example, public transport, the diplomatic service, or the military (Roche & Blaine, 2014). All these examples show that company culture is critical for organizational intelligence development, seen as the collective organizational ability to adapt to changes and improve internally. Such abilities matter for organizational resilience to business environmental turbulences.

Thus, summing up, we know that the KLC approach fosters collective organizational intelligence (Kucharska & Bedford, 2024), but what we do not know how to implement the KLC to adhocracies, clans, markets, or hierarchies to gain the best benefits, and enhance organizational intelligence development. Consequently, we know that organizational levels can reveal different culture types (Strengers et al., 2022), but we do not know how inconsistent organizational culture affects organizational collective intelligence. Therefore, this book is dedicated to filling this knowledge gap.

Moreover, bearing in mind that company culture type may affect multilevel organizational learning (Moonen, 2017) and the ability to adapt to changes (Rass et al., 2023), this book examines and translates into practice on how KLC-culture synergy affects organizational intelligence. This is viewed through the prism of different organizational culture types: adhocracy, clan, market, and hierarchy (Cameron & Quinn, 2006) and, at different organizational levels, namely, division and team.

References

Cameron, K. S., & Quinn, R. E. (2006). Diagnosing and changing organizational culture: Relationships to effectiveness. *Research in Organizational Change and Development*, *5*, 23–58.

Cannon, F. (2017). *The agility mindset: How reframing flexible working delivers competitive advantage*. Springer.

Chatterjee, A., Arun, P., & Reid, B. (2018). Impact of individual perception of organizational culture on the learning transfer environment. *International Journal of Training and Development*, *22*(1), 15–33. https://doi.org/10.1111/ijtd.12116

Denning, S. (2020). How the C-suite is embracing agile. *Strategy & Leadership*, *48*(5), 19–24. https://doi.org/10.1108/SL-06-2020-0084

Eilers, K., Simmert, B., Peters, C., & Leimeister, J. M. (2020). Doing agile vs. being agile: Understanding their effects to improve agile work. In *Proceedings of international conference of information systems, India* (pp. 1–17). https://aisel.aisnet.org/icis2020/is_development/is_development/6

Feuerstein, R., Feuerstein, S., Falik, L., & Rand, Y. (1979). *Dynamic assessments of cognitive modifiability*. ICELP Press.

Gao, A., Zhao, K., & Qu, Q. (2020). Linking person–organization adhocracy value congruence to creativity. *Journal of Managerial Psychology*, *35*(7–8), 603–615. https://doi.org/10.1108/JMP-08-2019-0448

Graham, J. R., Grennan, J., Harvey, C. R., & Rajgopal, S. (2022). Corporate culture: Evidence from the field. *Journal of Financial Economics*, *146*, 552–594.

Haapasaari, A., & Kerosuo, H. (2015). Transformative agency: The challenges of sustainability in a long chain of double stimulation. *Learning, Culture and Social Interaction*, *4*, 37–47. https://doi.org/10.1016/j.lcsi.2014.07.006

Hofstede, G., Hofstede, G. J., & Minkov, M. (2010). *Cultures and organizations: Software of the mind* (Rev. ed.). McGraw-Hill.

Kangas, L. M. (2009). Assessing the value of the relationship between organizational culture types and knowledge management initiatives. *Journal of Leadership Studies*, *3*(1), 29–38.

Kesterson, R. K. (2015). *The basics of Hoshin Kanri*. CRC Press/Taylor & Francis.

Kim, T., & Chang, J. (2019). Organizational culture and performance: A macro-level longitudinal study. *Leadership & Organization Development Journal*, *40*(1), 65–84.

Kucharska, W., Balcerowski, T., Kucharski, M., & Jussila, J. (2024a). Who is an agile leader? Technological vs. non-technological mindset employees' views. *20th European Conference on Management, Leadership and Governance*, *20*(1), 397–404. https://doi.org/10.34190/eckm.25.1.2367

Kucharska, W., Balcerowski, T., Kucharski, M., Jussila, J., & Laanti, M. (2024b). Why does the Agile leader mindset matter the most? Polish-Finnish, technological and non-technological perspectives on agile and non-agile mindset employees and organizations. *Heliyon*. https://ssrn.com/abstract=4988722

Kucharska, W., & Bedford, D. A. D. (2023). *The cultures of knowledge organizations: Knowledge, learning, collaboration (KLC)*. Emerald Publishing Limited.

Kucharska, W., & Bedford, D. A. D. (2024). The KLC cultures' synergy power, trust, and tacit knowledge for organizational intelligence. *Electronic Journal of Knowledge Management*, *22*(2), 18–35.

McIntosh, S. (2016). What exactly is the agile mindset? *InfoQ*. https://www.infoq.com/articles/what-agile-mindset

Moonen, P. (2017). The impact of culture on the innovative strength of nations: A comprehensive review of the theories of Hofstede, Schwartz, Boisot and Cameron and Quinn. *Journal of Organizational Change Management*, *30*(7), 1149–1183. https://doi.org/10.1108/JOCM-08-2017-0311

Moreira, M. E. (2013). *Being agile: Your roadmap to successful adoption of agile*. Apress.

Parikh, M. (2016). Move over Mintzberg, let adhocracy give way to ambidexterity. *Management Decision*, *54*(5), 1047–1058. https://doi.org/10.1108/MD-07-2014-0483

Parolini, J. L., & Parolini, M. D. (2012). Moving from maturity to renewal: An investigation of culture and innovation. *International Journal of Organization Theory & Behavior*, *15*(2), 200–238. https://doi.org/10.1108/IJOTB-15-02-2012-B003

Rass, L., Treur, J., Kucharska, W., & Wiewiora, A. (2023). Adaptive dynamical systems modelling of transformational organizational change with focus on organizational culture and organizational learning, *Cognitive Systems Research*, *79*, 85–108.

Rigby, D., Elk, S., & Berez, S. (2020). *Doing agile right: Transformation without chaos*. Harvard Business Review Press.

Roche, E. M., & Blaine, M. J. (2014). The intelligence gap: What the multinational enterprise can learn from government and military intelligence organizations. *Thunderbird International Business Review*, *57*(1), 3–13. https://doi.org/10.1002/tie.21675

Sahoo, C. K., & Chaubey, A. (2024). Evolution of organizational agility research: A retrospective view. *Benchmarking: An International Journal*, *31*(4), 1181–1224. https://doi.org/10.1108/BIJ-02-2023-0086

Senge, P. M. (1992). Mental models. *Planning Review*, *20*(2), 4–44. https://doi.org/10.1108/eb054349

Strengers, J., Mutsaers, L., van Rossum, L., & Graamans, E. (2022). The organizational culture of scale-ups and performance. *Journal of Organizational Change Management*, *35*(8), 115–130. https://doi.org/10.1108/JOCM-09-2021-0268

Wiewiora, A., Smidt, M., & Chang, A. (2019). The ‘how’ of multilevel learning dynamics: A systematic literature review exploring how mechanisms bridge learning between individuals, teams/projects and the organization. *European Management Review*, *16*, 93–115. http://dx.doi.org/10.1111/emre.12179

2 From company culture to organizational intelligence—conceptual framework

2.1 Intelligence-driven organizations. Why are they in focus?

Collective intelligence is seen in this book as an organization's collective ability to adapt to change (Kucharska & Bedford, 2023). This topic is of great interest because developing such a collective skill enables organizations to solve problems and accomplish tasks more effectively and efficiently in a fast-changing environment. This collective adaptability skill is possible to gain thanks to collaboration and knowledge sharing, which results exceed any effects that any individual could accomplish alone (Leimeister, 2010; Malone et al., 2008; Secundo et al., 2016). This collective ability is relevant in the hyperdynamic conditions of the current economy. To survive, organizations must adapt quickly and create new, up-to-date solutions that bring value to customers and ensure competitiveness and growth. Collective intelligence development is more and more often identified as an essential condition to sustain competitiveness through its significant contribution to value capture (Issam et al., 2023; Rae & Blenker, 2023). Digital innovations can undoubtedly support organizational intelligence processes (Volberda et al., 2021). However, at the same time, Ardichvili (2022) stresses that AI systems can doom organizational intelligence through the loss of organizational expertise of the most experienced members. This is because of reduced opportunities for collaborative learning from those members and, generally, the lower possibility of working on progressively more complex tasks and deliberate practice. Ardichvili (2022) suggests that promoting organizational culture conducive to expertise development can prevent organizational intelligence loss. Tacit, intuitive, and strongly contextual knowledge is beyond AI reception. This book follows this line of thought; it posits that to support organizational intelligence development, it is necessary to consider KLC functional culture synergy, which supports tacit and explicit knowledge creation and sharing to the next build collective intelligence (Kucharska & Bedford, 2023, 2024). Tacit knowledge is a base for any innovation. Therefore, it is a "must have" resource. Tacit knowledge development is precisely the advantage that human intelligence has over artificial. Tacit knowledge is created and stored in the human mind thanks to contextual learning by doing and social interactions supported by the solid,

DOI: 10.4324/9781003485230-4

explicit knowledge base and trust among coworkers (Kucharska & Erickson, 2023). So, collective intelligence in organizations grows when the team favors tacit knowledge creation and smooth (agile) circulation. Tacit knowledge creation and sharing cannot be forced by anyone or anything (*Can we force someone to share knowledge that only this person knows she/he has?*). Company culture is the only tool that can create the facilitating conditions in which an organization acts as a network of brilliant minds that agilely cooperate.

In other words, this book addresses the problem of the hitherto unclear relations of the KLC approach—a synergy of functional cultures of knowledge, learning, and collaboration dedicated to knowledge-driven organizations if these organizations represent different culture types. Thus, summing up, we know that the KLC approach fosters collective organizational intelligence (Kucharska & Bedford, 2023, 2024). However, we do not know if adhocracies, clans, markets, or hierarchies enhance organizational intelligence development equally through the implementation of the KLC approach or if some of these culture types perform better with the KLC approach. Consequently, we know that managerial levels can reveal different culture types (Strengers et al., 2022), but we do not know how inconsistent organizational culture affects intelligence. Therefore, this book aims to fill this knowledge gap. Such knowledge from a comparative perspective from different culture types (hierarchy, adhocracy, clan, and market) and other management levels (organization, division, team) will interest intelligence-driven organizations enthusiasts and strategists interested in long-range planning. Also, human resource development researchers and practitioners focused on human factor enhancement in organizations will find this book relevant to the change adaptability problem that organizations face today.

2.2 Company culture taxonomy. Why do company cultures differ?

Cameron and Quinn (2006) introduced four company culture types to which this study refers: adhocracy, clan, market, and hierarchy. Their taxonomy is embedded in the competing values framework (CVF), where values such as stability and control are opposed to flexibility and discretion, and similarly, external focus and differentiation are opposed to internal focus and integration. As a result, hierarchy culture opposes adhocracy and consequently markets to the clan.

Hierarchy culture is defined through stability and control, formalization and bureaucracy, and internal solid focus. This culture values efficiency, reliability, predictability, and standardization. Fast and smooth operations are maintained by strict adherence to the numerous formal rules, policies, and procedures. The employees throughout the multiple hierarchical levels typically have no discretion and are simply expected to obey rules. Leaders in hierarchical cultures are expected to be good organizers and coordinators who focus on effectiveness, so they usually expose fixed mindsets (Dweck, 2017; Moonen, 2017; Strengers et al., 2022). Hierarchical culture is often characteristic of big, mature organizations whose market offers are effects of complex internal operations. They are oriented to deliver repetitive quality standards effectively. Professional skills in hierarchies are more critical than social.

Adhocracy, in opposition to hierarchy, exposes differentiation, flexibility, and discretion at all levels and is externally focused on growth and innovation, and their employees are ready to think critically, learn, take risks, and dynamically change the course of action if necessary. Adhocracy exposes a dynamic, entrepreneurial, and creative course of action that thrives well in an uncertain, ambiguous, and turbulent environment. The common values are constant learning, innovation, flexibility, adaptability, risk-taking, experimentation, and initiative. Adhocracies leaders are then expected to be visionary, innovative, and ready to take a risk if necessary (but it does not mean they do not manage risks thoroughly—on the contrary, they do!). They expose a constantly learning growth mindset (Dweck, 2017; Moonen, 2017; Strengers et al., 2022). Agile mindset leaders would be a perfect match for adhocracies (Kucharska et al., 2024a, 2024b). Adhocracies are characteristic of dynamic small or medium entities that are constant development oriented. They "never have enough" of intellectual challenge. Curiosity and breaking conventions characterize their members. Members collaborate to solve problems, gain knowledge, break conventions, up horizons, and discover novelty. Growth drives them. The constant increase in intellectual capital is a shared aim that drives and bonds them.

Clan culture exposes internal focus, flexibility, and discretion, as well as a great concern for people, loyalty, affiliation, open communication, and overall community feeling. The clan culture is often compared to a family. This culture emphasizes teamwork (self-managed work teams), employee inclusion, empowerment, cohesion, participation, and company commitment to employees. Loyalty and tradition constitute a clan community. In this context, leaders are expected to simultaneously be mentors who act as excellent, caring, and demanding fathers. They are expected to empower employees, create social bonds among workmates, and facilitate their commitment and loyalty toward a company that opposes market culture (Dweck, 2017; Moonen, 2017; Strengers et al., 2022). Clans' leaders are expected to be good organizers and efficient coordinators who focus on effectiveness and usually expose fixed mindsets. However, it might be that they act agilely, too. The leader's mindset powerfully shapes the shared mindset of the entire clan. Clans are often observed in small or medium organizations. However, those organizations that develop strong brand citizenship behaviors among employees often act as clans, even if they are big and mature. The essence of clan culture is a robust and easy-to-observe bond among employees who care about one another, the brand's reputation, and the company. Social skills are equally critical to professional skills in clan culture.

Market culture is similar to hierarchies about control seeking but is externally (market) oriented and focuses on winning, gathering market knowledge, focusing on task accomplishment, and orienting toward market achievements. Therefore, market culture organizations are ready to change constantly—internally and externally. Those are the most agile. Hierarchies are internally oriented (they want to be the best version of themselves). Markets—externally (they want to be who they need to be to win). They focus on customers, their own productivity, business profitability, and market gains. Employees can cooperate smoothly to gain value. The common goals matter more than personal dislikes (winning and value gaining are strong motivators of cooperation). Leaders in this culture are expected to be formidable players and top winners, so they often are exposed to fixed mindsets (Dweck, 2017; Moonen, 2017; Strengers et al., 2022), but fast reactive kind to deliver a spectacular, however short-run success. However, to achieve mastery, market culture companies' leaders must be proactive, predictive, and pragmatic visionaries. So, they must have an agile mindset to lead the company to constant wins and long-run success.

At first glance, adhocracies seem potentially the most beneficial from the implementation of the KLC approach. However, many knowledge-driven organizations today still expose strong clans, markets, or hierarchy cultures, and they perform with success, for example, Toyota. It is also observed that many public organizations usually operate as hierarchies and, similarly to adhocracies, can also be very innovative and collectively intelligent, for example, public transport companies, diplomacy, or military (Roche & Blaine, 2014; Kucharska & Bedford, 2023). So, it is worth studying more in-depth if adhocracies, clans, markets, and hierarchies enhance organizational intelligence development equally through the KLC-approach implementation or if some of these types perform with the KLC approach better. We need to know this to prepare a plan of collective intelligence development for each culture type. Such a plan, considered from the managerial level, might be extremely useful in business practice. This book precisely serves this purpose.

Additionally, Appendix 1 provides a bibliometric analysis to verify which contexts of adhocracy, hierarchy, clan, and market cultures have been more frequently researched so far. Moreover, all the visualizations given in Appendix 1 prove that the study on which this book is based is unique.

2.3 Knowledge, learning, and collaboration approach essence. Why is the KLC approach beneficial?

The KLC approach refers to the implementation of a set of functional cultures knowledge, learning, and collaboration whose synergy supports knowledge-driven organizations' intelligence building (Kucharska & Bedford, 2023, 2024). The essence of these functional cultures' synergy recognition is first the understanding of the functional meaning of each culture separately as well as its synergic relations.

A knowledge culture dominates in knowledge-oriented organizations, which usually focus on verified explicit knowledge exploitation rather than new tacit knowledge seeking or creation (Kucharska & Bedford, 2023, 2024; Van Wijk et al., 2012). In contrast, learning culture dominates in dynamic organizations that constantly focus on new tacit knowledge creation and seeking new solutions, constantly disrupting the status quo. What links both is that knowledge culture is a base for learning culture. More specifically, knowledge culture creates the motivation for learning. This is because only those who understand that knowledge is power look for new knowledge when facing new problems in new contexts.

However, developing a *knowledge culture* is not the same as developing the motivation for learning. To develop such a mental state, a learning culture is needed. According to Garvin (1993), a culture of learning is an organization's ability to create, acquire, and exchange knowledge, modify organizational behaviors and choices, and integrate the new knowledge and insights into its organizational knowledge and aims. It is easy to predict that if any organization is stuck in the knowledge-orientation stage, where static exploitation of knowledge and control of the proper use of knowledge dominates, the new knowledge will usually be rejected as too risky. Relying only on old, verified knowledge and solutions gives such organizations the illusion of safety. Thus, the repetitive control of explicit knowledge distribution and application gives the illusion of organizational safety. For this reason, tried and tested methods of acting are valued over seeking new solutions, and any risk is rejected. Consequently, any risk of mistakes associated with these new ways of acting is avoided. Organizations based chiefly on proven knowledge prefer to "keep things as they are." Thus, focusing on safe, well-known routines and a control-oriented acting might block desired development. Hierarchies often act this way. In contrast, Moonen (2017) and Strengers et al. (2022) believe that adhocracies are in a constant learning mode.

A learning culture leads to constant and dynamic knowledge acquisition, driven by "intelligence in action" (Erickson & Rothberg, 2012). A pervasive and persistent learning culture is essential for the development and growth of learning organizations in the current economic climate of continuous change (Maes & Van Hootegem, 2019; Rass et al., 2023). An organizational learning culture can facilitate the creation and sharing of tacit knowledge while discouraging the hoarding or hiding of such knowledge (Weinzimmer & Esken, 2017). By itself, a knowledge culture does not have this effect, although it can foster curiosity and expose knowledge gaps that lead to learning. This finding is consistent with the research of Webster and Pearce (2008), who highlight the importance of situational learning, which is essential to active learning. Situational learning is aligned with the current context. It is especially relevant today in a dynamic and rapidly changing business environment. Acting in such a dynamic business environment is a kind of constant experiment or "first-time" acting, which may naturally result in mistakes. However, in this context, mistakes are seen as a potential source of learning. It does not mean that learning organizations do not try to avoid mistakes. They do care about their performance but they are realistic and accept the fact that mistakes happen; as Senge (1992, 2006) claims, we can learn only when we are ready to be wrong. In this way, a learning culture must include the acceptance of mistakes. Further, Kucharska and Bedford (2020) empirically proved that this organizational ability to learn and develop intelligence depends on two components: learning climate and acceptance of mistakes as a potential source of learning. The learning climate component reflects a positive attitude and motivation to learn. The mistake-acceptance component reflects the essential learning attitude of being ready to realize being wrong which is a base for a re-framing mindset and learning.

A collaboration culture is the most critical functional culture of any organization. This is because an organization is defined as a group of people coordinated to achieve aims that none of them can achieve alone. Thus, collaborative culture is the essence of any organization's efficacy, and whatever an organization aims to achieve, smooth collaboration is required (Kucharska & Bedford, 2023). Collaboration strongly supports collective learning (Nugroho, 2018). It is the core competency that enables organizations to create relational capital. Therefore, collaboration culture is essential ingredient of the KLC culture's synergy needed to create organizational intelligence, understood as the ability to collectively adapt to any change needed. Collective adaptability requires collective thinking, learning, and acting. Clan culture seems to reflect best the organizational disposition to act collectively (Moonen, 2017; Strengers et al., 2022), which potentially is a solid foundation for collective intelligence building. However, it does not diminish the efforts of other cultures to gain collective intelligence, either. The culture type adapted to the particular organization is often affected by the aim this company serves, the company's size, operational complexity, maturity, sector, national context, leadership type, and so on. The fact is that company culture affects leadership, and the opposite is also true (leadership and culture determine one another). So, in this book, I am far away from judging which culture type is better or worse because the answer is simple—it depends on what aims in which sector, country, and conditions the organization wants to achieve.

In summary, based on the above justification, it is assumed that the KLC approach has the powerful potential to support change adaptability in any type of culture. Thus, we formulate the following hypothesis:

H1: KLC cultures support change adaptability (collective intelligence) in organizations.

2.4 Collective intelligence (change adaptability) and innovativeness. Why are they in high demand?

Adaptability is seen as a proxy for intelligence (Feuerstein et al., 1979). Organizational adaptability reflects the collective ability of an organization's members to respond to changes by managing stress and uncertainty, demonstrating flexibility or resilience, and supporting those who tackle problems to face the change (Reupert, 2020). Martin et al. (2013) define adaptability as "appropriate cognitive, behavioral and/or emotional adjustment in the face of uncertainty and novelty" (p. 1). An organization is composed of people; therefore, the essence of the organization's adaptability is collective adaptability. The ability to collectively adapt to or drive change reflects collective intelligence at the organizational, unit, group, and individual levels (Kucharska & Bedford, 2023). It is based on the higher-level social and intellectual capital mix.

Change is a characteristic of the current reality. Consequently, creating new solutions and, through these, adapting to change is what organizations and individuals must do to deliver value in a fast-changing reality and win the market (Rass et al., 2023). Existing in a fast-changing environment requires making change a part of shared habits and daily organizational routines. How organizations deal with the need for adaptability and respond to surrounding change determines their survival and development. Naveed et al. (2022) demonstrate that organizational culture positively influences organizational effectiveness through internal innovation, which is precisely an effect of the organizational ability to constantly improve its own actions (processes, procedures, policies, etc.). The collective capability to adapt constantly pays. Those organizations that adapt through constant internal improvement are also better at external (market) innovation implementation, which helps them to sustain competitiveness (Hagedoorn & Wang, 2012; Jiménez-Jiménez & Sanz-Valle, 2011; Kucharska, 2021). Thus, we formulate the following hypothesis:

H2: Change adaptability fosters internal innovation.

2.5 Why do culture types differ among managerial levels in the same company? Multilevel analysis: organization, division, team

The culture type may differ among managerial levels of the same company primarily for two reasons—both are related. First, it is a function of the particular division or team. Second, it is a leadership style performed in this team or division. Precisely, both are related. Let us compare the production division to the R&D division. Production must efficiently and effectively deliver a repetitive quality. Tasks interdependence push cooperation to the perfect level of cooperation that is formalized by the sequence and hierarchy of processes. The know-how (explicit knowledge) sharing is secured through procedures. Learning happens mostly in single or double loops—employees learn how to do perfectly what they used to do or do it even better (Argyris & Schon, 1978). The best employees for production are those who obey orders, love routines, and accept constant control. Best leaders—the humanized type of optimizing commanders-controllers. Meanwhile, the R&D division is oriented toward delivering novelty, searching for new solutions, and breaking conventions. Invention processes are critically based on tacit knowledge sharing that is out of any control. The best leaders set up challenging tasks but offer the freedom to think outside the box. Lead others by mentoring and inspiring; supportive control focuses on progress. They build teams composed of people who do not compete; they collaborate because they need each other complementary competencies. Learning happens in R&D in double and triple-loops. The best employees are intelligent professionals driven by challenge and curiosity, with failure-resistant rebel souls and social skills. So, this comparison exposes the aim to which achievement the particular division or team is dedicated to determines the leadership and culture type that best serves this aim. So, the bigger and more complex the company, the more options of leadership/culture we can observe even in the same organization. Therefore, the adapted culture and leadership type are often affected by the aim to which the organization, division, or team serves, its size, operational complexity, maturity, sector, national context, business context, etc.

Returning to the conceptual framework of the focal point for this book research, managerial level division and team are inputted into the given theoretical model as control variables. A control variable (CV) signifies an additional factor third variable that may have a significant impact on a particular relationship between two variables. A CV may act as a confounder, moderator, or suppressor; therefore, CVs are not the focal part of the investigation, but from a theoretical perspective, they are nonetheless important (Becker et al., 2016; Nielsen & Raswant, 2018). Thus, the inclusion of a CV may change the power or significance of the assumed in the theoretical model relationships between variables. In this study, the managerial level is perceived as a CV. So, the inclusion of division and team as CVs matters to obtain an in-depth understanding of how the KLC supports organizational intelligence in organizations of different culture types and managerial levels. More specifically, Kucharska and Bedford (2023) point out that company culture may differ across organizational levels, while Wiewiora et al. (2019) affirm that it matters for organizational learning. Moreover, Rass et al. (2023) maintain that multilevel organizational learning also affects change adaptability. Regarding the knowledge we have about company culture and managerial level, Wiewiora et al. (2013, 2019) stress that company cultures that exhibit flexibility and discretion (e.g., adhocracy culture) are better than market, hierarchy, or clan cultures for multilevel organizational learning. Finally, Strengers et al. (2022) note that employees working at different organizational levels of the same organization report different culture types, but we do not know how this fact affects organizational intelligence. All above justifies the idea of controlling the organizational level in this study to explore how different organizational levels (team, division) moderate the focal relation between the KLC-culture components and change adaptability (intelligence-IQ). To explore this, each of the theoretical models (separate models for each culture type) is run with and without a CV imputation (Becker et al., 2016). The comparison of the quality of the models obtained with and without the CVs imputation gives us clear information on the appropriateness of the multilevel analysis.

Figure 2.1a, b illustrates all the above-elaborated sets of assumptions given earlier. Moreover, as a base, Model B (Figure 2.1b) demonstrates when KLC cultures directly influences organizational intelligence. In contrast, Model A (alternative) exposes the structure where these cultures influence one another as the KLC approach (Kucharska & Bedford, 2023), as shown in Figure 2.1a. Such

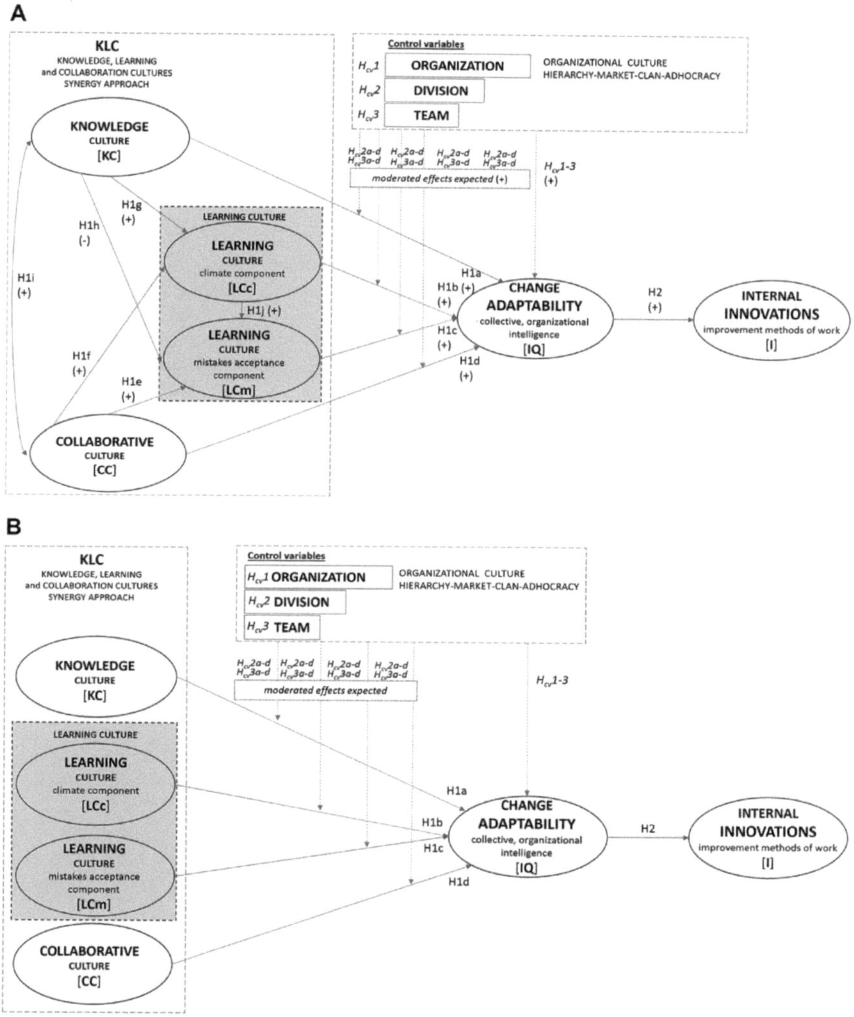

Figure 2.1 Theoretical framework: (a) Model A (b) Model B

Note: CC—collaborative culture; KC—knowledge culture; LCc—learning culture climate component; LCm—learning culture mistake-acceptance component; IQ—collective intelligence of the organization; and I—internal innovation.

a comparison (Tables 4.1 and 4.2a, b, Chapter 4) adds value to the analysis by showing exactly how the KLC-approach components (knowledge, learning, and collaboration cultures) interact with one another. This provides a better understanding of the KLC approach's powerful significance.

The next chapter exposes the method of the empirical verification of the theoretical model given in Figure 2.1a, b.

References

Ardichvili, A. (2022). The impact of artificial intelligence on expertise development: Implications for HRD. *Advances in Developing Human Resources*, *24*(2), 78–98. https://doi.org/10.1177/15234223221077304

Argyris, C., & Schon, D. A. (1978). *Organisational learning*. Addison Wesley.

Becker, T. E., Atnic, G., Breaugh, J. A., Carlson, K. D., Edwards, J. R., & Spector, P. E. (2016). Statistical control in correlational studies: 10 essential recommendations for organizational researchers. *Journal of Organizational Behavior*, *37*(2), 157–167. https://doi.org/10.1002/job.2053

Cameron, K. S., & Quinn, R. E. (2006). Diagnosing and changing organizational culture: Relationships to effectiveness. *Research in Organizational Change and Development*, *5*, 23–58.

Dweck, C. S. (2017). *Mindset*. Brown, Little Book Group.

Erickson, G. S., & Rothberg, H. (2012). *Intelligence in action: Strategically managing knowledge assets*. Springer.

Feuerstein, R., Feuerstein, S., Falik, L., & Rand, Y. (1979). *Dynamic assessments of cognitive modifiability*. ICELP Press.

Garvin, D. (1993, July–August). Building a learning organization. *Harvard Business Review*, 78–91.

Hagedoorn, J., & Wang, N. (2012). Is there complementarity or substitutability between internal and external R&D strategies? *Research Policy*, *41*(6), 1072–1083.

Issam, A., Nylund, P. A., & Brem, A. (2023). Who captures value from hackathons? Innovation contests with collective intelligence tools bridging creativity and coupled open innovation. *Creativity and Innovation Management*, *32*(2), 266–280. https://doi.org/10.1111/caim.12552

Jiménez-Jiménez, D., & Sanz-Valle, R. (2011). Innovation, organizational learning and performance. *Journal of Business Research*, *64*(4), 408–417. https://doi.org/10.1016/j.jbusres.2010.09.010

Kucharska, W. (2021). Do mistakes acceptance foster innovation? Polish and US cross-country study of tacit knowledge sharing in IT. *Journal of Knowledge Management*, *25*(11), 105–128. https://doi.org/10.1108/JKM-12-2020-0922

Kucharska, W., Balcerowski, T., Kucharski, M., & Jussila, J. (2024a). Who is an agile leader? Technological vs. non-technological mindset employees' views. *20th European Conference on Management, Leadership and Governance*, *20*(1), 397–404. https://doi.org/10.34190/eckm.25.1.2367

Kucharska, W., Balcerowski, T., Kucharski, M., Jussila, J., & Laanti, M. (2024b). Why does the Agile leader mindset matter the most? Polish-Finnish, technological and non-technological perspectives on agile and non-agile mindset employees and organizations. *Heliyon*. https://ssrn.com/abstract=4988722

Kucharska, W., & Bedford, D. A. D. (2020). Love your mistakes! They help you adapt to change. How do knowledge, collaboration and learning cultures foster organizational intelligence? *Journal of Organizational Change Management*, *337*, 1329–1354. https://doi.org/10.1108/JOCM-02-2020-0052

Kucharska, W., & Bedford, D. A. D. (2023). *The cultures of knowledge organizations: Knowledge, learning, collaboration (KLC)*. Emerald Publishing Limited.

Kucharska, W., & Bedford, D. A. D. (2024). The KLC cultures' synergy power, trust, and tacit knowledge for organizational intelligence. *Electronic Journal of Knowledge Management*, *22*(2), 18–35.

Kucharska, W., & Erickson, G. S. (2023). Tacit knowledge acquisition & sharing, and its influence on innovations: A Polish/US cross-country study. *International Journal of Information Management*, *71*, 102647. https://doi.org/10.1016/j.ijinfomgt.2023.102647

Leimeister, J. M. (2010). Collective intelligence. *Business Information Systems Engineering, 24*, 245–248.
Maes, G., & Van Hootegem, G. (2019). A systems model of organizational change. *Journal of Organizational Change Management, 32*(7), 725–738. https://doi.org/10.1108/JOCM-07-2017-0268
Malone, T. W., Atlee, T., & Lévy, P. (2008). *Collective intelligence: Creating a prosperous world at peace*. Earth Intelligence Network.
Martin, A. J., Nejad, H., Colmar, S., & Liem, G. A. D. (2013). Adaptability: How students' responses to uncertainty and novelty predict their academic and non-academic outcomes. *Journal of Educational Psychology, 105*(3), 728–746. https://doi.org/10.1037/a0032794
Moonen, P. (2017). The impact of culture on the innovative strength of nations: A comprehensive review of the theories of Hofstede, Schwartz, Boisot and Cameron and Quinn. *Journal of Organizational Change Management, 30*(7), 1149–1183. https://doi.org/10.1108/JOCM-08-2017-0311
Naveed, R. T., Alhaidan, H., Al Halbusi, H., & Al-Swidi, A. K. (2022). Do organizations really evolve? The critical link between organizational culture and organizational innovation toward organizational effectiveness: Pivotal role of organizational resistance. *Journal of Innovation & Knowledge, 7*(2), Article 100178. https://doi.org/10.1016/j.jik.2022.100178
Nielsen, B. B., & Raswant, A. (2018). The selection, use, and reporting of control variables in international business research: A review and recommendations. *Journal of World Business, 53*(6), 958–968. https://doi.org/10.1016/j.jwb.2018.05.003
Nugroho, M. A. (2018). The effects of collaborative cultures and knowledge sharing on organizational learning. *Journal of Organizational Change Management, 31*(5), 1138–1152. https://doi.org/10.1108/JOCM-10-2017-0385
Rae, D., & Blenker, P. (2023). The role of collective intelligence and collective agency in enterprising communities. *Journal of Enterprising Communities: People and Places in the Global Economy*. https://doi.org/10.1108/JEC-09-2022-0141
Rass, L., Treur, J., Kucharska, W., & Wiewiora, A. (2023). Adaptive dynamical systems modelling of transformational organizational change with focus on organizational culture and organizational learning, *Cognitive Systems Research, 79*, 85–108.
Reupert, A. (2020). Change and (the need for) adaptability: The new normal. *Advances in Mental Health, 18*(2), 91–93. https://doi.org/10.1080/18387357.2020.1792633
Roche, E. M., & Blaine, M. J. (2014). The intelligence gap: What the multinational enterprise can learn from government and military intelligence organizations. *Thunderbird International Business Review, 57*(1), 3–13. https://doi.org/10.1002/tie.21675
Secundo, G., Dumay, J., Schiuma, G., & Passiante, G. (2016). Managing intellectual capital through a collective intelligence approach: An integrated framework for universities. *Journal of Intellectual Capital, 17*(2), 298–319. https://doi.org/10.1108/JIC-05-2015-0046
Senge, P. M. (1992). Mental models. *Planning Review, 20*(2), 4–44. https://doi.org/10.1108/eb054349
Senge, P. M. (2006). *The fifth discipline. The art & practice of the learning organization*. Crown Business.
Strengers, J., Mutsaers, L., van Rossum, L., & Graamans, E. (2022). The organizational culture of scale-ups and performance. *Journal of Organizational Change Management, 35*(8), 115–130. https://doi.org/10.1108/JOCM-09-2021-0268
Van Wijk, R., Jansen, J. J., Van Den Bosch, F. A., & Volberda, H. W. (2012). How firms shape knowledge to explore and exploit: A study of knowledge flows, knowledge stocks and innovative performance across units. *Technology Analysis and Strategic Management, 24*(9), 929–950. https://doi.org/10.1080/09537325.2012.718666

Volberda, H., Khanagha, S., Baden-Fuller, C., Mihalache, O. R., & Birkinshaw, J. (2021). Strategizing in a digital world: Overcoming cognitive barriers, reconfiguring routines and introducing new organizational forms. *Long Range Planning*, *54*(5), 102110. https://doi.org/10.1016/j.lrp.2021.102110

Webster, J., & Pearce, G. (2008). Crossfire: Knowledge sharing should focus on learning culture, rather than the generation of knowledge. *Waterlines*, *27*(2), 97–103. https://doi.org/10.3362/1756–3488.2008.012

Weinzimmer, L. G., & Esken, C. A. (2017). Learning from mistakes: How mistake tolerance positively affects organizational learning and performance. *The Journal of Applied Behavioral Science*, *53*(3), 322–348. https://doi.org/10.1177/0021886316688658

Wiewiora, A., Smidt, M., & Chang, A. (2019). The 'how' of multilevel learning dynamics: A systematic literature review exploring how mechanisms bridge learning between individuals, teams/projects and the organization. *European Management Review*, *16*, 93–115. http://dx.doi.org/10.1111/emre.12179

Wiewiora, A., Trigunarsyah, B., Murphy, G., & Coffey, V. (2013). Organizational culture and willingness to share knowledge: A competing values perspective in Australian context. *International Journal of Project Management*, *31*, 1163–1174. http://dx.doi.org/10.1016/j.ijproman.2012.12.014

3 Methodology—study method

3.1 Sampling method

This study is based on Polish knowledge workers. Respondents were qualified to participate in the survey when they declared that their critical input and output at work was knowledge. It was critical because the KLC approach explored in this research is dedicated to knowledge-driven organizations. Moreover, to secure the respondents' familiarity with their organization's issues, I qualified only those who worked a minimum of one year for the same employer. A questionnaire was designed to measure all latent variables included in the conceptual framework (Figure 2.1a, b). The used measurement scales, their statements, and sources are given in Table 3.1. Respondents referred to given scale statements using a 7-point Likert scale. Besides, organizational culture type was identified through the respondents' nominal declaration of which culture type (Cameron & Quinn, 2006) best fits the particular level of organizations they are working for. Respondents were provided with definitions of these cultural types. Data collection took place in March 2023 using the computer-assisted web interviewing method. Scale reliabilities, basic statistics, and obtained correlations between constructs are presented in Table 4.2a, b, Chapter 4. Additionally, Table 3.2 presents the cross-loadings matrix, indicating that the applied scales do not overlap. Structural equation modeling (SEM method) was used to analyze the structure of relations visualized in Figures 2.1a, b (Kline, 2005; Byrne, 2016). The software selected to support the data analysis were SPSS Amos version 26 and SPSS Process version 3.4 (Hayes, 2018).

3.2 Sample quality

Sample quality assessment started with the Kaiser–Meyer–Olkin test, determining how suited data is for factor analysis; the obtained result, KMO .946, is assessed as very good (Hair et al., 2010). Total Variance Extracted: 74%, common method bias (CMB) was tested using the common latent factor method, which is 51%. So, it suggests that the sample is biased. There might be some potential sources of this bias. The first potential source might come from the observed strong correlation

DOI: 10.4324/9781003485230-5

Table 3.1 Scales and their sources

Construct and source	*Statements*
Change adaptability (org. intelligence—IQ) (Kucharska & Bedford, 2020)	• We are flexible to changes. • We can adjust ourselves to changes. • We adapt to changes easily.
Learning culture (Kucharska & Bedford, 2020)	*Learning climate component* • All staff demonstrates a high learning disposition. • We are encouraged to engage in personal development. • We are encouraged to implement new ideas every day. • We are encouraged to engage in seeking new solutions. *Mistake-acceptance component* • People know that mistakes are a learning consequence and tolerate it up to a certain limit. • Most people freely declare mistakes. • We discuss problems openly without blaming others. • Mistakes if happen are used as a source of learning.
Collaborative culture (Kucharska & Bedford, 2020)	• My company supports cooperation between workers. • Cooperation among the different duties, teams, and departments was encouraged. • Coworkers volunteer their support even without being asked. • People support each other.
Knowledge culture (Kucharska & Bedford, 2020)	• All employees perceive knowledge as a valuable resource. • We have a common language to support knowledge exchange. • We are encouraged to share knowledge, ideas, and thoughts. • We care about the quality of knowledge that we share.
Organizational Innovativeness—internal processes improvement (Kucharska & Erickson, 2023)	• We constantly improve the way we work. • We are good at managing changes. • We are highly disposed to introduce new methods and procedures. • We are highly disposed to accept new rules.

between collaboration culture and organizational collective intelligence (IQ) and with the collaboration culture and learning climate (LCc) component of the learning culture (Table 4.3, Chapter 4). So, it might be that collaborative culture in Polish knowledge-driven organizations indeed is a key driver, or it might be that it is a general characteristic independent of nationality. It might be, because collaboration is a driver of any organization. It requires further studies. Moreover, Kucharska and Kopytko (2024), regarding the acceptance of mistakes as a source of potential learning component of a learning culture measurement, exposed that it is usually affected by the bias of mistakes (BM).

Table 3.2 Cross-loadings matrix

	Loadings					
	1	*2*	*3*	*4*	*5*	*6*
LCm 3	**,934**					
LCm 4	**,892**					
LCm 2	**,879**					
LCm 1	**,824**			,128		
IQ1		**,904**		,163	-,201	
IQ 3		**,690**				,147
IQ 4		**,672**				
IQ 2		**,545**		-,119	,218	,116
KC 1			**,919**			
KC 2			**,867**			
KC 3			**,698**	,161		
LCc 4				**,866**		
LCc 3				**,692**		,214
LCc 1		,131	,175	**,544**		
C2				-,115	**,969**	
C3		,212		,228	**,558**	-,110
C4		,187		,108	**,493**	
I3		,261				**,647**
I2						**,636**
I1		,303				**,570**

Note: Loadings extraction method–Maximum Reliability. Rotation method–Promax with Kaiser normalization. Convergence was reached in six iterations.

The essence of this bias is the contradiction between the positive attitude toward learning from mistakes and the negative consequences experienced because of the mistake event. Mistakes are seen as an indicator of negligence. Mistakes are often seen negatively, so expecting the positive outcome of mistakes as a potential source of learning can be cognitively problematic. This bias is usually doubled when the lack of mistakes is seen in a particular organization, society, or community as a critical credential of a "good leader" or "good manager." The dominating doubled bias of mistakes (DBM) leads to mistakes hiding and creates the illusion of perfection, which jeopardizes organizational learning.

Since the mistake-acceptance component of a learning culture (LCm) is also included in the given research, it is reasonable to assume that this study probably also handles this bias. The cross-loading matrix (Table 3.2) clearly exposed that the measurement of the constructs went well. So, the identified bias comes from this cognitive bias rather than measurement problems. This sounds reasonable, especially since the previously mentioned strong correlation between the culture of cooperation, collective intelligence, and learning climate (Table 4.2a, b, Chapter 4) is not due to measurement bias (loadings do not overlap). It is therefore assumed that the identified bias may be caused by the measurement of the mistake-acceptance component of learning culture and it will be analyzed in the further part of the study.

3.3 Sample characteristics

The study sample is composed of 640 cases (fully completed and valid questionnaires with SD>.4) representing Polish knowledge workers: 159 specialists and 481 managers, 329 women and 311 men working mostly in private (76%) companies in different sectors and almost equally represented by micro (3%), small (31%), big (35%), and large companies (31%). The sector-mixed and company-size-mixed sample was dedicated to this study to illustrate the general view of the KLC cultures synergy approach for organizational intelligence and innovation growth in Poland analyzed through the prism of company culture type. Therefore, dominating sectors in the study sample were knowledge-intensive sectors: IT (8%), finance (8%), higher education (8%), healthcare (8%), trade (8%), and construction (8%)—together 48%—but also production (17%), public services (9%), and other services (24%). Summing up, this study verifies the hypothesized structures of relations among variables (Figure 2.1a, b) based on Polish, highly-qualified, and knowledge-oriented organizations and employees.

Moreover, this study focuses also on the organizational culture type. Therefore, the analysis of culture type frequency per organizational level is included in Table 3.3. This analysis showed that adhocracies and clans are the most consistent culture types across organizational levels (team, division, and organization) in Polish knowledge-driven organizations. Hierarchies and markets—opposite. Organizations with dominance of market or hierarchy culture characterize the strong mix of cultures developed across organizations in particular divisions or teams. As stated earlier, the adapted culture and leadership type are often affected by the aim, to which the organization, division, or team serves. Moreover, the company size, its operational complexity, maturity, particular sector specifics, the national and business context, impact the culture mix observed in the particular organization. This is in line with Kucharska and Bedford's (2023) suggestions that the corporate culture type observed in practice often varies between managerial levels (team, division, and organization). So, based on this study sample, it is an evident characteristic of hierarchies and markets. Therefore, this lack of cultural consistency (congruence) across the organization will be analyzed more in-depth in further parts of this research when examining the impact of the influence of the KLC functional cultures on organizational intelligence per culture type and level. It is essential to find how congruence or lack of it may impact the efficacy of strategies and methods of collective intelligence development.

In summary, this study is based on the structure of Polish knowledge-driven organizations, which cumulate the higher-level intellectual capital mainly into the following cultural types: hierarchies (29%), markets (33%), clans (23%), and adhocracies (15%). So, it is unknown if the lack of congruence observed in markets and hierarchies comes from their higher-level management skills open to multicultural management or if those organizations are "under transition." It requires further studies.

Table 3.3 Organization culture type frequency in the sample per organizational level: a) culture-type consistency across organizational levels (team, division, and organization) and b) culture type per company size

a) Culture-type consistency across organizational levels (team, division, and organization)

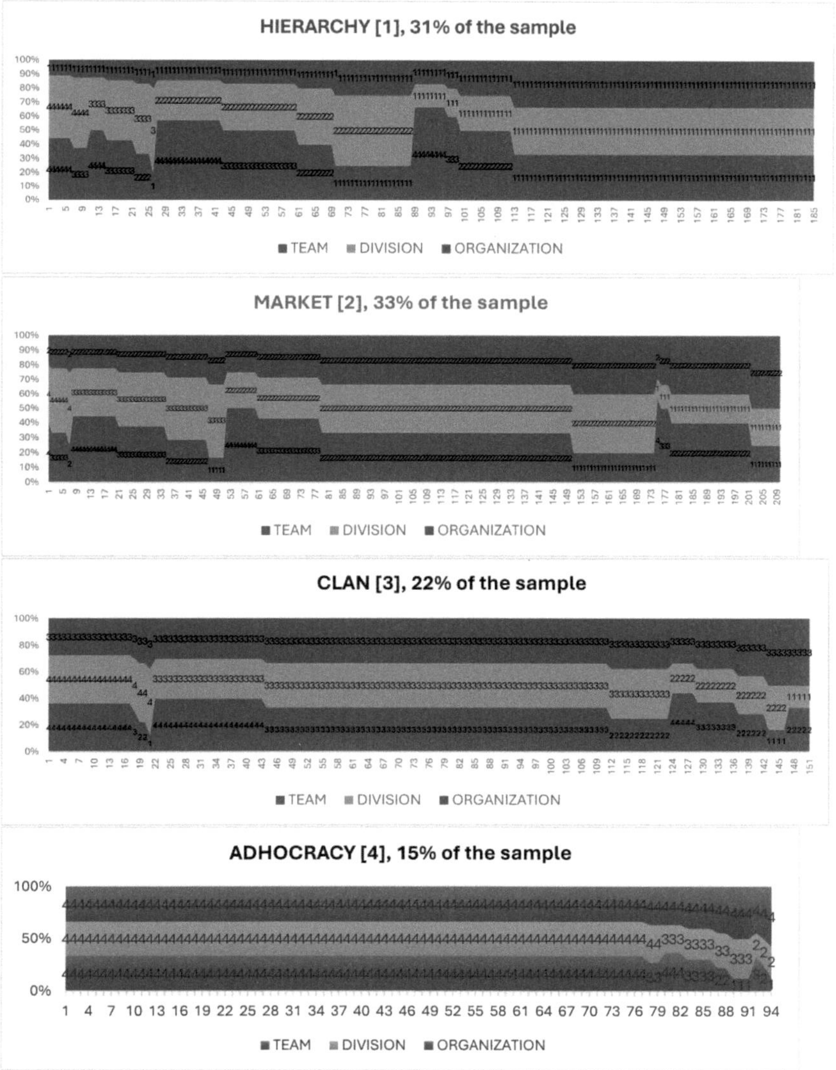

(*continued*)

Table 3.3 (Continued)

b) Culture type per company size

		Culture type			
		Hierarchy	*Market*	*Clan*	*Adhocracy*
Company size	Micro	1%	0%	1%	1%
	Small	6%	8%	9%	8%
	Big	11%	12%	8%	4%
	Large	13%	12%	4%	2%

Note: 4—Adhocracy; 3—Clan; 2—Market; and 1—Hierarchy

References

Byrne, B. M. (2016). *Structural equation modeling with Amos*. Routledge. https://doi.org/10.4324/9781315757421

Cameron, K. S., & Quinn, R. E. (2006). Diagnosing and changing organizational culture: Relationships to effectiveness. *Research in Organizational Change and Development*, *5*, 23–58.

Hair, J. F., Anderson, R. E., Babin, B. J., & Black, W. C. (2010). *Multivariate data analysis: A global perspective*. Pearson Education.

Hayes, A. (2018). *Introduction to mediation, moderation and conditional process analysis: A regression-based approach* (2nd ed.). Guilford Press.

Kline, R. B. (2005). *Principles and practice of structural equation modeling*. Guilford Press.

Kucharska, W., & Bedford, D. A. (2020). Love your mistakes!—They help you adapt to change. How do knowledge, collaboration and learning cultures foster organizational intelligence? *Journal of Organizational Change Management*, *33*(7), 1329–1354.

Kucharska, W., & Bedford, D. A. D. (2023). *The cultures of knowledge organizations: Knowledge, learning, collaboration (KLC)*. Emerald Publishing Limited.

Kucharska, W., & Erickson, G. S. (2023). Tacit knowledge acquisition & sharing, and its influence on innovations: A Polish/US cross-country study. *International Journal of Information Management*, *71*, 102647.

Kucharska, W., & Kopytko, A. (2024). Double bias of mistakes: Essence, consequences, and measurement method. *Electronic Journal of Business Research Methods*, *22*(1), 26–42. https://doi.org/10.34190/ejbrm.22.1.3320

4 Empirical evidence—study results

4.1 Knowledge, learning, and collaboration cultures' impact on organizational intelligence and innovativeness

The theoretical models' verification (Figures 2.1a, b) starts with the justification of control variables inclusion (Becker et al., 2016; Carlson & Wu, 2012; Nielsen & Raswant, 2018). So, both theoretical models, Model A and Model B, visualizing the different structures of the KLC cultures relation (Figure 2.1a, b) are created with the CVs (organization, division, team) inclusion. Therefore, the first step of analysis is the justification of this inclusion correctness for both. To do so, I ran and compared quality indicators obtained for the models with and without the CVs to compare their qualities (Becker et al., 2016; Nielsen & Raswant, 2018). Table 4.1 shows that the quality of both models A and B with CVs is better than the quality of models without CVs. So, the inclusion of CVs gives the model a better quality, so CVs inclusion is fully justified (Carlson & Wu, 2012). Therefore, further analyses are based only on models with CVs.

Table 4.1 shows models with and without CVs quality assessment and comparison.

Comparing the indicators obtained for Models A and B with CVs, the quality of both explored structures of the relation between all KLC cultures components is quite similar. But there is still a lesson that can be taken from the comparison of both structures' results (Figure 4.1a, b, Table 4.2a, b). Precisely, structure B (Model B base), where all KLC-culture components are considered as direct influencers of the organizational change adaptability (collective intelligence), exposes that the knowledge culture is not significant for change adaptability, which can seem to be a bit controversial. Especially since the sample this research is based on comprises knowledge workers employed in knowledge-based organizations. So, more light on it puts the structure A (Model A alternative) that findings expose that indeed knowledge culture matters for the organizational intelligence creation, but its influence is not direct, but indirect. That is in line with the knowledge, learning, and collaboration cultures synergy theory (the KLC approach) introduced by Kucharska and Bedford (2023, 2024). They stated that knowledge culture alone leads to static exploitation of the existing knowledge (explicit knowledge) and is

DOI: 10.4324/9781003485230-6

Table 4.1 Models: basic and alternative, with and without CVs—comparison

n = 640		*Chi-sq*	*Freedom degrees*	C_{min}/df	*RMSEA*	*CFI*	*TLI*
Base Model	without CVs	408.99	139	2.94	.055	.965	.957
B	with CVs	428.42	161	2.66	.051	.969	.960
Alternative Model	without CVs	323.67	122	2.65	.051	.972	.965
A	with CVs	450.31	167	2.67	.051	.967	.959

not efficient for innovation creation, change adaptability, or sustainability building because all those actions require a fresh view and novelty. So, new knowledge (tacit knowledge) is critical. It comes from exploring new areas and from formal and informal constant learning. So, the learning culture is in light of this critical as change adaptability and intelligence stimuli. However, there is always a risk connected with learning. New approaches are usually promising, but old ones are verified; this way, they are more reliable. This is why learning culture is much more difficult to develop than knowledge culture, which gives the illusion of effects predictability, stability, and control. However, it is worth highlighting that learning culture is rooted in knowledge culture. Without knowledge appreciation, there is no motivation to learn. This is why both knowledge and learning cultures must be developed to achieve smooth change adaptability.

Moreover, the comparison between models A and B enabled us to expose how powerful learning culture is and how inefficient knowledge culture is if applied as a "standalone." The synergy of knowledge, learning, and collaboration cultures means that none of the KLC cultures alone is as powerful as all these cultures are together. The comparison between models A and B proves this.

Table 4.3a, b and Figure 4.1a, b present the hypotheses verification based on the model with CV inclusion—base and alternative.

Table 4.3 shows hypotheses verification—model with CVs includes (a) Model A (alternative) and (b) Model B (base).

Summing up, generally, the results presented earlier (Figure 4.1a, b, Table 4.3a, b) exposed the essence of the knowledge, learning, and collaboration cultures' synergic influence on organizational intelligence (IQ R^2=.84) and through it also on organizational innovativeness (H2, β = .85***; I R^2=.74). Furthermore, the given results also confirmed that the organizational level, represented by the control variables, matters for the relationships between knowledge, learning, and collaboration cultures and change adaptability (Model A/B; $H_{cv}1$=.19***/.19***; $H_{cv}2$=.22***/.23***; $H_{cv}3$=.17***/.18***).

Continuing, the vital issue to solve by this study is the exploration of how the company culture type (adhocracy, clan, market, and hierarchy) supports or blocks the particular KLC functional culture and how it responds to the management level (organization, division, team), which we found as indeed, significant

Table 4.2 Basic statistics, average variance extracted (AVE) root square, and correlations between variables. (a) Alternative Model A. (b) Base Model B

a)

Model A alternative	*Mean*	*SD*	*AVE*	*CR*	*Cronbach alpha*	*Cv org*	*CV div*	*CV team*	*CC*	*LCm*	*LCc*	*KC*	*IQ*	*I*
Cv org	3.58	2.13	-	-	-	-								
CV div	3.55	2.03	-	-	-	0.674	-							
CV team	3.45	2.09	-	-	-	0.544	0.649	-						
CC	3.58	2.03	0.61	0.83	.804	0.597	0.603	0.596	**0.783**					
LCm	3.13	1.7	0.82	0.93	.94	0.362	0.35	0.434	0.648	**0.904**				
LCc	3.7	2.15	0.62	0.83	.788	0.486	0.486	0.508	0.827(*)	0.719	**0.789**			
KC	4.27	2.5	0.66	0.85	.881	0.402	0.407	0.399	0.672	0.415	0.614	**0.923**		
IQ	3.63	2.04	0.58	0.81	.814	0.719	0.75	0.715	0.836(*)	0.594	0.747	0.607	**0.898**	
I	3.59	2.04	0.58	0.81	.809	0.62	0.646	0.616	0.721	0.512	0.644	0.523	0.862	**0.764**

b)

Model B basic	*Mean*	*SD*	*AVE*	*CR*	*Cronbach alpha*	*CV org*	*CV div*	*CV team*	*CC*	*LCm*	*LCc*	*KC*	*IQ*	*I*
CV org	3.58	2.13	-	-	-	-								
CV div	3.55	2.03	-	-	-	0.674	-							
CV team	3.45	2.09	-	-	-	0.544	0.649	-						
CC	3.58	2.03	0.62	0.81	.804	0.573	0.582	0.583	**0.790**					
LCm	3.13	1.7	0.80	0.94	.94	0.446	0.479	0.436	0.637	**0.893**				
LCc	3.7	2.15	0.60	0.82	.788	0.533	0.496	0.512	0.804(*)	0.606	**0.776**			
KC	4.27	2.5	0.68	0.86	.881	0.357	0.35	0.435	0.637	0.407	0.72	**0.929**		
IQ	3.63	2.04	0.58	0.81	.814	0.723	0.754	0.716	0.806(*)	0.63	0.756	0.591	**0.898**	
I	3.59	2.04	0.58	0.81	.809	0.623	0.65	0.617	0.695	0.543	0.652	0.51	0.862	**0.764**

Note: $n = 640$; CC—collaborative culture; KC—knowledge culture; LCc—learning culture climate component; LCm—learning culture mistake-acceptance component; IQ- collective intelligence of organization; I—internal innovations; *LCc and IQ correlations with CC exceed AVE root square, but these constructs' meanings are clearly different, and their scales do not overlap (Table 3.2, Chapter 3). So, it should be interpreted not as a measurement instrument error but as a natural correlation between measured phenomena (Ronkko & Cho, 2020).

Table 4.3a Model A (alternative) with CVs—hypotheses verification

Hypothesis	*β*		*Verification*	
H1a	.06(.178)		*Rejected*	
H1b	.14(*)		*Sustained*	
H1c	.07 (*)		*Sustained*	
H1d	.29(***)		*Sustained*	
H1e	.54(***)		*Sustained*	
H1f	.62(***)		*Sustained*	
H1g	.32(***)		*Sustained*	
H1h	−.11(*)		*Sustained*	
H1i	.65(***)		*Sustained*	
H1j	.24(**)		*Sustained*	
H2	.85(***)		*Sustained*	
$H_{cv}1$	.19(***)		*Sustained*	
$H_{cv}2$	.23(***)		*Sustained*	
$H_{cv}3$	.18(***)		*Sustained*	
Indirect (mediated) effects analysis				
Mediation expected	*Direct influence*	*Indirect influence*	*Total influence*	*Mediation type*
KC->LCa->IQ	06(.161)	*.06(*)*	*.10 (*)*	*Full mediation*
KC->LCm->IQ		*−.012(*)*		
KC->LCa->LCm->IQ		*.014 (**)*		

Note: $n = 640$; χ^2=450(167); $C_{min}/df = 2.67$; RMSEA = 0.51; CFI = 9.67; TLI = 9.59; ML—maximum likelihood; *$p < .05$; **$p < .01$; ***$p < .001$; ns: not significant result. The indirect effects were measured through a bootstrap approximation obtained by constructing two-sided bias-corrected confidence intervals.

Table 4.3b Model B (base) with CVs—hypotheses verification

Hypothesis	*β*	*Verification*
H1a	.06(.161)	*Rejected*
H1b	.16(**)	*Sustained*
H1c	.08 (*)	*Sustained*
H1d	.25(***)	*Sustained*
H2	.85(***)	*Sustained*
$H_{cv}1$	.19(***)	*Sustained*
$H_{cv}2$	.23(***)	*Sustained*
$H_{cv}3$	.18(***)	*Sustained*

Note: $n = 640$; $\chi^2 = 428$ (161); $C_{min}/df = 2.66$; RMSEA = 0.51; CFI = 9.69; TLI = 9.60; ML—maximum likelihood; *$p < .05$; **$p < .01$; ***$p < .001$; ns: not significant result.

for the focal interaction between the KLC cultures components and the change adaptability (organizational intelligence development). The organizational level was exposed in the main models (Figure 4.1a, b). Figures 4.2–4.5 visualize the moderated effects of managerial levels: division and team considered for the relation between the KLC and IQ separately for each culture type. Precisely,

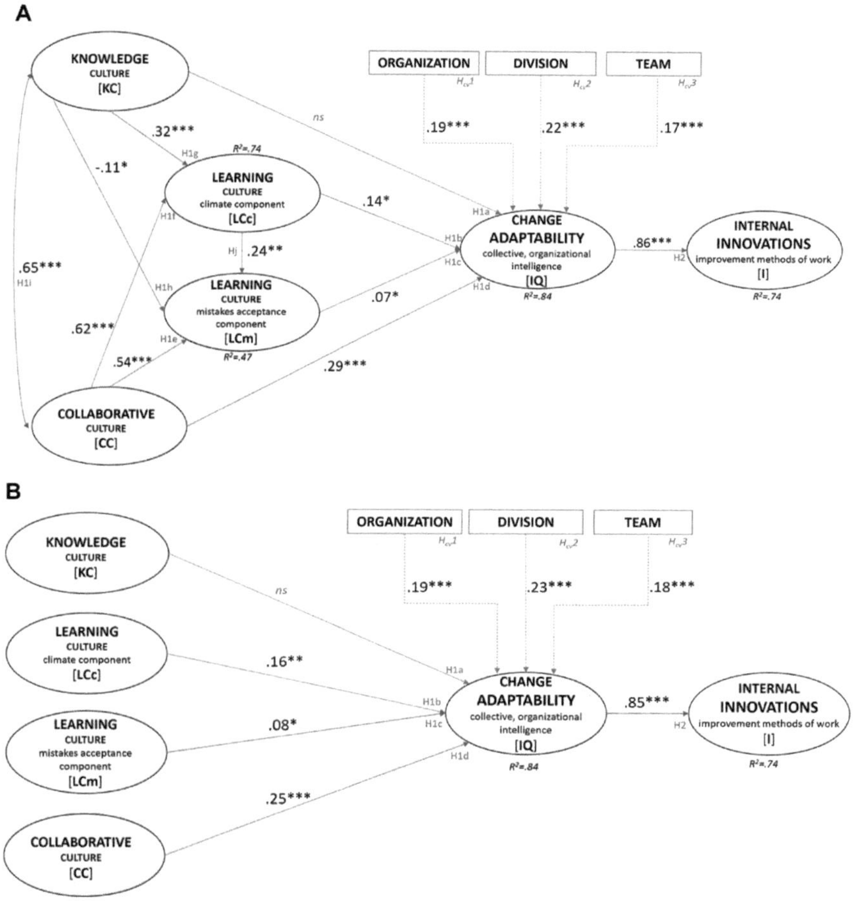

Figure 4.1 Results visualization: (a) Model A (b) Model B

these figures visualize the influence of knowledge, learning, and collaboration cultures on organizational change adaptability made from the perspective of each organizational culture type (adhocracy, clan, market hierarchy) moderated by division and team.

Technically, first, based on the organizational level culture type, the sample was divided into four culture-type sub-samples. Next, for each of the sub-samples, moderated by the team and division effect of each of the KLC components, impact on organizational intelligence was analyzed.

Table 4.3 and Appendix 2 present statistical details of the analyzed moderations through OLS regression made using SPSS PROCESS (Hayes, 2018). Consequently, Figures 4.2–4.5 visualize these effects.

4.2 Knowledge, learning, and collaboration cultures' impact on organizational intelligence analyzed per culture type

4.2.1 Hierarchy culture

Figures 4.2a–c visualize the impact of knowledge, learning, and collaboration cultures on change adaptability (organizational intelligence IQ) moderated by

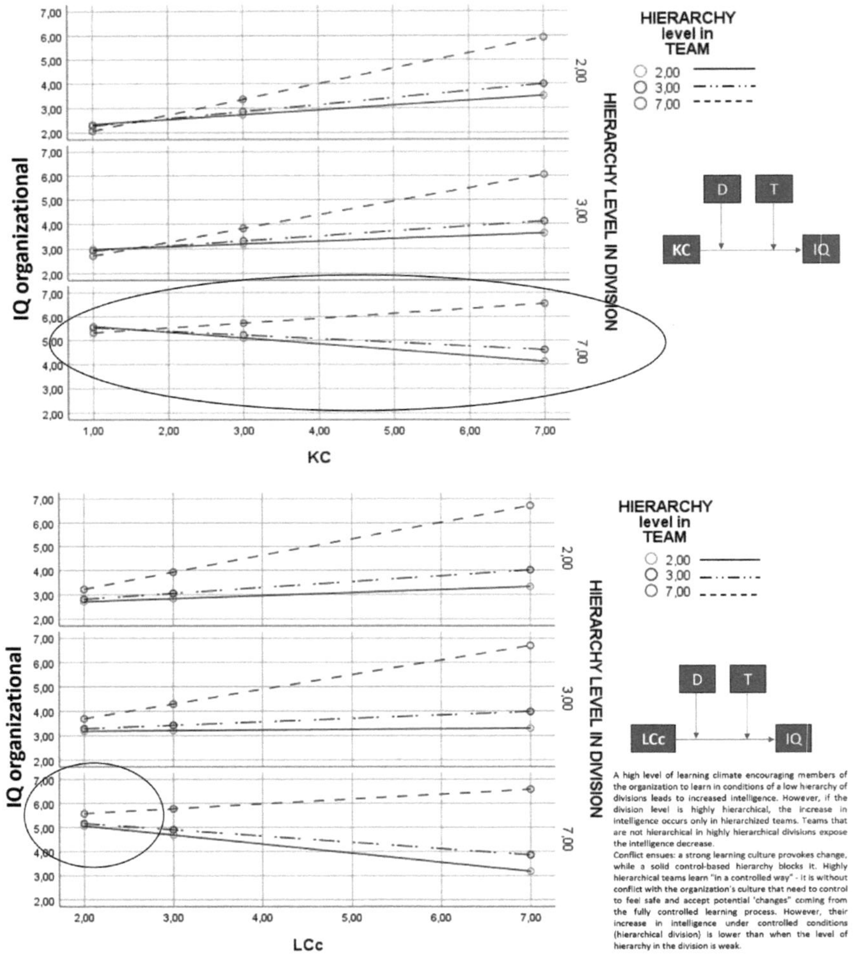

Figure 4.2 Hierarchy: a) knowledge culture—KC; b) learning culture climate component—LCc; and c) collaborative culture—CC

Note: n = 185; learning culture mistake-acceptance component was found insignificant in hierarchy organizations; therefore, its' moderated effect is not presented here. Hierarchy levels: 2—very low; 3—low; and 7—high.

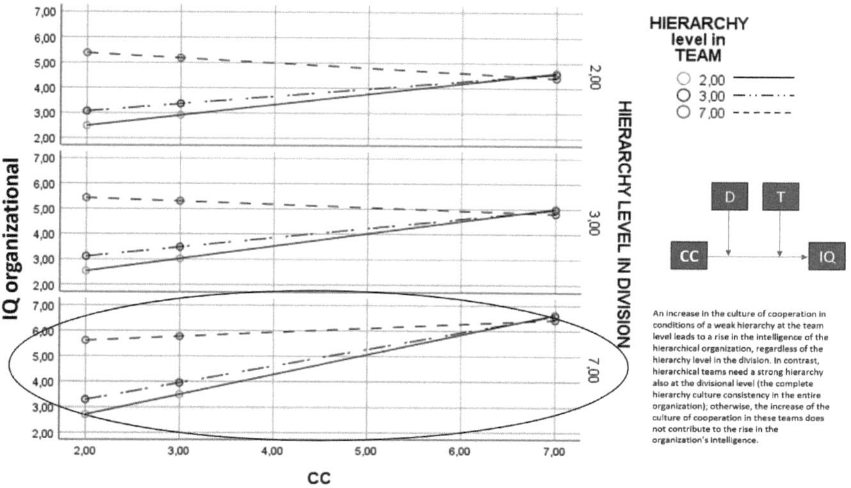

Figure 4.2 (Continued)

team and division. The figures specifically expose how the hierarchy level in teams corresponds with the hierarchy level in divisions when it comes to the impact of the KLC on organizational IQ. These levels are considered: 2—very low; 3—low; 7—high.

The knowledge culture in hierarchical organizations increases organizational intelligence if the team and division level represent a very low or low hierarchy level (Figure 4.2a). If the hierarchy culture in a division is high, then the organizational intelligence goes down for teams that are not hierarchical, but it goes up if the hierarchy in the team is high (effect highlighted by the ellipse in Figure 4.2a). So, the hierarchy culture consistency across levels gives the best effects in organizational intelligence growth thanks to the knowledge culture implementation. So, the hierarchy culture can be efficient for organizational intelligence building through the knowledge culture if all managerial levels respect the hierarchy. If not, hierarchy culture does not work in the collective IQ favor through knowledge culture (KC) implementing.

The same conclusions concern the learning culture climate component (Figure 4.2b), but regarding the collective culture (Figure 4.2c), conclusions for hierarchies are pretty opposite. The stronger the collective culture, the stronger the collective intelligence of the entire hierarchically consistent organization. The exception is the situation observed when the hierarchy level in the team is high, but in the division is very low or low. In such a case, the stronger the collective culture, the lower the intelligence level in strongly hierarchical teams. It aligns with the conclusion that hierarchical organizations' intelligence depends strongly on its consistency (congruence) across the entire organization. So, hierarchy obedience is critical for collective intelligence building. The simultaneous lack of a strong hierarchy at the team and division levels can disturb the strict marching after the leader. It is easy to assume—the more intelligent the hierarchical organization leader, the more intelligent the entire organization. If the leader falls, the organization falls. Furthermore, it is worth stressing that in hierarchical knowledge-driven organizations, the knowledge of culture dominates above the culture of learning, and as a result, mistakes are not seen as a potential source of learning as much as they are seen as a problem (Kucharska & Bedford, 2023; Kucharska & Kopytko, 2024). In the given study, the mistake-acceptance component of learning culture was found insignificant; therefore, its moderated effect is not visualized here. The learning culture is vital if both components are developed in organizations. In hierarchies based on control, there is no space for acceptance of learning from mistakes because there is no tolerance for mistakes. It is why hierarchies are bureaucratic—all the procedures, rules, and procedures are aimed at serving uncertainty avoidance and facilitating full control. Therefore, knowledge culture in hierarchies dominates above learning culture. Moreover, it is worth highlighting that low and very low hierarchical teams, even in a high learning climate, do not perform in favor of collective intelligence if such a team is located in a highly hierarchical division. In fact, the higher the learning climate, the worse the effect is observed (effect highlighted by the ellipse in Figure 4.2b).

Conflict ensues: a strong learning culture provokes change, while a solid control-based hierarchy blocks it. Highly hierarchical teams learn "in a controlled way"—it is without conflict with the organization's culture that needs to be controlled to feel safe and accept potential "changes" coming from the fully controlled learning process. However, their increase in intelligence under controlled conditions (hierarchical division) is lower than when the level of hierarchy in the division is weak. So, hierarchy does not serve well for collective, spontaneous, informal learning, which is precisely the best source of tacit knowledge. So, hierarchies do not serve this way well in terms of innovativeness.

In summary, hierarchies must expose hierarchy congruity and have extremely intelligent leaders to build collective intelligence supported by the KLC approach, but since they have serious trouble with the strong learning culture development, they will never be as intelligent as adhocracies, clans, or markets.

4.2.2 Market culture

Figures 4.3a–d visualize the impact of knowledge, learning, and collaboration cultures on change adaptability (organizational intelligence IQ) moderated by team and division in market culture-dominated organizations. The figures specifically expose how the market culture level in teams corresponds with the market culture level in divisions regarding the impact of the KLC on organizational IQ. These levels are considered: 2—very low; 3—low; 4—middle.

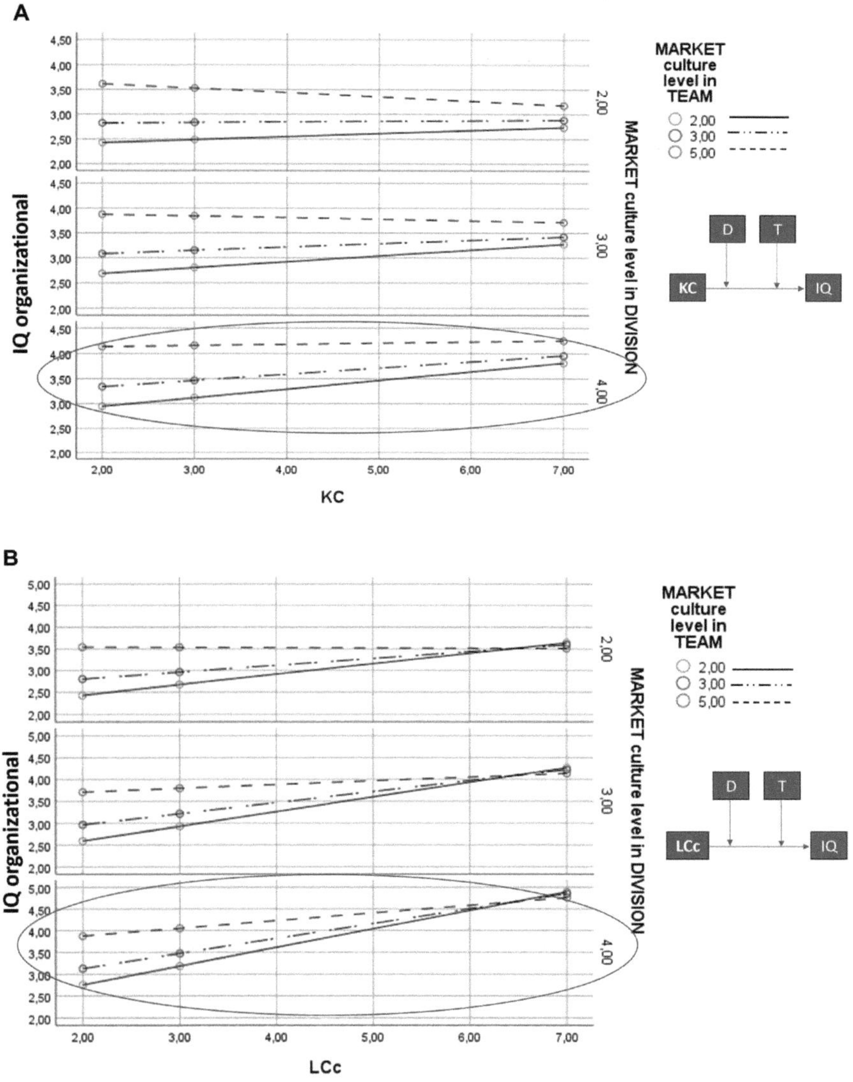

Figure 4.3 Market: a) knowledge culture; b) learning culture climate component—LCc; c) learning culture mistake-acceptance component—LCm; and d) collaborative culture—CC

Note: n = 210; knowledge culture moderated, BOTH team and division effect on organizational intelligence in market organizations was found insignificant; therefore, this effect is not presented here. Market culture levels: 2—very low; 3—low; and 4—middle.

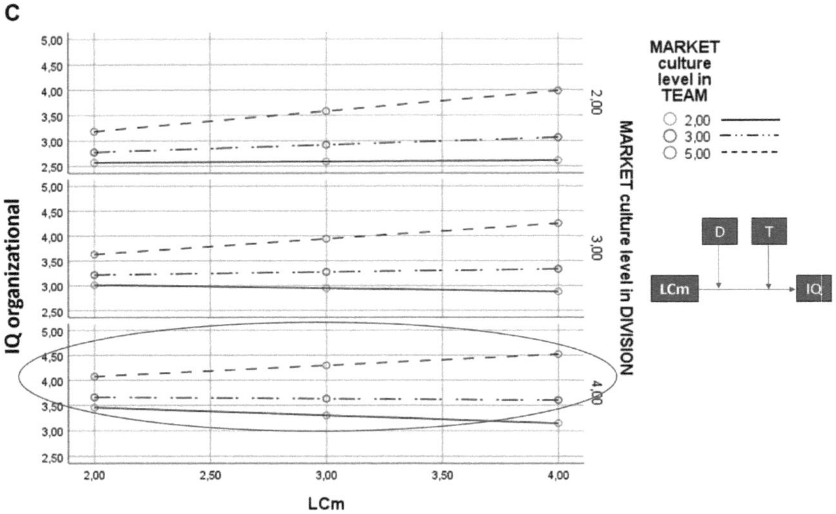

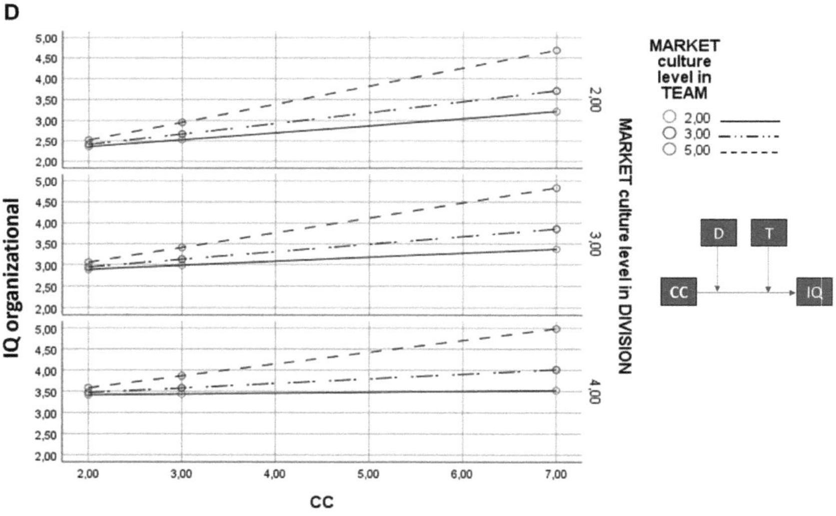

Figure 4.3 (Continued)

Generally, market culture in the given sample is not strong at the division or teal level. Regarding knowledge culture (Figure 4.3a), it supports organizational IQ if the team-division culture is consistent (the effect is highlighted by the ellipse in Figure 4.3a). If not, if the team exposes a higher market culture than division, the effect is negative (the positive KC impact on IQ is decreasing). So, cultural congruence matters.

Regarding the learning culture climate component (Figure 4.3b) and the collaborative culture (Figure 4.3d), the effect is similar: the stronger these functional cultures are, the higher organizational intelligence is observed at all levels. Regarding the mistake-acceptance component (Figure 4.3c), the same pattern is observed but only for the highest level of market culture in teams. For a low level, the mistake-acceptance component development does not enhance organizational intelligence growth.

Regarding collective culture, it serves best to increase IQ when the market culture in division and team is low (Figure 4.3d)—the highest growth is observed. However, the highest IQ level is noted for the opposite—the teams operating in higher observed level 4 of market culture in divisions. Unfortunately, the sample does not allow us to verify how strong the market culture (e.g., 7 level) works with the high level of collaborative culture. However, based on the highest possible observation in our sample levels of the market culture in the team and division, it can be assumed that the highest market culture in the team and division (congruency) is the best effect of the collaboration cultural impact on the organizational IQ is observed. Again, cultural congruence matters in market culture.

4.2.3 *Clan culture*

Figures 4.4a–c visualize the impact of knowledge, learning, and collaboration cultures on change adaptability (organizational intelligence IQ) moderated by team and division in clan culture-dominated organizations. The figures specifically expose how the clan culture level in teams corresponds with the clan

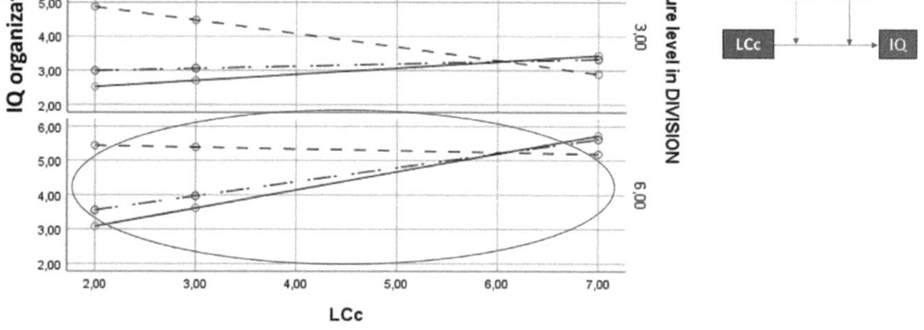

Figure 4.4 Clan: a) learning culture climate component—LCc; b) learning culture mistake-acceptance component—LCm; and c) collaborative culture—CC

Note: $n = 151$; knowledge culture moderated, by BOTH team and division effect on organizational intelligence in clan organizations was found insignificant; therefore, this effect is not presented here. Clan culture levels: 2—very low; 3—low; and 7—high.

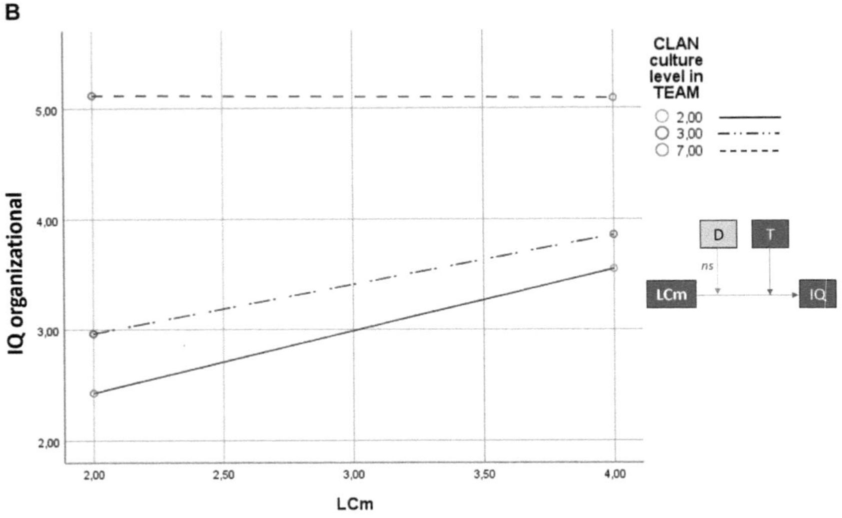

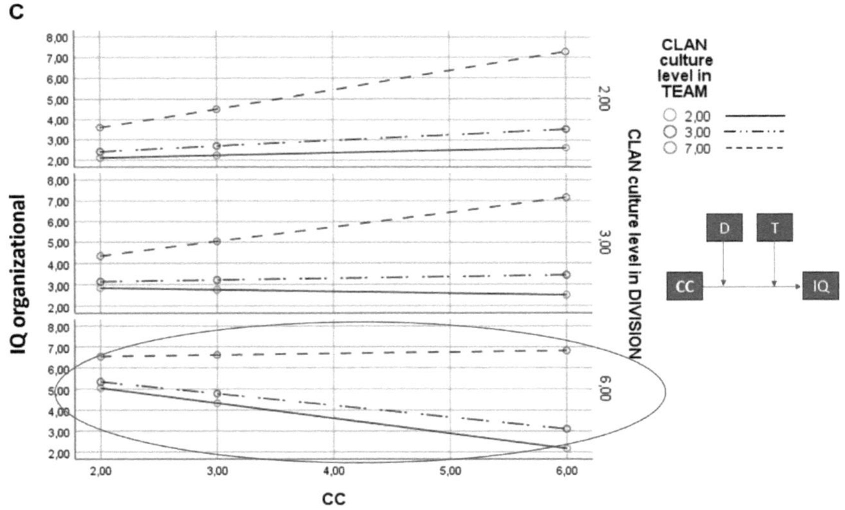

Figure 4.4 (Continued)

culture level in divisions regarding the impact of the KLC on organizational IQ. These levels are considered: 2—very low; 3—low; 7—high.

Knowledge culture moderated by both team and division effect on organizational intelligence in clan culture-dominated organizations was found insignificant. Therefore, this effect is not presented. It suggests that knowledge culture is not powerful in clan culture-dominated knowledge-driven organizations exposed by the study sample.

The learning culture components in clan organizations (Figure 4.4a, b) both support the organizational intelligence if its level of development in teams is low; if its level is high, it works rather opposite. It suggests that clans' characteristic behaviors jeopardize learning. The exception is the situation when the division is also high. In such a case learning culture climate component supports organizational intelligence in clans. Division level is not significant for mistake-acceptance component, but at the team level, indeed it supports the organizational intelligence growth.

Regarding collaborative culture (Figure 4.4c), its high level of development in teams supports organizational intelligence growth. If the clan culture level in teams is low, then the effect is rather opposite—the intelligence decreases. So, for the organizational intelligence growth in clans is critical to develop learning and collaborative cultures in teams and divisions simultaneously. Again, cultural congruence division-team matters, also in clans.

4.2.4 Adhocracy culture

Figures 4.5a–d visualize the impact of knowledge, learning, and collaboration cultures on change adaptability (organizational intelligence IQ) moderated by team and division in adhocracy culture-dominated organizations. The figures specifically expose how the adhocracy culture level in teams corresponds with the clan

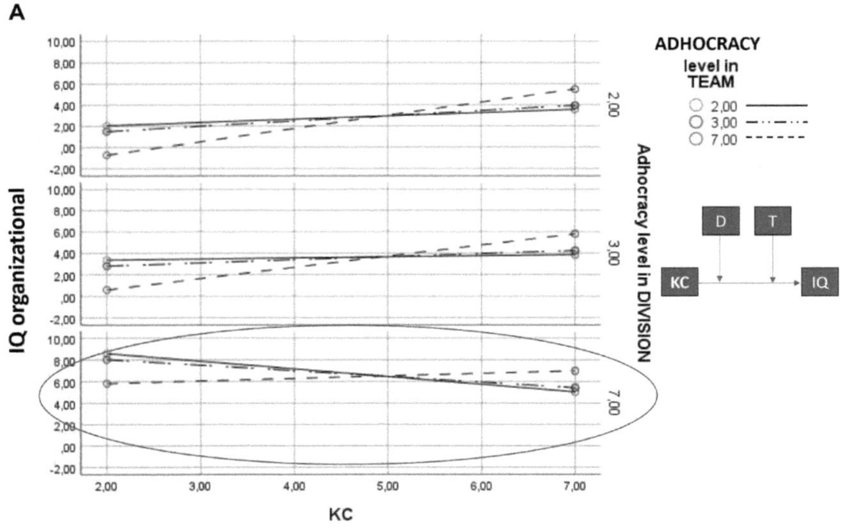

Figure 4.5 Adhocracy: a) knowledge culture—KC; b) learning culture climate component—LCc; c) learning culture mistake-acceptance component—LCm; and d) collaborative culture—CC

Note: n = 94 Clan culture levels: 2—very low; 3—low; and 7—high.

B

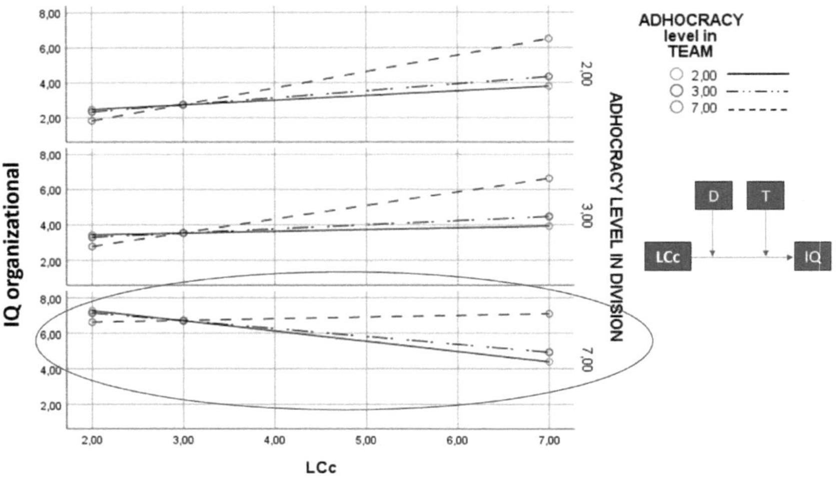

C

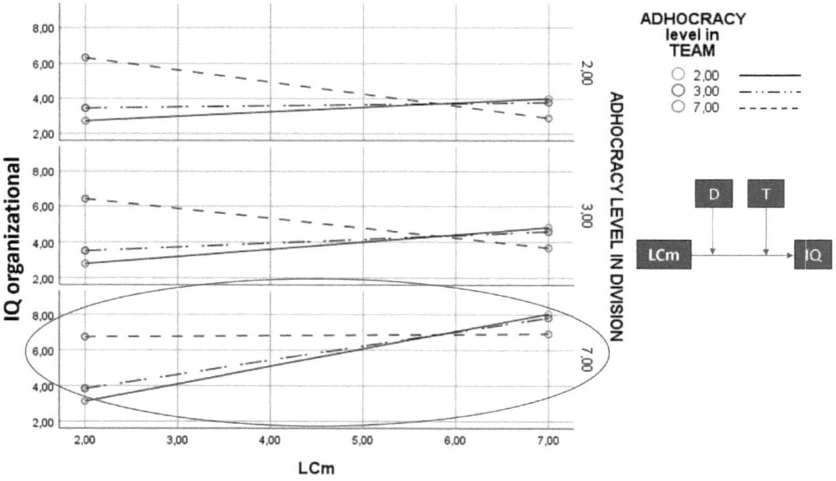

Figure 4.5 (Continued)

culture level in divisions regarding the impact of the KLC on organizational IQ. These levels are considered in the study sample: 2—very low; 3—low; 7—high.

The knowledge culture in adhocracy organizations increases organizational intelligence if the team and division level represent a high adhocracy (Figure 4.5a). If the adhocracy level in the team is low, the knowledge culture does not support intelligence in high-level adhocracy divisions (effect highlighted by the ellipse in Figure 4.5a).

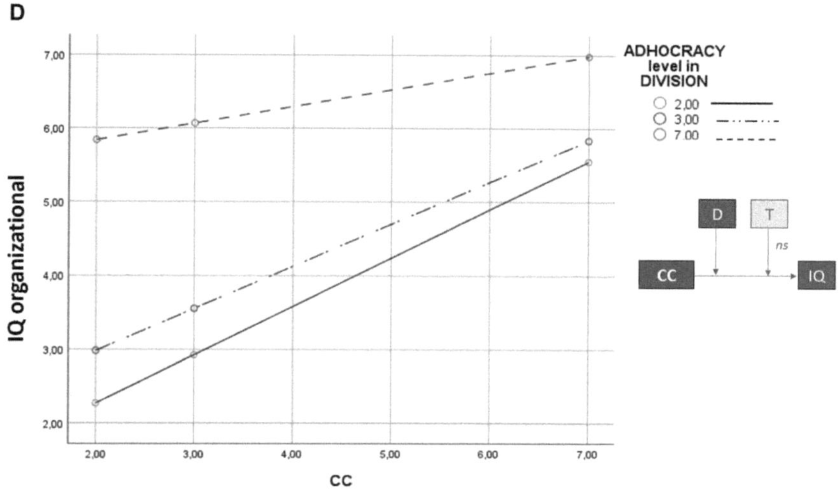

Figure 4.5 (Continued)

The learning culture component of climate (Figure 4.5b) pattern is similar to knowledge culture, but for mistake-acceptance component (Figure 4.5c), it is quite the opposite. In a high level of adhocracy divisions, the developed component of mistakes acceptance supports organizational intelligence even in teams with low adhocracy levels. So, it suggests that the strong adhocracies in divisions are critical for functional knowledge, learning, and collaboration cultures implementation to create organizational intelligence in adhocracy organizations. The collaborative culture's influence on organizational intelligence (Figure 4.5d) confirms this conclusion. Indeed, the moderated effect of the organizational level observed for the collaborative culture influence on organizational intelligence is significant only for the division level, and it is not significant for the team level. So, in light of this, adhocracy culture seems to be the most favorable for implementing the KLC approach to facilitate organizational intelligence and innovativeness development.

In summary, the above analysis of the knowledge, learning, and collaboration cultures on organizational intelligence through company culture typology revealed that the KLC approach best works in adhocracies and exposes a quite promising potential in market culture organizations. Clans and hierarchies can also benefit from KLC implementation however, only if their leaders value the collective intelligence. If not, if the leader prefers to remain the only mind responsible for critical thinking in the organization, then clans and hierarchies would rather have no chance to benefit from the KLC. However, clans seem to have a better disposition to adopt the KLC approach and gain its benefits than hierarchies. Hierarchical cultures develop their intelligence mainly through the cultures of knowledge and collaboration, but only if the hierarchy culture is solid and consistent at all levels. The situation is very similar in clans, but knowledge culture alone is not strong enough to develop intelligence in clans. Learning and collaborative cultures developed simultaneously at team and division level and are critical for intelligence development in clans, which must be promoted by learning-oriented leaders.

Naturally, the attitude toward collective intelligence of market cultures dominated organizations' leaders, and adhocracies leaders matters too. Overall, leaders are those who are the most impactful individuals who can create the company culture. However, in contrary to hierarchies and clans, the characteristics of markets and adhocracies embed the need for collective intelligence.

So, all the given results showed that apart from the studied model elements, the omitted in the model leadership is critical for formulation strategies for implementing the KLC approach to drive adhocracy-, market-, clan-, and hierarchy-dominated cultures to create collective intelligence, sustain openness to changes, and develop agility. Moreover, results showed that culture-type consistency congruency across managerial levels facilitates intelligence building through the KLC approach in all culture types. However, it is much easier to maintain cultural congruency in small organizations, adhocracies, and clans than in medium and large organizations' hierarchies and markets. Given that markets and adhocracies are the most favorable for implementing the KLC approach to promote organizational intelligence and innovativeness, company culture congruency seems to be an efficient facilitator of intelligence building, probably because it is much easier to implement any tactic, plan, or strategy when it is communicated to people with a similar mindset. So, altogether above precisely exposes that the collective intelligence building in clans, hierarchies, adhocracies, and markets requires different strategies and methods.

4.3 The double bias of mistakes views per culture type

The initial data analysis revealed a slight bias in this study sample. It might be caused by the high correlation between the collective motivational learning climate component of learning culture with collaborative culture and collaborative culture and change adaptability high correlation. However, the loading of these scale constructs does not overlap. Therefore, the doubled cognitive bias of mistakes was suspected as potentially responsible for this.

Briefly, the essence of the bias of mistakes (BM) is the contradiction between an often-declared positive attitude toward learning from mistakes—we all know that there is no learning without mistakes, and at the same time the experience of companying them, negative consequences (Kucharska & Kopytko, 2024). Financial and personal consequences, shame, and blame force desperate employees to hide their mistakes. Mistakes hidden or repressed can't be a lesson for anyone—not for the mistake maker or the organization. These adverse outcomes are doubled in organizations by the widespread belief that managers, especially top-level, should never make mistakes, which makes the DBM even more harmful. There is no learning without mistakes. Double bias-affected leaders do not learn from mistakes. They select only easy tasks to secure their "success image" and positions (Dweck, 2017). Double bias affects employees who want to be endorsed to higher positions and hide their mistakes to keep their self-image of a "perfect employee." Diminishing the risk of failure is generally very positive and desired as long as doing so does not block organizational growth. So the DBM can block it.

Authors who explored the bias of mistakes so far studied first the impact of mistake-acceptance component of learning culture (Kucharska & Bedford, 2020; Kucharska & Rebelo, 2022a, 2022b), mistakes bias of mistakes (Rass et al., 2023; Samhan et al., 2023a, 2023b), especially double bias of mistakes (DBM) on organizations (Hosseini et al., 2023; Kucharska & Kopytko, 2024; Kucharska & Bedford, 2024; Kucharska & Karwowska, 2025) and found that it might severely affect intellectual capital, organizational learning, dynamic capabilities, intelligence building, innovativeness, sustainability, and entire organizational growth. Moreover, Kucharska and Kopytko (2024) discovered that gender and position matter for the perception of mistake-acceptance component of the learning culture view. The impact of the DBM on culture type has not yet been studied. So, verifying the post-hoc hypothesis that the bias in the study sample is the effect of the DBM. To verify this, the samples of each culture type were divided into DBM-biased and free-from-bias sub-samples following the procedure by Kucharska and Kopytko (2024) to next compare the effects for each culture type. So, to check on how DBM or lack of it moderates (or not) the relationship between learning culture components (collective, motivational climate for learning component and acceptance of mistakes as a source of learning component), analyses were provided using SPSS PROCESS (Hayes, 2018).

Adhocracy culture was noted as free from the DBM, so this sub-sample was excluded from the analysis. Figures 4.6a–c visualize findings obtained for hierarchy, clan, and market cultures. Appendix 2 presents the statistical details of this analysis.

Regarding Kucharska and Bedford's (2020) study, the relation between motivational climate for learning components and acceptance of mistakes as a source of learning components is that the climate component fosters the acceptance of the mistakes (as a source of learning) component. It is confirmed for the hierarchy culture sub-sample (Figure 4.6a). Precisely, in hierarchy culture, the "collective climate motivator for learning" component fosters the "mistakes acceptance as a source of learning" component stronger for biased employees than for those who are free from bias. So, it can be concluded that the climate component is this way a critical factor in hierarchical cultures. No-biased sub-sample supports mistake-acceptance component even if the "climate" component is zero. However, the best effects are observed precisely for the biased group. It means that the collective climate motivating for learning in hierarchical organizations is a

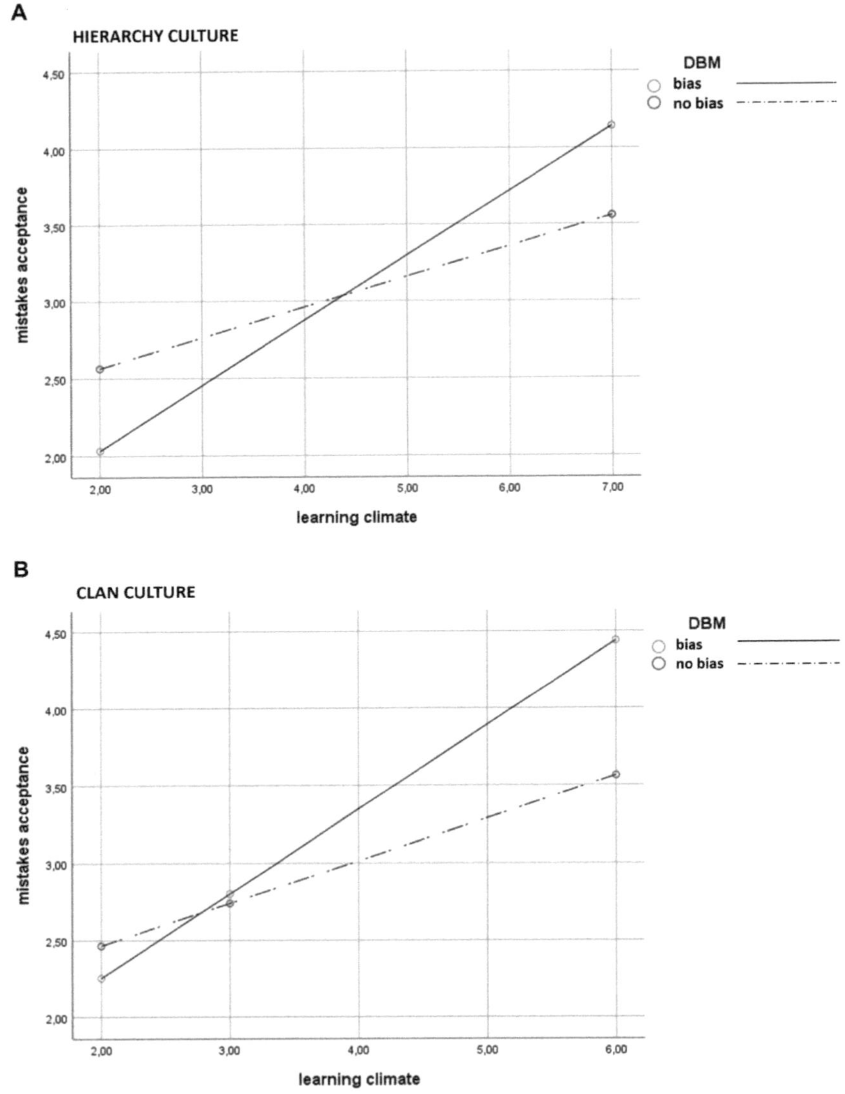

Figure 4.6 Double bias of mistakes tests per culture type: (a) hierarchy culture; (b) clan culture; and (c) market culture

Note: a) $n = 200$; b) $n = 138$; and c) $n = 208$. Adhocracy culture was noted as free from the DBM; therefore, it was excluded from this analysis.

pre-step to enhance the particular hierarchical organization to accept the fact that mistakes happen and if happen should be a source of lessons.

This analysis exposes the potential threat posed by the double bias of mistakes to organizational learning and organizational intelligence. Therefore, it is essential to

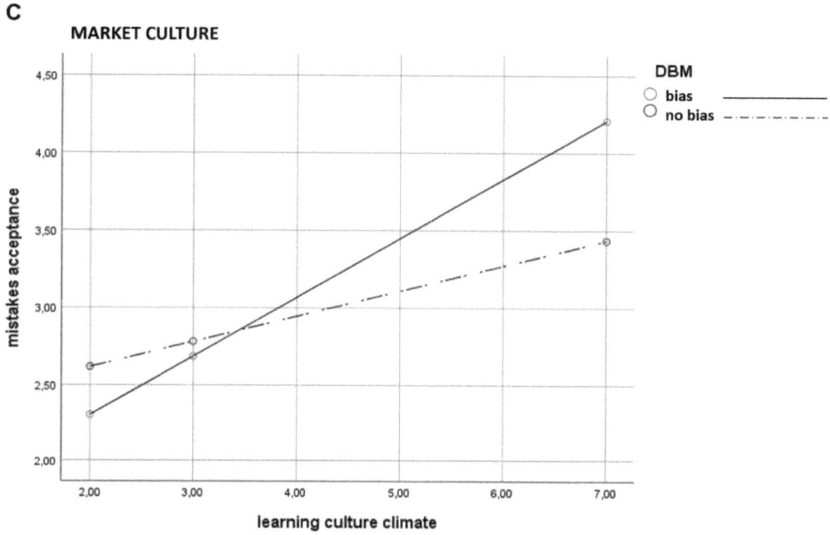

Figure 4.6 (Continued)

understand the phenomenon of the cognitive bias of mistakes and its consequences. Without it, there is a risk that the entire idea of accepting mistakes as a potential source of learning will be simplified by biased minds to mistake tolerance and rejected as ridiculous. Therefore, it is critical to highlight that "mistake-acceptance component" of learning culture is not about promoting mistake tolerance. It is about accepting that even if we remain diligent, we can be mistaken, especially when we dynamically and contextually explore new areas of knowledge instead of statically exploiting old ones and keeping our "comfort zone." Organization needs a culture that promotes diligence but, at the same time, supports critical and creative thinking and acting that is risky by nature. In practice, accepting that mistakes can be a source of valuable learning is not the same as being tolerant of mistakes. On the contrary, it is the first step to managing errors and creating effective systems to avoid mistakes through efficient lessons learned. For hierarchies to develop, a strong learning climate is needed first—it is critical.

The same is observed for clans (Figure 4.6b). However, the distance between the biased and non-biased groups when the learning climate is low is not as big as it is observed in hierarchies, and the effect of the climate component support observed for the biased group is stronger in clans than observed in hierarchies. For market culture organizations (Figure 4.6c), non-biased employees accept learning from mistakes on the higher level than clans and hierarchies, even if the climate component is low. When the climate component is high, no biased group accepts the learning from mistakes component at the same high level as other non-biased employees in hierarchies or clans. Nevertheless, regarding the biased group, most culture employees' effect is lower than the observed for clans.

In summary, the worse the initial conditions for developing acceptance of learning from mistakes, the more efforts must be made to develop a motivational climate for collective learning.

So, the biggest DBM is observed for hierarchy culture. Adhocracy culture does not expose the DBM at all. These cultures are opposite in their natural predispositions to collective formal and informal learning. Markets expose higher natural predispositions to collective learning from mistakes, but clans are those who can benefit the most in collective learning from mistakes acceptance, but only if they put a significant effort in a motivational climate for collective learning development.

References

Becker, T. E., Atnic, G., Breaugh, J. A., Carlson, K. D., Edwards, J. R., & Spector, P. E. (2016). Statistical control in correlational studies: 10 essential recommendations for organizational researchers. *Journal of Organizational Behavior*, *37*(2), 157–167. https://doi.org/10.1002/job.2053

Carlson, K. D., & Wu, J. (2012). The illusion of statistical control: Control variable practice in management research. *Organizational Research Methods*, *15*(3), 413–435.

Dweck, C. S. (2017). *Mindset*. Brown, Little Book Group.

Hayes, A. (2018). *Introduction to mediation, moderation and conditional process analysis: A regression-based approach* (2nd ed.). Guilford Press.

Hosseini, M., Treur, J., & Kucharska, W. (2023). An adaptive network model for a double bias perspective on learning from mistakes within organizations. In *International conference on complex networks and their applications* (pp. 91–103). Springer Nature.

Kucharska, W., & Bedford, D. A. D. (2020). Love your mistakes! They help you adapt to change. How do knowledge, collaboration and learning cultures foster organizational intelligence? *Journal of Organizational Change Management*, *337*, 1329–1354. https://doi.org/10.1108/JOCM-02-2020-0052

Kucharska, W., & Bedford, D. A. D. (2023). *The cultures of knowledge organizations: Knowledge, learning, collaboration (KLC)*. Emerald Publishing Limited.

Kucharska, W., & Bedford, D. A. D. (2024). The KLC cultures' synergy power, trust, and tacit knowledge for organizational intelligence. *Electronic Journal of Knowledge Management*, *22*(2), 18–35.

Kucharska, W., & Karwowska, E. (2025). Company culture matters! Knowledge-driven companies' way to innovations and sustainability. *Social Sciences & Humanities Open*, 11. Article 101268. https://doi.org/10.1016/j.ssaho.2024.101268

Kucharska, W., & Kopytko, A. (2024). Double bias of mistakes: Essence, consequences, and measurement method. *Electronic Journal of Business Research Methods*, *22*(1), 26–42. https://doi.org/10.34190/ejbrm.22.1.3320

Kucharska, W., & Rebelo, T. (2022a). Transformational leadership for researcher's innovativeness in the context of tacit knowledge and change adaptability. *International Journal of Leadership in Education*, 1–22. https://doi.org/10.1080/13603124.2022.2068189

Kucharska, W., & Rebelo, T. (2022b). Knowledge sharing and knowledge hiding in light of the mistakes acceptance component of learning culture-knowledge culture and human capital implications. *The Learning Organization*, *29*(6), 635–655.

Nielsen, B. B., & Raswant, A. (2018). The selection, use, and reporting of control variables in international business research: A review and recommendations. *Journal of World Business*, *53*(6), 958–968. https://doi.org/10.1016/j.jwb.2018.05.003

Rass, L., Treur, J., Kucharska, W., & Wiewiora, A. (2023). Adaptive dynamical systems modelling of transformational organizational change with focus on organizational culture and organizational learning. *Cognitive Systems Research*, *79*, 85–108.

Rönkkö, M., & Cho, E. (2022). An updated guideline for assessing discriminant validity. *Organizational research methods*, *25*(1), 6–14. https://doi.org/10.1177/1094428120968614

Samhan, N., Treur, J., Kucharska, W., & Wiewiora, A. (2023a). An adaptive network model simulating the effects of different culture types and leader qualities on mistake handling and organisational learning. In H. Cherifi, R. N. Mantegna, L. M. Rocha, C. Cherifi, & S. Miccichè (Eds.), *Complex networks and their applications. Studies in computational intelligence* (Vol. 1077). Springer. https://doi.org/10.1007/978-3-031-21127-0_19

Samhan, N., Treur, J., Kucharska, W., & Wiewiora, A. (2023b). Computational simulation of the effects of different culture types and leader qualities on mistake handling and organisational learning. In *Computational modeling of multilevel organisational learning and its control using self-modeling network models* (pp. 363–408). Springer International Publishing.

5 Meaning of the given findings—discussion

Based on the results presented earlier, this study brought novelty in the following areas:

1. The KLC culture's significant impact on organizational intelligence and innovativeness is confirmed for all culture types.
2. The KLC-approach components' impact on intelligence varies between company culture types and management levels (team, division, and organization); the culture-type consistency (congruence) is the potential facilitator of the organizational IQ.
3. The biggest doubled bias of mistakes is observed for hierarchy culture. Adhocracy culture does not expose DBM at all. These cultures are opposite in their natural predispositions to collective formal and informal learning. Markets expose higher natural predispositions to collective learning from mistake acceptance, but clans are those who can benefit the most in collective learning from mistake acceptance, but only if they put a significant effort into a motivational climate for collective learning development.

In the following, each of these key findings is discussed more in depth.

5.1 Knowledge, learning, and collaboration cultures significantly affect organizational intelligence

The essence of the KLC culture's synergy idea is the simultaneous implementation of functional cultures of knowledge, learning, and collaboration to grow knowledge-driven organizations (Kucharska & Bedford, 2023). Authors claim that these cultures support and strengthen one another to develop favorable conditions for new knowledge creation and utilization, which impacts the organizational ability to adapt to externally induced changes. This organizational change adaptability is rooted in collective organizational intelligence, which simultaneously is potent to internally dedicated changes oriented to organizational efficacy improvements. The KLC culture's synergy was assumed to be

DOI: 10.4324/9781003485230-7

extremely powerful for strengthening the collective intelligence-building behaviors (Kucharska & Bedford, 2023) that are focal for human and relational capital development, and this is also true for organizational intelligence. The given study results confirmed it.

Therefore, KLC cultures are worth to be implemented simultaneously. Moreover, there is a risk that organizations with a learning culture developed without collaboration are stuck at the individual level of learning only. Similarly, it is clear that a knowledge culture developed without a multilevel learning culture jeopardizes the organization's growth. In such a case, only old, proven knowledge exploitation is accepted. That extreme situation leads to the rejection of new knowledge that is usually rationalized by the need for business safety security—that is nothing more than a ruse for intellectual laziness or personal barriers of fixed-minded managers. Similarly, knowledge culture rejects the mistake-acceptance component of learning culture that makes learning problematic. Can we learn without mistakes? Obviously, we cannot. So, a knowledge culture without learning and collaboration also jeopardizes organizational development. There is no development without learning. Moreover, the learning climate component of learning culture is insufficient for explicit knowledge sharing, and collaboration is needed to make learning and sharing happen. So, knowledge sharing, organizational intelligence, and innovativeness are vital benefits of the synergy that offers the KLC-culture simultaneous implementation and cultivation. Trust strengthens this effect.

Many organizations assume that if they espouse and even live a knowledge culture, by definition, they have a learning culture and a collaboration culture. It is more apparent than expected. Each of the KLC- sub-cultures requires attention and some effort to be implemented. All of these functional company cultures can exist independently. The effect will be subliminal—but such existence is possible and happens. Collaboration alone creates organizations where everybody feels good, but the company needs to perform. Knowledge culture alone can create organizations that focus too much on perfectionism and control the "status quo" that blocks development. Learning culture alone can focus too much on constantly seeking new, better solutions. Such a constant state can be problematic for organizational learning and development if we omit transforming new knowledge into new organizational rules, procedures, and daily routines. So, the KLC cultures approach can be implemented by having a complete organizational understanding of how all its components affect one another.

Company culture is an asset that requires design, implementation, and management to leverage the company by supporting its strategy. If company culture and strategy misalign, there is no chance for success in the long run. So, knowledge-driven organizations that develop their intellectual capital should implement KLC cultures and take full advantage of the synergy needed for organizational innovativeness. There is no chance for innovativeness without collective intelligence.

KLC cultures significantly impact organizational intelligence—this study confirmed the synergic influence of knowledge, learning, and collaboration cultures (the KLC approach) on organizational intelligence (collective change adaptability). This confirmation means that the entire company as a community should show respect for knowledge and be brave in seeking new knowledge that is up to date in new contexts instead of ignoring new reality and rejecting new knowledge due to intellectual and operational laziness.

Intellectual laziness can keep an organization away from any change implementation that always requires some effort to be done with success. It is why the lack of collective intelligence is equal to intellectual laziness. It is much easier to "keep things as they are" in organizations and repeat the same way of action every day and create the illusion of safety. Intelligent organizations change themselves internally—it is a natural consequence of adaptability.

Learning individually and collectively is an intellectual effort. Intelligent organizations are those that make this effort and develop collectively. Such organizations are open to growth and development, constantly learn from positive and negative experiences, and collaborate smoothly. So, knowledge, learning, and collaboration in functional cultures are needed to support organizational intelligence in knowledge-driven organizations.

5.2 The impact of the different components of the KLC approach on intelligence varies depending on company culture type and management level (team, division, and organization), and culture-type consistency (congruence)

Consistency was noted in the section of results as a potential facilitator of the KLC-approach implementation in any organizational culture. This finding is in opposition to Cameron and Freeman's (1991) study, which, based on the higher education sector in the US, did not notice any significant differences in organizational effectiveness between organizations with and without congruent cultures. It might be that this difference between Cameron and Freeman (1991) and the current study comes from sample issues (the current sample is half bigger, and it represents mixed sectors, almost equally small as big companies), or it might be that this difference comes from the congruency measurement method. Cameron and Freeman (1991) assessed congruency as high if relations, leadership style, strategic focus, and culture type are aligned. In this research organizational culture is assessed as congruent if respondents for all managerial levels (team, division, and organization) reported the same culture type.

Sample characteristics analysis (Table 3.3b, Chapter 3), exposed that hierarchical organizations dominate in the sample and that these organizations are usually not consistent in their culture and, these organizations are mostly big and large. So, it is totally clear that it is much more difficult to keep organizational consistency in big and large companies (markets and hierarchies) than in micro and small (adhocracies and clans). However, the fact is that this lack of congruency can cause some managerial troubles (Akpa et al., 2021). So, it is assumed that this lack of cultural consistency across the entire organization (team, division, and organization) as well as the hierarchy culture characteristics can probably be the root of hierarchical organizations' troubles in change adaptability achievements because hierarchies can't be learned out of control. Such kind of controlled learning is based on explicit knowledge mostly. So, hierarchies usually learn of what is perfectly known, which Argyris and Schon (1978) named competency of a single loop of learning—hierarchies learn to perfectly repeat actions (rules, procedures, policies) to secure the achievement of the expected, predictable result.

But at the same time, market culture organizations (Table 3.3b, Chapter 3) are similarly inconsistent in teams and divisions as hierarchies in this study sample. However, all the KLC-approach components serve in markets much better than hierarchies. This might be because market cultures perform better knowledge management than other cultures (Kangas, 2009). Market organizations focus on external market changes more strongly than other cultures. They focus on the market and care about market knowledge, so they learn. Knowledge management is a focal part of organizational intelligence building (Jarrahi et al., 2023; Rothberg & Erickson, 2017). So, to understand this seemingly controversial effect, we must compare the key focus of market organizations and the key focus of the hierarchical cultures. Precisely, hierarchical cultures focus on uncertainty avoidance and see a sense of security in procedures, ordering working conditions, and order and control. Market culture focuses on the value. So, if market culture members see the value in knowledge, learning, and collaboration—then they follow it. In a hierarchy culture, if the knowledge, learning, and collaboration are not included in company policies or are not executed—hierarchy company members do not care about it. This is also the essence of why markets and clans are more efficient in intelligence building than hierarchies. Markets and clans can learn from contextual events, can gain active knowledge from unexpected actions and improve their courses of action, including entire business models (double-loop learning; Argyris & Schon, 1978).

Clan cultures focus on relationships among members, so clans build their intelligence mostly thanks to a culture of collaboration and learning, including the acceptance of mistakes.

Collaboration matters in hierarchies, but it is extremely powerful in clans.

Hierarchies do not accept mistakes and focus mostly on static explicit knowledge that can be controlled rather than on dynamic learning and tacit knowledge discovery that consequences are not predictable as perfectly as solutions based on many times verified (procedural) knowledge. What is important, in hierarchical organizations, the higher level of hierarchy in the division the stronger organizational intelligence is even if the knowledge culture is low. What is worth to stress, this organizational level of collective intelligence stimulated by the hierarchy obeys is quite strong. It means that hierarchical organizations' intelligence comes mostly from their leaders, not from collective cooperation. As is observed based on this research, an increase in the culture of cooperation in conditions of a weak hierarchy at the team level leads to a rise in the intelligence of the hierarchical organization, regardless of the hierarchy level in the division. In contrast to low hierarchical teams, the strong hierarchical teams need a strong hierarchy also at the divisional level (the complete hierarchy culture consistency in the entire organization); otherwise, the increase of the culture of cooperation in these teams does not contribute to the rise in the organization's intelligence.

So, the conclusion is that hierarchical organizations to be intelligent must be consistent in the hierarchy at the organizational and division level and must be led by an intelligent leader. These factors seem to be critical for intelligence building in hierarchies. They are, because hierarchies face troubles in learning outside of hierarchies. It is observed based on this research (Figure 4.2b, Chapter 4) that a high level of learning climate encouraging members of the organization to learn in conditions of a low hierarchy of divisions leads to increased intelligence. However, if the division level is highly hierarchical, the increase in intelligence occurs only in hierarchized teams. Teams that are not hierarchical in highly hierarchical divisions expose the intelligence decrease when the climate of learning grows. It is probably because the cultural conflict ensues: a strong learning culture provokes change, while a solid control-based hierarchy blocks it. Highly hierarchical teams learn "in a controlled way"—it is without conflict with the organization's culture that need to be controlled to feel safe and accept potential "changes" coming from the fully controlled learning process. However, their increase in intelligence under controlled conditions (hierarchical division) is lower than when the level of hierarchy in the division is weak. The practical implications of such a situation might be severe. Details are presented in Section 6.3 (Chapter 6).

So, going back to the culture consistency issue—adhocracies and clans are the most consistent across levels, but at the same time, those culture types are represented mostly by the small organizations. So, keeping culture consistency in a small organization is easier than in big entities. Market culture-dominated organizations, in this study sample is represented mostly by big and large entities The most favorable for the KLC approach are markets and adhocracies—then consistency in organizational culture can be seen as KLC-approach and organizational IQ relation facilitator, probably because culture congruency makes any tactic, plan, or strategy implementation much easier when it is communicated with people reflecting the similar mindset. Another important issue is the company culture-strategy alignment (Kucharska & Bedford, 2023). It might be that hierarchies' troubles with organizational intelligence buildings come from the company-culture-strategy misalignment. It happens when ambitious strategic aims surpass the cultural capacity of the organization reflected in its members' shared mindset.

Summarizing, the essence of this study was an insight into organizational IQ building through the KLC approach by focusing on the particular culture type. From this perspective market culture and adhocracies are the most efficient in the KLC-approach implementation—these types can select those of functional cultures that support their strategic aims and bring themselves and their organizations value. Adhocracies and markets assess this value mostly from the external perspective, which naturally requires intelligence building. So, these cultures, through their external focus, are naturally motivated to build intelligence.

Figure 5.1 visualizes all the results obtained in Chapter 4 regarding the impact of the KLC and company culture type on organizational intelligence. The empirical research summary exposes that the synergy of knowledge, learning, and collaboration functional cultures (the KLC approach) impact organizational intelligence, and this impact varies depending on company culture type (adhocracy, clan, bureaucracy, and market) and management level (team, division, and organization).

The figure exposes each KLC component's impact on the intelligence building in the particular culture-type condition. The broad arrows expose a strong impact, which is understood as the summary of its impact (β) and its significance

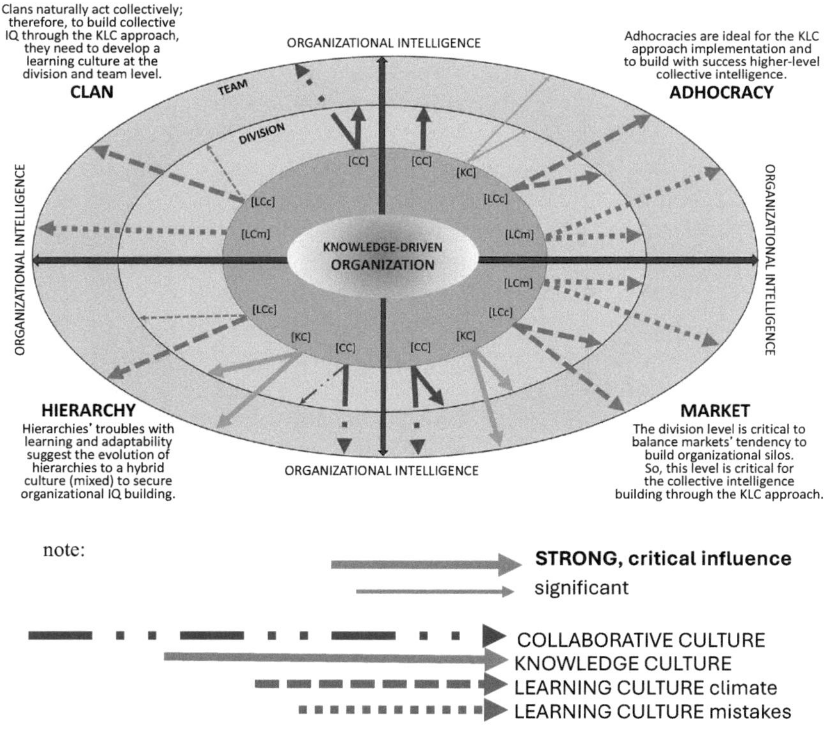

Figure 5.1 KLC and company culture type impact on organizational intelligence—summary

(p). Those KLC components that direct impact revealed to be insignificant for the particular culture type were excluded from this visualization. It is the LCm impact on intelligence building in hierarchies and KC impact in clan culture-dominated organizations. The fact that those KLC components' direct impact is not significant suggests that hierarchical and clan organizations require specific methods of fostering these cultures indirectly. Moreover, the fact that some KLC components impact some culture types stronger and others weaker in teams and divisions also suggests that implementing the KLC approach in each of the given company culture types requires different methods tailored to the management level to gain the competency of smooth adaptability. Part II of this book provides these methods.

5.3 Double bias of mistakes impact on collective intelligence and culture type—discussion

The essence of the DBM is the contradiction between an often-declared positive attitude toward learning from mistakes and the experience of companying them and negative consequences. This chapter investigates the potential threat posed by the double bias of mistakes (DBM) to organizational learning and, finally, organizational intelligence. Therefore, it is essential to understand the phenomenon of the cognitive bias of mistakes and its consequences. Without it, there is a risk that the entire idea of accepting mistakes as a potential source of learning will be simplified by biased minds to mistake tolerance and rejected as ridiculous. Therefore, it is critical to highlight that this study is not about promoting mistake tolerance. It is about accepting that even if we remain diligent, we can be mistaken, especially when we dynamically and contextually explore new areas of knowledge instead of statically exploiting old ones and keeping our "comfort zone." Organization needs a culture that promotes diligence but, at the same time, supports critical and creative thinking and acting that is risky by nature. In practice, accepting that mistakes can be a source of valuable learning is not the same as being tolerant of mistakes. On the contrary, it is the first step to managing errors and creating effective systems to avoid mistakes through efficient lessons learned.

The Double Bias of Mistakes Theory (Kucharska & Kopytko, 2024) posits that the conflict between positive attitudes and beliefs regarding learning processes and negative attitudes and beliefs toward mistakes experiences, particularly evident among control managers, may impede organizational learning from mistakes. Consequently, this obstacle can adversely impact organizational intelligence (Kucharska & Bedford, 2024). DBM is a particularly threatening factor that can jeopardize the deep, contextual, and lifelong learning of knowledge workers, especially experts. In biased business environments, even if knowledge is gained from mistakes, this knowledge can be hidden because of the mistake's shame (Kucharska & Rebelo, 2022a). Financial and personal repercussions, shame, and blame compel employees to conceal their errors. These adverse effects are exacerbated by the prevalent belief within organizations that managers are infallible, thereby intensifying the detrimental impact. Leaders influenced by this double bias tend to select only straightforward tasks to safeguard their positions, while employees aspiring for promotion conceal their mistakes to uphold the image of the "ideal employee." Although avoiding the risk of failure is not inherently problematic, it becomes detrimental when it impedes organizational growth. There is no learning without mistakes. So, how can then experts and leaders learn? The mastery of being an outstanding expert comes from experience, precisely from constant contextual lifelong learning from all experiences—from successes and failures. Double bias-affected leaders do not learn from mistakes. Diminishing the risk of failure is generally very positive and desired as long as doing so does not block organizational growth. So, the DBM can block it. Former studies showed that acceptance of mistakes as a source of learning differs among genders (Kucharska & Rebelo, 2022b; Kucharska, 2024). Therefore, because of its potentially severe consequences, this phenomenon is worth exploring, especially in the context of gender differences.

This research has several practical implications. First, since the DBM can severely jeopardize organizational learning, it must be neutralized. The best way to do this is to implement both components containing the learning culture: the learning climate (shared motivation to learn) and the acceptance of mistakes as a source of learning. It is worth highlighting that we do not promote negligence. We promote humanity (on the contrary to exaggerated perfection). We promote the attitude of acceptance that mistakes happen when we act in dynamic and high-uncertainty conditions, even if we are perfectly diligent, which is the essence of learning from experience in a changing context. That is how experts learn at work—they gather tacit knowledge from dynamically changing contexts. This way, gained tacit knowledge can also be called knowledge-based intuition—a skill precisely desired by experts; it is intelligence gained thanks to years of contextual, practical experiences. Experts are leaders of intelligence, so the shared intelligence-building essence is the shared collective learning, also from mistakes. This is why the primary practical implication of this study is implementing the learning culture. This study showed that both learning culture components mediate explicit and tacit knowledge sharing driven by knowledge culture and supported by collaboration. Any culture should be implemented by exposing leaders to desired behaviors. The desired behavior regarding learning culture is the constant, contextual learning from good and bad experiences. If a mistake is made, then it should be claimed, reported, and discussed to avoid similar events in the future by proper procedural corrections. Mistakes are harsh, sometimes costly lessons, so neither individual nor the organization can waste the knowledge they bring. Therefore, to implement the learning culture, leaders should be first who expose the good examples, and admit mistakes, and share the knowledge gained thanks to this harsh event. Immediately implemented improvements enable us to avoid similar mistakes in the future. Accepting mistakes as a learning source is not to promote negligence among knowledge workers, it is about promoting constant learning from all possible sources and contexts (long-life contextual learning). Experts and organization leaders should be the best examples of learning behaviors they want to see among your organization members. An organization is a group of people who want to achieve together an aim that each member cannot complete alone. So, for any organization's success, it does not matter what people can achieve alone. The essence of organizational success is what people can achieve together. So, collective instead of individual growth matters more. Therefore, if you want your organization to grow, enhance the multilevel, collective learning. Organizational intelligence is not the sum of individual iQs but a collective ability to adapt smoothly together as a community

DBM represents the negative perception of mistakes that might cause troubles in gaining new knowledge from mistakes that is doubled by the common belief that the legit for power holding (being a boss) is being perfect and never making mistakes. Precisely if mistakes are seen negatively in the particular society then shame blocks collective learning—people hide mistakes or blame others to avoid shame. Moreover, shame can block a personal learning. Some popular strategies of coping with shame are, for example, rejection shame through trying to forget the mistake event, ignorance through the rationalization that "nothing really happened," rejection the reflection though diminishing consequences "there is nothing to think about," and other attempts to withdraw the event from active consciousness. Therefore, the culture of the continuous learning should develop not only the component encouraging learning (the climate component) but also the component of mistakes acceptance as a source of learning. So, both these components matters to support collective learning. Figures 4.6a–c exposed clearly that the climate component supports mistake-acceptance component, and this support is very important for societies, communities, groups, or teams affected by the mistakes' cognitive bias, especially if it is doubled (DBM). The common mistakes bias blocks mainly personal learning, whereas DBM strongly impacts organizational learning. Precisely, managers select easy tasks to avoid any errors. In such a case organization avoids any risk, and their development is jeopardized in the long run (Kucharska & Bedford, 2023). The remedy for the double bias of mistakes is a strong culture of learning with the mistake-acceptance component as a potential source of learning development.

References

Akpa, V. O., Asikhia, O. U., & Nneji, N. E. (2021). Organizational culture and organizational performance: A review of literature. *International Journal of Advances in Engineering and Management*, *3*(1), 361–372.

Argyris, C., & Schon, D. A. (1978). *Organisational learning*. Addison Wesley.

Cameron, K. S., & Freeman, S. J. (1991). Cultural congruence, strength and type: Relationships to effectiveness. *Research in Organizational Change and Development*, *5*, 23–58.

Jarrahi, M. H., Askay, D., Eshraghi, A., & Smith, P. (2023). Artificial intelligence and knowledge management: A partnership between human and AI. *Business Horizons*, *66*(1), 87–99. https://doi.org/10.1016/j.bushor.2022.03.002

Kangas, L. M. (2009). Assessing the value of the relationship between organizational culture types and knowledge management initiatives. *Journal of Leadership Studies*, *3*(1), 29–38.

Kucharska, W. (2024). Self-perceived personal brand equity of knowledge workers by gender in light of knowledge-driven organizational culture: Evidence from Poland and the United States. *SAGE Open*, *14*(1). https://doi.org/10.1177/21582440241227280

Kucharska, W., & Bedford, D. A. D. (2023). *The cultures of knowledge organizations: Knowledge, learning, collaboration (KLC)*. Emerald Publishing Limited.

Kucharska, W., & Bedford, D. A. D. (2024). The KLC cultures' synergy power, trust, and tacit knowledge for organizational intelligence. *Electronic Journal of Knowledge Management*, *22*(2), 18–35.

Kucharska, W., & Kopytko, A. (2024). Double bias of mistakes: Essence, consequences, and measurement method. *Electronic Journal of Business Research Methods*, *22*(1), 26–42. https://doi.org/10.34190/ejbrm.22.1.3320

Kucharska, W., & Rebelo, T. (2022a). Knowledge sharing and knowledge hiding in light of the mistakes acceptance component of learning culture-knowledge culture and human capital implications. *The Learning Organization*, *29*(6), 635–655.

Kucharska, W., & Rebelo, T. (2022b). Transformational leadership for researcher's innovativeness in the context of tacit knowledge and change adaptability. *International Journal of Leadership in Education*, 1–22. https://doi.org/10.1080/13603124.2022.2068189

Rothberg, H., & Erickson, G. S. (2017). Big data systems: Knowledge transfer or intelligence insights? *Journal of Knowledge Management*, *21*(1), 92–112. https://doi.org/10.1108/JKM-07-2015-0300

6 What else do we need to know?—emerging questions raised from limitations and implications

6.1 Knowledge, learning, and collaboration approach, intelligence, and company culture type relations—what else do we need to know?

1. The study results showed that culture-type congruency across managerial levels facilitates intelligence building through the KLC approach for all culture types. It is very true. But at the same time, we know that, for example, production division aims, strategies, and working methods significantly differ from the R&D division. It might be that in the same company, we have both of them and even more functional divisions that consequently have their own specific aims, strategies, and working methods. That logically can require specific cultures that align with these aims, strategies, and methods. So, the question arises: how can the culture of a multi-functional, complex company be managed to secure its efficacy?
2. It has been discovered that culture-type consistency across the management level (team, division, and organization) matters for the organizational IQ, so consequently also for innovativeness. Therefore, it would also be beneficial for better strategic guidelines formulation to explore this issue more in depth. Precisely, it is still unknown; if indeed, some of the culture types as, for example, hierarchy, will always be less intelligent than adhocracies or markets, and it is still not verified empirically; however, it is assumed in this chapter that hierarchies should evolve to hybrid forms to be able to build their change adaptability and innovativeness that are necessary today not only to successfully compete but to simply survive in a dynamically changing world and critically needed to grow. Summing up, it is also not known what kind of hybrids are possible in hierarchy of reality and efficient for intelligence building and how to manage such hybrids, especially since the current study exposed that cultural-type consistency is the most efficient. Does it make sense to create hybrids? Such a question remains open.
3. The study showed that the KLC-approach components' impact on intelligence varies between company culture types and management levels (team, division, and organization). So, the practical question arises of how to implement

DOI: 10.4324/9781003485230-8

the KLC in each type of culture and how to manage it to gain the best benefits. Part II of this book will deliver some guidelines.

4. Conclusion from the results section suggested that the omitted in the model leadership is critical for formulation strategies for implementing the KLC approach to drive adhocracy-, market-, clan-, and hierarchy-dominated cultures to create collective intelligence. It was highlighted that leaders who want to implement the KLC must first expose the KLC cultures and, next, execute it. But the question arises if any other critical skills, habits, and behaviors of the potential "dream leader" that could best serve a particular culture type for collective intelligence building are omitted.
5. It is proved in this chapter that, indeed, the KLC cultures significantly impact organizational intelligence. But at the same time, it is also exposed that the KLC-approach components' impact on intelligence varies between company culture types and management levels (team, division, and organization)—this study revealed this very clearly. Based on this, the conclusion has been formulated that the implementation of the KLC requires different methods of implementation, and the effect of the KLC implementation visible in change adaptability and innovativeness will not be equal. Unfortunately, this study sample size did not enable to verify of this statement directly empirically through constructing four separate SEM models representing each type of culture but concluding from all results given, it seems to be clear that the effects of this implementation visible in internal innovativeness will not be equal. So, a deeper exploration is needed to expose these differences and formulate more precise practical guidelines.
6. It was also exposed that the cognitive double bias of mistakes (DBM) varies per culture type. The most biased type is a hierarchy; the less is adhocracy. Since there is no learning without mistakes, and based on the presented findings, it was concluded that hierarchies will expose the biggest problems with learning and change adaptability which is in line with the existing literature (Rass et al., 2023; Wiewiora et al., 2019), there is a question about the future of hierarchies. Should they evolve into hybrids as it is suggested earlier in this chapter or should they simply be dedicated to entire organizations operating in sectors based on the repeatable actions that to be competitive should achieve perfection but do not require learning, a higher-level change adaptability skills or innovativeness? This is a question that also remains open.
7. Apart from the studied model elements, the omitted in the model leadership is critical for formulation strategies for implementing the KLC approach to drive adhocracy-, market-, clan-, and hierarchy-dominated cultures to create collective intelligence, sustain openness to changes, and develop agility. So, culture type determine a different leadership (Klein et al., 2013; Kargas & Varoutas, 2015; Gao, 2017; Koehn, 2022). Generally speaking, leadership seeks to foster an atmosphere conducive to implementing organizational goals and strategies (Kotter, 1996).

8. Moreover, the study results given in this book showed that culture-type consistency congruency across managerial levels facilitates intelligence building through the KLC approach in all culture types. However, it is much easier to maintain cultural congruency in small organizations, adhocracies, and clans than in medium and large organizations' hierarchies and markets. Given that markets and adhocracies are the most favorable for implementing the KLC approach to promote organizational intelligence and innovativeness, company culture congruency seems to be an efficient facilitator of intelligence building, probably because it is much easier to implement any tactic, plan, or strategy when it is communicated to people with a similar mindset. So, altogether above precisely exposes that the collective intelligence building in clans, hierarchies, adhocracies, and markets require different strategies and methods.

6.2 Future study directions based on research limitations

Based on the study limitations, some ideas for further studies arise as follows:

1. There are three key limitations of this research: only one country-based sample, the sample size, and the sample sectors. Precisely, it is known that the country's culture and company culture are related (Ghali et al., 2022; Hofstede & Hofstede, 2005; Kucharska & Bedford, 2023; Lewis, 1999). This study sample was collected in Poland, which is still an economy in transition, especially when it comes to company cultures (Kochanowicz, 2004; Hofstede Insights, 2020). So, the given findings are novel, interesting, and inspiring but might be that Polish results may differ not only when compared to other European economies and not only to other East European economies but definitely when compared to Asian or American realities (Lewis, 1999). Therefore, similar studies based on samples coming from different countries can be very useful.
2. Moreover, not only countries but also sectors have their cultural specifics, for example, the public sector (Kucharska & Bedford, 2023). So studies of this topic across sectors are also needed. Finally, a bigger sample size (400 cases per culture type and up) would enable us to compare the KLC approaches impact on change adaptability and innovativeness, including the more profound DBM assessment.
3. In summary, this study is based on the structure of Polish knowledge-driven organizations, which cumulate the higher-level intellectual capital mainly into the following cultural types: hierarchies (29%), markets (33%), clans (23%), and adhocracies (15%). So, it is unknown if the lack of congruence observed in markets and hierarchies comes from their higher-level management skills open to multicultural management or if those organizations are "under transition." It requires further studies.
4. Sample quality assessment started with the Kaiser–Meyer–Olkin test, determining how suited data is for factor analysis; the obtained result, KMO .946,

is assessed as very good (Hair et al., 2010). Total Variance Extracted: 74% CMB was tested using the common latent factor method, which is 51%. So, it suggests that the sample is biased. There might be some potential sources of this bias. The first potential source might come from the observed strong correlation between collaboration culture and organizational collective intelligence (IQ) and with the collaboration culture and learning climate (LCc) component of the learning culture (Table 4.3, Chapter 4). So, it might be that collaborative culture in Polish knowledge-driven organizations indeed is a key driver, or it might be that it is a general characteristic independent of nationality. It might be, because collaboration is a driver of any organization. It requires further studies.

6.3 Practical implications—general ideas

Company culture is an intangible asset that requires design, implementation, and management to leverage the company knowledge strategy. If company culture and knowledge strategy are misaligned, there is no chance for successful knowledge management from a long-run perspective. The long-run perspective management requires organizational innovativeness and collective intelligence development.

Based on the above, the KLC-approach implementation best practices are as follows:

1. Appreciate new knowledge and seek new understanding when the business context changes. Never reject new knowledge only because the old ways of acting are solid. Old solutions might not work best in new times. Intellectual laziness can cost you the market. Therefore, always keep your mind open to a deep contextual understanding of "what is going on" and "what any new reality means for your internal and external clients and your business." Remember that what fitted yesterday or today might not be relevant tomorrow. Stay open-minded.
2. Learn constantly. Constant learning focus helps you balance knowledge exploitation and exploration. To do it perfectly, you must recognize context changes and their meaning for your people, clients, and business. So, constantly analyze the context, your actions, and their effects. Improve yourself and your team, division, and organization. Think critically, learn, and constantly align your actions with the context change—it is the essence of agility skills.
3. Learn from your good and bad experiences, from successes and failures. Remember, mistakes are harsh, sometimes costly lessons, so you cannot waste the knowledge they bring you. Therefore, be the first to admit mistakes and share the knowledge gained thanks to this harsh event; immediately implement improvements to avoid similar mistakes in the future. Be the best example of learning behaviors you want to see among your organization members.

4. Learn collectively. An organization is a group of people who want to achieve together an aim that each member cannot complete alone. So, for your organization's success, it does not matter what you or one of your workmates or employees can achieve alone. The essence of organizational success is what you can achieve together. So, collective instead of individual growth matters more. Therefore, if you want your organization to grow, then enhance the multilevel, collective growth. Organizational learning is not the sum of individual learning but a collective learning issue. If you do not develop it—you do not have a chance for collective intelligence. There is no intelligence without constant critical thinking and learning.
5. The collective intelligence of knowledge-driven organizations results from the smooth cooperation of brilliant minds. To achieve this, the KLC approach is very helpful. We learn about company culture from our experiences, not from formal statements. Employees mirror leaders' behaviors (Badrinarayanan et al., 2019; Hosseini et al., 2023). That is why, as a manager, you must expose it first. You need to create the KLC cultures' synergy experiences among your employees. Without the positive experience of the KLC, your employees will not absorb the KLC. The only way to successfully implement any behavior is to be the perfect example of behavior you want to see around you.
6. Collective intelligence understood as a network of knowledge workers and brilliant minds that collaborate smoothly, is a severe organizational potency that needs to be activated. KLC cultures' synergy facilitates this activation significantly. Knowledge sharing, organizational intelligence, and innovativeness are key benefits of the synergy that offers the KLC cultures' simultaneous implementation and management. According to (Kucharska & Bedford, 2024) trust strengthens this effect.
7. Trust the people you work with (Kucharska & Bedford, 2024). If you cannot trust them, find others worth your trust. We rarely accept support from someone we do not trust and vice versa. We do not support people we cannot trust. That is why trust matters so much for learning organizations. Trust is challenging to earn and easy to lose. It is precious because it determines collective acting, especially tacit knowledge sharing. Trust comes from positive mutual experiences. Do not be surprised if your people do not trust you and do not engage at work when you expose overcontrol and treat them like cheaters. Knowledge workers' brilliant minds to engage at work need challenges and trust. Give it to them if you want your organization to grow.
8. To thrive and survive in the knowledge economy, managers must "see" their company culture's power to shape the company's course and learn to gain and sustain knowledge, learning, and collaboration cultures synergy. A culture mediates the relationship between a leader and an organizational performance (Tichy & Cohen, 1997). Therefore, company culture is a leader's essential resource for making their strategies happen. Nowadays, hyperdynamic business reality requires intelligent actions. When managers "see"

their cultures as assets, they can shape and use them for the company's best (Kucharska & Bedford, 2023).

9. Moreover, to use the company culture as a tool supporting the strategy, the cultural type ought to be examined to reveal the distance between the existing culture and the culture required. Sometimes, some changes in company can be implemented by the changes in culture. So, to secure their collective intelligence building, innovativeness, and agility implementing the KLC approach should be very supportive in knowledge-driven organizations. The implementation process should be diligently tailored to the particular organization's realities. Otherwise, resistance to culture change and friction may occur. To implement the KLC approach successfully, organizations need first to select leaders reflecting the KLC approach at all managerial levels through their own behaviors (Samhan et al., 2023; Wiewiora et al., 2019). Without leaders, exposing and executing the KLC approach, any changes in organizational behavior is possible. Organizational cultures start with leaders who impose their own personal values and assumptions on a group (Schein, 1992). Organizations interested in collective company intelligence building should employ only those leaders who reflect (exposed by their behavior) the KLC approach—those who act oppositely to the KLC should not be leaders at any level in knowledge-driven organizations.

Based on the identified challenges with the KLC implementation regarding company culture types, best practices are as follows:

10. For adhocracies: focus intensely on collectivism at the team level. Adhocracies are ideal for implementing the KLC approach and successfully building higher-level collective intelligence. What they can do to improve their efficacy in collective IQ building is collectivism. The positive attitudes and behaviors toward knowledge and learning, including learning from mistakes, are remarkable in adhocracies. So, to avoid potential competitiveness coming from personal ambitions, it is important to employ those who can, like, and want to collaborate. Apart from employing team players, it is essential to reward employees not for their individual achievements but for their collective ones—this directly supports teamwork. However, it makes sense only if the team shares values and aims and it is tailored diligently to supplement the team's knowledge, competencies, and skills. However, a reward for the collective, instead of the individual performance, should not be understood as a reward equal to all members. Recognition also matters in adhocracies, but it should be gained for contributing to the team's performance. Precisely for the positive impact on the team's efficacy. Individual ambitions over teams' are the biggest potential threat in adhocracies.
11. For Markets: focus intensely on collectivism at the division level. The division level is critical to balance markets' tendency to build organizational silos, which is the biggest challenge of its culture type. Precisely this level is

critical for collective intelligence building. Market culture is not collectivistic by nature, but this culture can collaborate when it pays. So, the cooperation between divisions should be rewarded. So, the lower the market culture in divisions, the better for an organization to build collective intelligence. In practice, leaders of functional divisions should constitute a solid collectivistic "management team" rewarded only partially for their division's achievements but mainly for general organizational achievements resulting from the cooperation between divisions. It can seem at first glance controversial, but it is the best way to avoid competitiveness between divisions leaders (usual silo builders) and secure their cooperation. Next to adhocracies, markets have great potential to implement collective intelligence through the KLC. It is critical to make it clear to all members that it pays. So, the vision of benefits that are possible to win only thanks to teamwork is the most persuasive way in this culture type to motivate collectivism. Divisions (silo building) ambitions over organizational' success are the most significant potential threat in market culture entities.

12. For clans, focus on leader selection. Clans naturally act collectively; therefore, to build collective IQ through the KLC approach, they need to develop knowledge and learning cultures at the division and team levels. Since clans strictly follow leaders, leaders are critical for learning, culture development, and the achievement of the entire KLC synergy. A leader who does not care about knowledge and learning is the biggest potential threat to clans. Clans, next to adhocracies, expose the high potential to develop the KLC.
13. For hierarchies: the leaders' problem noted for clans is equally critical for hierarchies. However, mature hierarchies operating for a significantly longer period are based more on their structured rules, procedures, norms, and traditions than on their leaders (Kucharska, 2021; Kargas & Varoutas, 2015). Additionally, in contrast to clans, hierarchies face serious troubles with collaboration (similarly to adhocracies and markets) and, specifically for themselves, overestimate static knowledge above dynamic, contextual learning. Hierarchies have troubles in collective learning, especially from mistakes (hierarchies do not accept the LCm component of LC and expose the strongest DBM), so the remedy for hierarchies is to face these troubles—there is no intelligence without learning, and there is no learning without accepting the option to be wrong. So, hierarchy obedience is critical for collective intelligence building. The simultaneous lack of a strong hierarchy at the team and division levels can disturb the strict marching after the leader. It is easy to assume—the more intelligent the hierarchical organization leader, the more intelligent the entire organization. If the leader falls, the organization falls. Furthermore, it is worth stressing that in hierarchical knowledge-driven organizations, the knowledge of culture dominates above the culture of learning, and as a result, mistakes are not seen as a potential source of learning as much as they are seen as a problem.

So, two critical challenges for collective intelligence in hierarchies are leadership (similar to clans) and the learning culture, which are even more problematic due to the lack of collectivism. Hierarchies are not as collective as clans. Hierarchy esteems knowledge culture, control, and focuses on uncertainty avoidance. Hierarchies' troubles with learning and adaptability suggest the evolution of hierarchies to a hybrid culture (mixed) to secure organizational IQ building. The biggest challenge to doing this is the inevitable, multilevel inner cultural collision that, as we know, can totally jeopardize any strategy—company culture eats strategy for breakfast—as Peter Drucker rightly noticed.

Part II delivers some propositions and guidelines for all culture types to face the above-described challenges and drive collective intelligence and organizational agility through the KLC-approach implementation.

References

Badrinarayanan, V., Ramachandran, I., & Madhavaram, S. (2019). Mirroring the boss: Ethical leadership, emulation intentions, and salesperson performance. *Journal of Business Ethics*, *159*, 897–912.

Gao, Y. (2017). Business leaders' personal values, organisational culture and market orientation. *Journal of Strategic Marketing*, *25*(1), 49–64.

Ghali, Z., Saidi, K., & Aman, A. (2022). Effects of national culture on adaptation of employees to the innovation in workplace: The case of the Middle East and North Africa region. In S. Sindakis & S. Aggarwal (Eds.), *Entrepreneurial rise in the Middle East and North Africa: The influence of quadruple helix on technological innovation (advanced strategies in entrepreneurship, education and ecology)* (pp. 181–200). Emerald Publishing Limited. https://doi.org/10.1108/978-1-80071-517-220221011

Hair, J. F., Anderson, R. E., Babin, B. J., & Black, W. C. (2010). *Multivariate data analysis: A global perspective*. Pearson Education.

Hofstede, G., & Hofstede, G. J. (2005). *Culture and organizations: Software of the mind* (2nd ed.). McGraw-Hill.

Hofstede Insights. (2020). *Country comparison*. https://www.hofstede-insights.com/country-comparison-tool?countries=poland

Hosseini, M., Treur, J., & Kucharska, W. (2023). An adaptive network model for a double bias perspective on learning from mistakes within organizations. In *International conference on complex networks and their applications* (pp. 91–103). Springer Nature.

Kargas, A. D., & Varoutas, D. (2015). On the relation between organizational culture and leadership: An empirical analysis. *Cogent Business & Management*, *2*(1), 1055953.

Klein, A. S., Wallis, J., & Cooke, R. A. (2013). The impact of leadership styles on organizational culture and firm effectiveness: An empirical study. *Journal of Management & Organization*, *19*(3), 241–254.

Kochanowicz, J. (2004). Trust, confidence, and social capital in Poland: A historical perspective. In I. Markova (Ed.), *Trust and democratic transition in post-communist Europe* (pp. 63–83). Oxford University Press.

Koehn, D. (2022). Ethical and leadership challenges by organizational culture type. In *Leadership and business ethics* (pp. 183–199). Springer.

Kotter, J. P. (1996). Why transformation efforts fail. *Harvard Business Review*. Leading Change: Why Transformation Efforts Fail. https://hbr.org/1995/05/leading-change-why-transformation-efforts-fail-2

Kucharska, W. (2021). Wisdom from experience paradox: Organizational learning, mistakes, hierarchy and maturity issues. *Electronic Journal of Knowledge Management*, *19*(2), 105–117.

Kucharska, W., & Bedford, D. A. D. (2023). *The cultures of knowledge organizations: Knowledge, learning, collaboration (KLC)*. Emerald Publishing Limited.

Kucharska, W., & Bedford, D. A. D. (2024). The KLC cultures' synergy power, trust, and tacit knowledge for organizational intelligence. *Electronic Journal of Knowledge Management*, *22*(2), 18–35.

Lewis, R. D. (1999). *When cultures collide: Managing successfully across cultures*. Nicholas Brealey Publishing.

Rass, L., Treur, J., Kucharska, W., & Wiewiora, A. (2023). Adaptive dynamical systems modelling of transformational organizational change with focus on organizational culture and organizational learning, *Cognitive Systems Research*, *79*, 85–108.

Samhan, N., Treur, J., Kucharska, W., & Wiewiora, A. (2023). An adaptive network model simulating the effects of different culture types and leader qualities on mistake handling and organisational learning. In H. Cherifi, R. N. Mantegna, L. M. Rocha, C. Cherifi, & S. Micciché (Eds.), *Complex networks and their applications. Studies in computational intelligence* (Vol. 1077). Springer. https://doi.org/10.1007/978-3-031-21127-0_19

Schein, E. (1992). *Organizational culture and leadership* (2nd ed.). Jossey-Bass.

Tichy, N. M., & Cohen, E. (1997). *The leadership engine: How winning companies build leaders at every level*. Harper-Collins.

Wiewiora, A., Smidt, M., & Chang, A. (2019). The 'how' of multilevel learning dynamics: A systematic literature review exploring how mechanisms bridge learning between individuals, teams/projects and the organization. *European Management Review*, *16*, 93–115. http://dx.doi.org/10.1111/emre.12179

Part II

Organizational intelligence activation through the KLC-approach implementation—manual

Part II presents strategies, methods, and techniques for implementing the KLC approach to drive adhocracy-, market-, clan-, and hierarchy-dominated cultures to create collective intelligence, sustain organizational openness to changes, and develop agility. So, all the knowledge gained from the research presented in Part I regarding challenges in KLC-approach implementation is the base for formulating strategies, methods, and techniques fostering organizational collective intelligence in the long-run perspective for each culture type.

DOI: 10.4324/9781003485230-9

7 Motivation matters—organizational change drivers impact the KLC-approach implementation methods

7.1 Motivational powers to sustain organizational openness to change and agility development

Motivation to sustain organizational openness to change and agility development differs among culture types. Adhocracies and market cultures seek opportunities to sustain organizational competitiveness and growth, so change is their natural response to opportunities and vice versa they search for solutions enabling to transform any market change into growth opportunity. So, they observe market and are ready to constantly adapt. On the contrary, hierarchies, and sometimes also clans see changes rather as threats for their stability than opportunities to develop. So, such a fundamental difference in motivation to identify and implement change must determine the methods of its introduction. These methods are determined by the change-agents. Change-agents are determined by the change motivation source (internal or external). The potential internal sources are employees, leaders, or shareholders, and external sources are market pressure (law regulations, competitors, and consumers) or stakeholder pressure. In the following, all these are discussed.

Market orientation (external pressure)

Market orientation motivates organizations to develop collective intelligence that facilitates innovations to secure market advantage and competitiveness. So, strongly market-oriented organizations are consequently strongly motivated to adapt smoothly to market changes and develop agility. Market orientation is composed of three components: customer orientation, competitor orientation, and inter-functional coordination, and two decision-making criteria: a long-term focus and a profit focus (Narver & Slater, 1990; Jaworski et al., 2000). It means "learning about market development, sharing knowledge with the team, and adapting offerings to a changing market" is what market-oriented companies do constantly.

DOI: 10.4324/9781003485230-10

However, market orientation is not a characteristic of only market culture organizations. Adhocracies are like market cultures seeking new opportunities and developing competitive advantages. Adhocracies support a dynamic, entrepreneurial, and creative place to work, focus on innovation, and are ready to take the risk of experimentation if necessary. A commitment to breaking conventions and thinking "out of the box" are what is characteristic of autocracies members. In the long term, they emphasize growth and constantly acquire new knowledge, methods, approaches, and technologies. Constant change is a "normal." It is why adhocracies naturally learn and appreciate the knowledge and are motivated to build collective intelligence to respond smoothly to market challenges. Success for adhocracies means introducing a new, unique offer and winning the market. Adhocracy culture is characteristic of highly innovative entities.

On the contrary, the market orientation of hierarchies and clan cultures organizations' is weak or nonexistent (Appiah-Adu & Blankson, 1998; Gao, 2017). It is why their motivation to develop collective intelligence is rarely motivated by external (market) pressure. Hierarchies and clans can ignore market pressure in favor of own stability and control. In fact, it is an illusion of stability and control. But what hierarchies and clans care the most is the "status quo security." Therefore, if a change need arise it usually is forced by the changing law requirements (externally) or it comes from leaders' ambitions (key internal source motivating to change). Grassroots initiatives for any changes rarely happen in hierarchies. Employees working in hierarchies absorb security feelings from repetitiveness and control, forming excellence in their daily performance. This is why any changes, especially hazardous ones, cannot be implemented without friction in hierarchies. Hierarchies love their traditions, procedures, rules, policies, and routines as much as adhocracies love to break them. Hierarchies are strongly oriented to inner governance order; clans are oriented to inner relationship power. Clans focus on loyalty, tradition, and interpersonal cohesiveness (Deshpande et al., 1993). Both clans and hierarchies tend to be ignorant of market changes as long as they are not radically impactful, which means their ignorance is no longer an option. Following this line, the frame for the KLC implementation must take into account the above way on how market (external) pressure can impact organization regarding its culture type.

Stakeholders (external pressure)

CSR theory and practice are modern concepts that focus on "doing well by doing good" (Falck & Heblich, 2007, p. 1). According to Falck and Heblich (2007), CSR is regarded as an unsolicited corporate commitment to fulfill the explicit and implicit duties imposed on a company by the expectations of institutions and society (Kowalczyk & Kucharska, 2020). Hence, CSR is a way of promoting social-friendly trends to enhance the order of society, which consists of obligations that cover both legal frameworks and social conventions.

CSR implementation is enhanced by groups that have an interest in the company. They are called stakeholders. Stakeholders comprise institutions, organizations, communities, and individuals who can affect or who are affected by this particular organization (Freeman, 1984). Story and Neves (2015) stressed that organizations might jeopardize their position if they ignore stakeholders' needs and do not engage in CSR practices. Porter and Kramer (2006) identified four key factors that motivate companies to implement CSR: moral obligation, sustainability, license to operate, and reputation. These motives are linked with one another and all are reflected in company culture.

Regarding the company culture type, Übius and Alas (2009) noted that the market culture type predicts the economic facet of corporate social responsibility: the firm's performance regarding social issues. Clans, hierarchies, and adhocracies also care about the company's performance regarding social issues; additionally, they respect other agents' interests. The forward-looking competence of the leaders is an additional motivation to develop in organizations sustainability focus. In the center of the sustainability achievement in knowledge-driven organizations is the tacit knowledge sharing that happens thanks to intensive social interactions (Kucharska & Karwowska, 2025). Following this line, again, adhocracies and markets are the cultural types where social interactions are expected to be friendly and unceremonious. Kucharska and Karwowska (2025) show that regarding the KLC approach, a knowledge culture is essential, but without a collaborative culture first and a learning culture second, it is insufficient for tacit knowledge-sharing development. This matters because tacit knowledge is a critical driver of dynamic capabilities and innovations development. Tacit knowledge gained from experiences and social interactions influences dynamic capabilities and change adaptability more robustly than explicit knowledge. Finally, change adaptability supports innovations and leads to sustainability. The value essence of such detailed empirical evidence delivery is to prove that sustainability achievement is all about the company culture that determines the collective development of the higher-level learning skills essential for sustainability. So, regarding stakeholders pressure and identified by Porter and Kramer (2006) key factors that motivate companies to implement CSR: moral obligation, sustainability, license to operate, and reputation. Concluding from all what was said so far about all culture types All of these CSR motives seem to be perfectly fitted to adhocracies. Partially to markets (sustainability, license to operate, and reputation) and clans (moral obligation, license to operate, and reputation) and less to hierarchies (license to operate, and reputation). It seems to be in line with the study by Dyck et al. (2019), who noted that (1) a hierarchy culture is associated with greater emphasis on financially sustainable organizing and with better financial outcomes, (2) a clan culture is associated with greater emphasis on socially sustainable organizing and with better social outcomes, (3) a market culture is associated with greater emphasis on ecologically sustainable organizing and with better ecological outcomes, and (4) an adhocracy culture is associated with greater emphasis on holistically sustainable organizing and with better holistic outcomes. In summary, regarding to sustainability—hierarchy culture focuses on financially sustainable organizing, the clan culture on socially sustainable organizing and, the market culture and ecologically sustainable outcomes (Dyck et al., 2019). Following this line, the frame for the KLC implementation must take into account the above way on how stakeholder (external) pressure can impact organization regarding its culture type.

Shareholders value orientation (internal pressure)

Shareholders value orientation (SVO) emphasizes profit maximization for the shareholders and it is generally associated with legitimacy in global financial markets (Ghoshal, 2005). Shareholders pressure to gain SVO is mostly related to long or short orientation toward expected profits, and this is often driven by the character of the organization—public or private.

Public organizations do not care about profits in a short perspective. They rather focus on social values and their profits are perceived in a long-socio-politics perspective. Public organizations serve society. Society vote. So, public organizations' shareholders are interested in introducing changes perceived as valuable by society—such changes will pay back. In fact, public organizations may adapt to changes and implement new ideas to promote societal legitimacy rather than efficiency Bezemer et al. (2015). Sometimes, it is efficient only to talk about changes, espousing the adoption of new normative beliefs without implementing them. It may already generate positive societal reactions because prevailing logics (strongly visible in financial markets) also tend to be socially constructed (Zajac & Westphal, 2004). So, public organizations—usually hierarchies, can be motivated to introduce changes by their shareholders if those changes are legitimized by the society. It sometimes matters more than the financial efficiency of these changes.

Private organizations (mostly adhocracies and markets) shareholders are usually interested in their profit's maximization in short run, and they can push to changes to maximize SVO or, equally they can avoid risks of losing profits because of costly investments. Details of these decisions will depend on the individual contexts.

However, family organizations (often exposing clan culture) are particularly specific in this matter because family owners might resist change oriented to immediate profits due to the fact they are risk averse and care more about the longevity of the company, rather than short-term profits. Indeed, loyalty, tradition, responsibility, long-term survival and prosperity of the family and their associates make clans philosophy of acting different from markets and adhocracies. Family owners often act as "protective stewards" of a firm (Miller et al., 2013). Independent institutional investors, that is, the ones that have no business relations with the company and a clear value maximization perspective, will be acting oppositely.

Leadership (internal pressure)

Based on the challenges identified in Part I regarding the implementation of KLC in hierarchies and clans, leaders were identified for these cultures as exceptionally critical for intelligence building in these culture's types of organizations. Partially it is justified by the market orientation that is weak in clans and hierarchies. So, any other external powers except of law obligations or reputation care, are inefficient to motivate hierarchies and clans to adapt constantly, build collective intelligence and agility skills to be more and more innovative. In fact, those are adhocracies and markets motives. It is why, in fact, leaders, especially transformational ones, are the best motivators for clans and hierarchies to build a collectively intelligent entity. The market orientation drives markets and adhocracies. Clans and hierarchies are not driven by the market pressure; rather by stake or shareholders pressures. So, keeping in mind the fact that organizational changes can be driven internally (cultures, leaders, employees, shareholders) or externally (market pressure, stakeholders), leaders are the very powerful motivators to collective intelligence building in all culture types'. But focusing on the triangle: leader-culture-organization where a culture mediates the relation between a leader and an organizational performance (Tichy & Cohen, 1997), we can see that these culture types (clans and hierarchies), which are not characterized by the natural market orientation and innovation seeking can be efficiently motivated to adaptability precisely by leaders.

Leaders who are open to change values form an adhocracy culture, while leaders who express conservative values promote a hierarchical or clan culture as those which help them to implement their strategies according to their values.

Managing corporate culture may entail members discarding old values and embracing new ones, learning new behaviors, and managing the anxiety associated with change. Leaders who possess the technical and interpersonal skills to shape the firm's culture are an essential ingredient in this equation. Leaders play critical roles in part because they are charged with selecting new firm members who will fit in and meet expectations. Leaders also have the legitimate authority to challenge existing norms that may impede the achievement of corporate goals. Although bottom-up transformations in values and behaviors do occur (Beer & Walton, 1990), strong leadership and acceptance of changes initiated from above seem to be critical for any changes initiated in hierarchies to gain legitimacy.

But for mature hierarchies with a long tradition of all rules and procedures that for decades shaped their own specific (often unworkable) system of beliefs, they usually see a very transformational, charismatic, agile mindset leaders not as a savior but as a threat to their collectively secured comfort zone built on a false assumption regarding a current business reality. This is why old hierarchies' employees can exclude the formal leader, which destroys this "safety illusion" created by collective blindness.

So, leaders are potentially the only source of pressure for clans and hierarchies to build organizational intelligence. But we must be aware that in extreme cases even skilled leaders may not be sufficient to change employee habits. The clash of mentalities is not easy to overcome.

Employees (internal pressure)

It is noted that many factors influence organizational culture, not just leadership. Organizational cultures emerge both from the bottom-up choices made by members and from the top-down decisions of management, and bearing in mind the fact that the significant impact of leadership styles on organizational culture and firm effectiveness indicates that the leadership skills of managers and supervisors are critical factors in the creation and reinforcement of cultural norms (Klein et al., 2024). It seems reasonable to assume that managing culture relies on effective leadership coupled with the commitment and capacity of members who occupy the culture (Block, 2003; Sarros et al., 2002; Schein, 1992).

Employees are a potentially very efficient power pressing to change in any culture type. However, clans seems to be an exception. Clan culture supports an open and friendly place to work where people share a lot of themselves. Group loyalty and a sense of tradition are strong. There is an emphasis on long-term benefits of development and great importance is given to group cohesion. There is a strong concern for people and the organization places a premium on teamwork, participation, and consensus.

Regarding market cultures employees need to see the value (monetary and social too). So, they can press the organization to improvements that will bring decent benefits to all parties involved. Employees that feel good in market culture have a natural skill to seek for shared value as a form of consensus.

Employees who feel fitted to adhocracies can press to changes when they will stop see the development opportunities or, will see that opportunities which arise are not used for common good understood as development. Adhocracy employees are resilient to turbulences they see as an intellectual challenge.

Employees who feel safe in hierarchies will press to change, seeking that their "comfort zone" can be jeopardized. They will fight to eliminate the threat and secure safety. Hierarchy employees are change-resilient.

7.2 Strategy-culture-structure alignment

Strategy, culture, and structure must align. No matter how brilliant a strategy is, it will have no chance of success if the right company culture does not support it and the company structure does not enhance it. So, the question arises which culture and structure are "the right one." But to answer correctly, we need to know the strategy.

This book focuses on knowledge-driven organizations. So, apart from strategic aims specific to the particular company's and its business context, the typical knowledge-related long-run strategic aim is to create and secure the efficiency of the knowledge management system.

A company's organizational culture affects information acquisition and its smooth transformation into knowledge, wisdom, and intelligence, which should be understood as the smooth use of apt knowledge, according to the business context. Such a system is efficient thanks to the efficiency of its key processes:

1. The identification of the knowledge needed and its sources—tacit and explicit (knowledge culture support)
2. Tacit knowledge creation and acquisition (consciously and unconsciously) thanks to "learning by doing" and "learning by social interactions" (learning culture support and collective culture support)
3. Tacit knowledge internalization and externalization to explicit form (learning culture support and collective culture support)
4. Explicit knowledge storage and security (technology support)
5. Explicit knowledge sharing (distribution) accordingly to authorization (technology and collective culture support)
6. Knowledge utilization in the current business context (tacit and explicit) through combination and internalization (knowledge, learning, and collaboration cultures synergy in action; technology support may increase the effect).

The smooth flow of these processes is essential to create and secure the efficiency of the knowledge management systems that is a base of even the most sophisticated knowledge strategy (Kucharska & Erickson, 2023; Nonaka & Takeuchi, 2007; Rowley & Slack, 2009; Rothberg & Erickson, 2005).

Based on the above given processes sequence and the analyzed earlier in this chapter potential motivation sources (internal and external) characteristic for each culture type to build the collective intelligence, it is easy to conclude that hierarchies ignoring tacit knowledge acquisition may face some difficulties in organizational intelligence development. Adhocracies markets and clans are unlimitedly open to all knowledge management processes. So, hierarchy as a culture and structure jeopardize collective intelligence building through its unfavorable conditions to tacit knowledge creation and acquisition.

Flat organizational structures help shorten the distance between employees, promoting their free interactions and creating an opportunity for tacit knowledge to circulate. The ideal structure of knowledge-driven organization is a network which is inclusive, where brilliant minds are equal and can freely cooperate, learn, and contextually stimulate one another to collectively create knowledge, wisdom, and extreme intelligence. So, adhocracy culture and network as a company structure seems to be a perfect composition to support knowledge-driven organizations aimed to agilely adapt to the market, constantly create innovativeness to be competitive and secure sustainability to be resistant.

Network structure fits to R&D organizations, divisions, and teams oriented to constant novelty. That need to secure a smooth tacit knowledge flow that happens thanks to the free cooperation of brilliant minds that are equal. It is what adhocracy culture can do. Hierarchy culture and structure fits to those organizations that need to secure order to deliver to the market the same, repetitive quality of products or services which production is complex. So, the steep hierarchy should reflect extreme complexity of the organization processes.

The structure of market-oriented organizations should be a mix of network and flat-functional hierarchy to avoid silos. The complexity of strategic aims should determine its final shape. What is critical—the company's' structure should always be designed to support the company's strategy. It is a huge mistake keeping the company structure in the same shape even if strategic aims have changed several times. The company's intelligence building pillars: strategy, culture, and structure must align. There is no excuse to keep a company structure frozen. If you do not align your company structure to your aims—sooner or later you will face troubles and be forced to re-structure your company to avoid bankruptcy. It is much better to smoothly align structure to strategic aims to make it supportive for communication and cooperation required to win the strategy. Consequently, company culture must strengthen those values, beliefs, and behaviors required to fulfill the strategy.

Company culture of knowledge-driven organization is an intangible asset that requires design, implementation, and management to leverage the company knowledge strategy. If company culture, structure, and knowledge strategy are misaligned, there is no chance for successful knowledge management from a long-run perspective. Knowledge management is a base for wisdom and intelligence development. The long-run perspective management today requires supporting organizational innovativeness, sustainability, and agility that never happen without a collective intelligence development.

7.3 The KLC implementation framework

The KLC approach, as the Part I study results exposed, fosters organizational intelligence in knowledge-driven organizations. But the KLC-approach components': knowledge, learning, and collaboration cultures impact on intelligence varies between company culture types and management levels (team, division, and organization). Moreover, the literature review opening the practical Part II of this book showed that company culture's type might determine the motivation to implement changes, and this way the general motivation to build organizational intelligence and consequently to implement the KLC (internal and external pressures). Moreover, the company's strategy-culture-structure alignment or misalignment level in the organizational culture type, also may impact on the efficacy and efficiency of the KLC-approach implementation, as Sections 7.1 and 7.2 clarified.

So, the given frame below summarizes all the knowledge gained form Part I study and from Sections 7.1 and 7.2 literature to serve with guidelines on which factors must be taken into account when implement the KLC in each type of culture and how to manage it to gain the best benefits.

Company culture is an asset that requires design, implementation, and management to leverage the company by supporting its strategy. If company culture and strategy misalign, there is no chance for success in the long run. So, knowledge-driven organizations that develop their intellectual capital should implement KLC cultures and take full advantage of the synergy needed for organizational innovativeness. There is no chance for innovativeness without collective intelligence. The given frame clearly exposes that the biggest challenge in implementing the KLC approach is expected for clans and hierarchies because these culture types do not represent a significant motivation to be innovative and their knowledge management strategies mostly relate on these knowledge processes that exploit an explicit knowledge instead of explore the new tacit.

So, design, implementation, and management of the company culture supporting organizational intelligence in clans and hierarchies are the most challenging and problematic. According to Deshpande et al. (1993), some culture types coexist in the organization. The given in Table 3.3a, b (Chapter 3) view on culture-type consistency across organizational levels (team, division, and organization) confirms it. Regarding the sample study presented in Part I, hierarchies and markets are the most frequent in big and large companies which also expose the highest rate of co-existence with other cultures' types. Referring to the given frame (Figure 7.1), it is easy to predict that some culture types' combination cannot coexist without frictions. So, culture type collisions, in light of the Part I study findings can jeopardize the organizational intelligence. Next chapters deliver solutions to all identified so far challenges regarding the KLC implementation to each culture type to support organizational intelligence.

A company culture must be first experienced to be next, learned. Therefore, the following chapters next to the practical guidelines also offer contextual case studies that serve as practical examples. Part II presents a compelling array of manuals and case studies that not only illuminate the concepts outlined in the book but also enrich our understanding of different culture types and the art of intelligence building. This invaluable resource is designed to inspire and empower educators and business professionals alike, ensuring the knowledge is both engaging and applicable in real-world settings.

Each of the following chapters starts with exposing key challenges specific to the particular company culture type when implementing the KLC identified through the Part I study results (Figure 5.1), and through broader motivational context analysis (Figure 7.1). Next, the remedy to these challenges is presented regarding managerial levels (organization, division, team, and leadership). Each chapter closes a case study illustrating the particular cultural challenges and the KLC-approach implementation remedies.

ORGANIZATIONAL INTELLIGENCE / COLLECTIVE CHANGE ADAPATBILITY

			KNOWLEDGE-DRIVEN ORGANIZATION			
			company culture type			
			adhocracy	market	clan	hierarchy
Motivation to implement changes	external	market pressure	*HIGH*	*HIGH*	*MODERATE*	*WEAK*
		stakeholders	moral obligation, sustainability, license to operate, reputation	sustainability, license to operate, reputation	moral obligation, license to operate, reputation	*license to operate, reputation*
	internal	shareholders	*HIGH*	*HIGH*	*MODERATE*	*WEAK*
		leaders	*HIGH*	*HIGH*	*HIGH*	*HIGH**
		employees	*HIGH*	*HIGH*	*MODERATE*	*WEAK*
Critical criterion: Strategy-Culture-Structure alignment						
Knowlede Management Strategy	knowlede focus		**tacit & explicit** knowledge focus	**tacit & explicit** knowledge focus	**tacit &** explicit knowledge focus	**explicit** knowledge focus
	knowledge processes expected outputs		**data information knowledge wisdom intelligence**	**data information knowledge wisdom intelligence**	**data information knowledge wisdom** intelligence	**data information knowledge** wisdom intelligence
Functional cultures			**Knowledge Learning** Cooperation	**Knowledge Learning Cooperation**	Knowledge Learning **Cooperation**	**Knowledge** Learning Cooperation
Favorable Structure			network	flat functional hierarchy	hierarchy	hierarchy

Figure 7.1 The general KLC implementation framework

Note: Bolded text exposes high intensity of the particular factor.

*—In extreme cases, hierarchies' leaders advocating changes may be seen as stability threats and eliminated.

References

Appiah-Adu, K., & Blankson, C. (1998). Business strategy, organizational culture, and market orientation. *Thunderbird International Business Review, 40*, 235–256.

Beer, M., & Walton, E. (1990). Developing the competitive organization: Interventions and strategies. *American Psychologist*, *45*(2), 154.

Bezemer, P. J., Zajac, E. J., Naumovska, I., Van Den Bosch, F. A., & Volberda, H. W. (2015). Power and paradigms: The Dutch response to pressures for shareholder value. *Corporate Governance: An International Review*, *23*(1), 60–75.

Block, L. (2003). The leadership-culture connection: An exploratory investigation. *Leadership & Organization Development Journal*, *24*(6), 318–334.

Deshpande, R., Farley, J. U., & Webster, F. E. (1993). Corporate culture, customer orientation, and innovativeness in Japanese firms: A quadrad analysis. *Journal of Marketing, 57*, 23–37.

Dyck, B., Walker, K., & Caza, A. (2019). Antecedents of sustainable organizing: A look at the relationship between organizational culture and the triple bottom line. *Journal of Cleaner Production, 231*, 1235–1247.

Falck, O., & Heblich, S. (2007). Corporate social responsibility: Doing well by doing good. *Business Horizons, 50*(3), 247–254. https://doi.org/10.1016/j.bushor.2006.12.002

Freeman, R. E. (1984). *Strategic management: A stakeholder approach*. Pitman.

Gao, Y. (2017). Business leaders' personal values, organisational culture and market orientation. *Journal of Strategic Marketing, 25*(1), 49–64.

Ghoshal, S. (2005). Bad management theories are destroying good management practices. *Academy of Management Learning & Education, 4*, 75–91.

Jaworski, B., Kohli, A. K., & Sahay, A. (2000). Market-driven versus driving markets. *Journal of the Academy of Marketing Science, 28*, 45–54.

Klein, N. D., Bravo, A. J., Conway, C. C., Keough, M. T., Pilatti, A., & Mezquita, L. (2024). Individualism, collectivism, and emotion regulation: A cross-cultural examination among young adults from seven countries. *Current Psychology, 43*(31), 26007–26018.

Kowalczyk, R., & Kucharska, W. (2020). Corporate social responsibility practices incomes and outcomes: Stakeholders' pressure, culture, employee commitment, corporate reputation, and brand performance. A Polish–German cross-country study. *Corporate Social Responsibility and Environmental Management, 27*(2), 595–615.

Kucharska, W., & Erickson, G. S. (2023). Tacit knowledge acquisition & sharing, and its influence on innovations: A Polish/US cross-country study. *International Journal of Information Management, 71*, 102647.

Kucharska, W., & Karwowska, E. (2025). Company culture matters! Knowledge-driven companies' way to innovations and sustainability. *Social Sciences & Humanities Open*, 11. Article 101268. https://doi.org/10.1016/j.ssaho.2024.101268

Miller, D., Le Breton-Miller, I., & Lester, R. H. (2013). Family firm governance, strategic conformity, and performance: Institutional vs. strategic perspectives. *Organization Science, 24*, 189–209.

Narver, J. C., & Slater, S. F. (1990). The effect of a market orientation on business profitability. *Journal of Marketing, 54*, 20–35.

Nonaka, I., & Takeuchi, H. (2007). The knowledge-creating company. *Harvard Business Review, 85*(7–8), 162.

Porter, M. E., & Kramer, M. (2006). Strategy and society: The link between competitive advantage and corporate social responsibility. *Harvard Business Review, 84*(12), 78–92.

Rothberg, H. N., & Erickson, G. S. (2005). *From knowledge to intelligence: Creating competitive advantage in the next economy*. Routledge.

Rowley, J., & Slack, F. (2009). Conceptions of wisdom. *Journal of Information Science, 35*(1), 110–119.

Sarros, J. C., Gray, J., & Densten, I. L. (2002). Leadership and its impact on organizational culture. *International Journal of Business Studies, 10*(2).

Schein, E. (1992). *Organizational culture and leadership* (2nd ed.). Jossey-Bass.

Story, J., & Neves, P. (2015). When corporate social responsibility (CSR) increases performance: Exploring the role of intrinsic and extrinsic CSR attribution. *Business Ethics: A European Review, 24*(2), 111–124. https://doi.org/10.1111/beer.12084

Tichy, N. M., & Cohen, E. (1997). *The leadership engine: How winning companies build leaders at every level*. Harper-Collins.

Übius, Ü., & Alas, R. (2009). Organizational culture types as predictors of corporate social responsibility. *Engineering Economics, 61*(1).

Zajac, E. J., & Westphal, J. D. (2004). The social construction of market value: Institutionalization and learning perspectives on stock market reactions. *American Sociological Review, 69*, 433–457.

8 Adhocracy culture

8.1 Key challenges in the KLC-approach implementation in adhocracies

Adhocracies are strongly motivated internally (shareholders, leaders, employees) and externally (market orientation, stakeholders) to smoothly implement changes and build the collective intelligence in organization. They have a strong knowledge, and focus on learning, including learning from mistakes.

Characteristics: Adhocracies characterize differentiation, flexibility, and discretion at all levels and is externally focused on growth and innovation, and their employees are ready to think critically, learn, take risks, and dynamically change the course of action if necessary. Adhocracy exposes a dynamic, entrepreneurial, and creative course of action that thrives well in an uncertain, ambiguous, and turbulent environment. The common values are constant learning, innovation, flexibility, adaptability, risk-taking, experimentation, and initiative. *Leaders:* Leaders who are open to change and expose an agile mindset (Kucharska et al., 2024a, 2024b) are perfect for adhocracies. Adhocracies leaders are then expected to be visionary, innovative, and ready to take a risk if necessary (but it does not mean they do not manage risks thoroughly—on the contrary, they do it perfectly!). They expose a constantly learning growth mindset (Dweck, 2017; Moonen, 2017), and very strongly affect organization (Kargas & Varoutas, 2015), however they are not the only pressure source motivating to change as it is observed in clans or hierarchies.

Employees: Extremely intelligent, always stay open-minded. Adhocracy employees are resilient to turbulences they see as an intellectual challenge. They "never have enough" of intellectual challenge. Curiosity and breaking conventions characterize their members. Members collaborate to solve problems, gain knowledge, break conventions, up horizons, and discover novelty. Growth drives them. The constant increase in intellectual capital is a shared aim that drives and bonds them. Adhocracies characteristics are ideal for the KLC-approach implementation.

DOI: 10.4324/9781003485230-11

Size: dynamic small or medium entities, highly innovative and constant development oriented.

Structure: network (smoothly cooperating network of brilliant minds constitute adhocracy collective intelligence). The alignment of knowledge strategy-culture-structure is perfectly reflected in the network of smoothly cooperating network of brilliant minds.

Strategy-Culture-Structure alignment criterion: Strategy always requires a long-run perspective. So, the KLC-approach implementation serves the organizational intelligence building in the long run. Since adhocracies are market-oriented then this purpose is clear and easy to accept for adhocracies members. Network structure secures smooth knowledge flow in adhocracies.

Critical asset: Relationships (social capital), trust, intellectual capital is critical but adhocracies usually have it.

Key Challenge: collective cooperation above individual ambitions. Highly self-aware, with a perfect understanding of all interdependencies, highly ambitious and brilliant individuals might jeopardize cooperation if they feel injustice, are manipulated, used or non-respected.

Remedy: Make people feel part of something important, an "extraordinary enterprise" that does not happen anywhere else. Let them know that this game is possible to win only together with those you have (they need to feel they need each other). You must feel and see that they accept this interdependency. If you can't feel this way about all members, let go of those who can jeopardize your team.

Priority actions (regarding the KLC): trust-building, team-building

Final advice for adhocracies leaders: focus intensely on trust and collectivism, especially at the team level. Adhocracies are ideal for implementing the KLC approach and successfully building higher-level collective intelligence. What they can do to improve their efficacy in collective IQ building is collectivism, but it requires trust (Kucharska & Bedford, 2019, 2024; Kucharska et al., 2017; Kucharska, 2017). The positive attitudes and behaviors toward knowledge and learning, including learning from mistakes, are remarkable in adhocracies. So, to avoid potential competitiveness coming from personal ambitions, it is important to employ those who can, like, and want to collaborate. Apart from employing team players, it is essential to reward employees not for their individual achievements but for their collective ones—this directly supports teamwork. However, it makes sense only if the team shares values and aims and it is tailored diligently to supplement the team's knowledge, competencies, and skills. However, a reward for the collective, instead of the individual performance, should not be understood as a reward equal to all members. Recognition also matters in adhocracies, but it should be gained to contribute to the team's performance. Precisely for the positive impact on the team's efficacy. Individual ambitions over teams are the biggest potential threat in adhocracies. So, build trust through teamwork, transparency, justice; support teamwork thorough shared responsibility, empowerment, inclusion, shared leadership and voice for all.

8.2 KLC implementation plan in adhocracies

As assumed, the collective cooperation above individual ambitions is potentially the key challenge that may disturb the collective intelligence building in adhocracies composed of extremely ambitious individuals. But, regarding the tailored plan of the KLC implementation, we need to remember that each company is specific, and only their members know these specifics—they know them best. So it might be that in your adhocracy culture-dominated organization, you will identify more than only the typical "individual ambitions over collective success" problem, or it might be that in your particular organization, a different challenge is a critical one. Therefore, below, next to the description of the fundamental KLC introduction steps, see some helpful (in italics) guidelines that will help you make your KLC implementation plan tailored to your organization and hopefully make it successful.

1. Start with the KLC-approach assessment tool (Appendix 3). Using this form, you can compare the KLC level expected by you to the level you observe in your organization. The discrepancy between the KLC-approach level desired and existing will show you clearly the required improvements direction.

   a) discrepancy in knowledge culture: the critical is the perception of employees, because employees, in fact, constitute the organization. So, if they see the culture stronger or weaker than leaders there is a space for critical thinking and strategizing. You need to find out the authentic root of this discrepancy. Remember that only authentic root will give you a chance for improvements. It might be that your employees have a false self-perception. But it is equally possible that your leaders too. I suggest the open discussion to identify roots and establish improvements steps.

      Generally, we implement knowledge culture through the making is a key factor, critical for making any decision. So, always before making decision be sure you have a required knowledge to make it. *If you do not have it, organize it. If you can't organize it—ask yourself why? Is it an intellectual laziness—very bad indicator. Is it a lack of resources—re-think your priorities. The knowledge-driven organization simply must make the access to knowledge required a priority.*

   b) discrepancy in learning culture components:

      - climate (collective motivation to learn)—as above: identify authentic roots of this discrepancy. *The collective motivation to learn is an engine for collective intelligence building. You need to know your collective intelligence drivers and blockers—so ask your employees what motivate them to support others learning and what block them to share knowledge with others or support others in growing and why. Is it again the ambition of "being the best"? If so—then reward your people for being "the best in supporting others." Be creative, find the solution. You not always can change the nature of people, but you can use their nature for common good. Be clever.*

- mistakes acceptance as a source of learning—as above: identify authentic roots of this discrepancy. *The double bias of mistakes makes this component of learning culture really problematic (Kucharska & Kopytko, 2024). First, check if there is a discrepancy between what your employees declare and do regarding claiming mistakes, learning, hiding or sharing knowledge from mistakes. Typically, fear and shame are key blockers of claiming mistakes and sharing knowledge gained from them. It is much better, cheaper, and more efficient if your employees share lessons taken from failures (if they do not, believe me others will do the same soon and it all costs the company more—it is much cheaper to pay once). So, ask yourself- do they my employees feel supported and safe in my company? Or do they feel controlled and hunt? Do we manage mistakes and use the knowledge from them to learn how to avoid them in a future? Or we play a "shame and blame" game? If people make mistakes but take their lessons and support others—it is a healthy growing process. If they hide mistakes, neither take their lessons nor support others—let such people go. The acceptance component of mistakes is not about negligence acceptance. It is about accepting how learning happens when we are brave enough to break conventions, search for new ideas, and accept uncertainties (as R&D entities should). There is no learning without mistakes. Be sure you do not expect the impossible.*

c) discrepancy in cooperation culture—as above: identify authentic roots of this discrepancy. Discuss openly and establish what is the shared vision of cooperation in your organization. *Do your company members trust one another? What make them trust? What blocks their trust? Knowledge is the power. You need to understand why some people do not want to share this power. Are their reasons ambitional or rational? If ambitional—use their ambitions to common good (be clever, e.g., "reward best collaborators") If their reasons are rational, then change rules, and make the collaboration rational, for example, reward instead individual—collective achievements or make a "collective achievements" a required minimum for positive appraisal (be clever—you know your people best, so find the tailored solution).*

2. Might be that sometimes the culture type is seen differently among company members. The observed discrepancies often occur due to the position of a division/team. So, Appendix 3 provides a short questionnaire that can help you assess the employee's perception of the company culture type. Again, the potential discrepancy between the perception of the company culture type per position or division/team will show you the potential discrepancy and, based on this, the direction of the required improvement. If leaders see the culture differently than employees, they have a lot of work to do, starting with their behaviors first. Remember the golden rule of the company culture implementation—leaders must reflect the company culture they want to see. It might be that some leader's self-awareness is low. I mean, they do not understand how their behavior impacts people. In these situations, I strongly encourage this type leaders to prioritize their personal development before gracefully stepping down from their leadership roles. This approach not only fosters growth but also sets a powerful example for others to follow. As a leader, name the change, you want to see and reflect it in own behavior. Why is this change beneficial for your organization? What precise benefits you want to gain. What are your priorities in doing this (follow the impact and tailor your solution to the organization).
3. Strategy always requires a long-term vision. So, consider the results of your organization's analytics in the context of building collective intelligence in the long term. With that in mind, you need to have a vision of creating and sustaining collective intelligence in your organization. So, ask yourself how to secure triple-loop learning in your organization (Argyris & Schon, 1978; Tosey et al., 2012). The triple-loop learning approach helps us understand why members in certain organizations behave as they do—we learn on how employees learn and unlearn and re-learn. It would be beneficial if you deeply understand what makes your employees' collective learning happen, what motivates them, and what supports them in caring about collective growth. It will give you a base for a long-term vision for your organizational intelligence development.
4. Establish and communicate clearly your aims through benefits you want to gain, *benefit example: I want to see people support one another in solving tasks*. Ask yourself: what must be done to gain these benefits in my organization*? Example: let's add the point to the appraisal form 360: IQ SUPPORT MASTER*. Next, ask yourself: What helps and what jeopardizes the implementation of these planned actions? *Example of jeopardizing factor: some people care about others naturally others simply not*. In light of this reflection, you may add some conditions that would help you to make IQ SUPPORT MASTER a company habit. *Example*: set up a minimum level, for example, 4 (scale 1–5) that is critical to gain a positive assessment. It will definitely help to create an IQ support behaviors toward others a habit.

5. Build a plan to foster divisions and teams' engagement in what you want to change.

    1. Introduce knowledge culture along with some knowledge culture application golden rules like, for example, "use knowledge you have, ask for knowledge you need; organize the knowledge needed that is missing in organization, be open to new knowledge, avoid intellectual laziness."

        Example: Organize, for example, a "knowledge week" when teams and divisions share their newly gained best practices supporting knowledge flow. It could also be an opportunity to identify "knowledge problems" and search for solutions for better knowledge flow between teams, divisions or departments. Solution-searching teams should be inter-unit, and the best solutions should be implemented. If the solution works, then it should be rewarded during the next "knowledge week" (let the solution be tested and optimized in the meantime; be sure that having a group of employees interested in this solution's efficacy is the best way to make it work).
    2. Introduce learning culture along with some learning culture application golden rules like, for example, "learn constantly and enhance others" or "the day without a new learning is a day lost" or "the mistake is a failure if there is no lesson taken from it."

        Example: Organize, for example, "learning week" when you will enhance formal and informal learnings through training and workshops organized in an inter-unit convention. Moreover, organize the "new collective learnings sharing" sessions when teams, departments, divisions can share their "best collective learnings" of a quoter (if your "learning weeks" are organized quarterly)—the most valuable learnings should be rewarded by audience (team can't vote for themselves). This way you will gain engagement and gamification.
    3. Introduce collective culture along with some golden rules for applying collaboration culture, such as "equity and inclusion over judging and exclusion," "shared values, aims and goals," and "shared problems are smaller and shared successes bigger, so share and be a part of the team."

        Consequently, you can organize the "cooperation weeks" when employee can share, they collective performance effects.

        You can organize such meetings more often in the first year of the KLC implementation, for example, monthly, each first Friday. When your organization becomes the KLC master, you can organize such events occasionally but remember to do this to sustain it. It matters for making the KLC permanent.

6. Going back to the identified by your discrepancies in the KLC-desired versus existing, you can frequently examine it to see the progress. You can also

dedicate a project supporting the entire KLC implementation or only the problematic component. To execute it establish: aim, scope, budget, and time. Do not forget about KPIs (key performance indicators). So, name precisely what changes in employees' behaviors' you want to see, or you want or eliminate and decide how you want to measure it and set up KPIs.

KPI example; Let's imagine you want to eliminate the situation when your organization repeats the same mistake. You aim is to eliminate this mistake. But you do not want people simply stop report it (hide it). You want them to take their lessons and implement improvements. So, your KPI are number of this particular problematic process improvements (not the number of the repeated mistake!). Remember: use your people nature for, "better good" and be clever!

7. Always identify risks, prepare a plane on how to mitigate the most probable-impactful ones.

   You know your company best. So, thing about events, factors, people who can jeopardize the KLC implementation and prepare remedies tailored to these particular events, factors, and people to mitigate or eliminate these risks.

8. Constantly analyze effects, reflect and learn, and constantly optimize focusing on benefits you want to gain form the KLC. It might be that if context change you will need to find another way to gain your benefits. Be ready on it. If something changed in your business environment (internal or external) revise your aims and plans to secure your KLC benefits. Might be you need to find another way to achieve them. So, adapt constantly your aims, plans, and methods to your expected gain—be agile.

   Remember, being a good manager or leader secret ingredient is a constant critical thinking, analyzing and improvement. So, constant adaptability. If you expect that there is a universal solution set up from now till forever; ready to apply for every organization—you are wrong. Such solutions do not exist. But you can be inspired by the examples given in this book to prepare your own solution tailored to your organization conditions. Be brave to do this.

9. Analyze leadership impact, remember the golden rule of the KLC implementation: if you are the leader—be the example of the KLC-approach highest level you want to see among your employees. The company culture must be experienced to be learned (absorbed). We do not learn about culture through the theory as best as through the experience and practice. Without leaders exposing and executing the KLC approach, any changes in organizational employee behavior are possible. Organizations interested in collective company intelligence building should employ only those leaders who reflect (exposed by their behavior) the KLC approach—those who act oppositely: do not apply knowledge, do not learn, do not collaborate—should not be leaders at any level in knowledge-driven organizations. It is a golden rule of the KCL implementation in any culture type, including adhocracy.

8.3 Case study

"My Wave" company

"My wave" is a clothing company founded by college friends in 2005 in California. They design, produce, and sell clothes for surfers. The company's mission is to provide a higher class of utility and design. That is why they are constantly looking for new technological innovations in fibers and sewing and new inspirations to express the happiness, freedom, extreme challenges, and supreme professionalism of surfers to make them feel good in their clothes. So, the "surfers' mindset" is in the center of this company's innovativeness and creativity. All of the owners, Ana, Thomas, Nico, and Julia are passionate surfers. They are also more likely to employ surfers than no-surfers to their teams. So, the company members generally do what they believe in and live their authentic lives.

Ana is responsible for the R&D and suppliers; Nico for production; Thomas for design and Julia is organizing distribution channels, and she is also the boss (CEO). They employ 50 people.

The problem they faced recently was Thomas's behavior. Thomas's team is pretty good. Their design is exceptional, and "My Wave" won the market a couple of years in a row, thanks to Thomas's team's creativity. Thomas was always a creative leader, but recently, the designs of Paola (young shark) and Eugine (old wolf) have been much better than those of Thomas, who can't accept the situation. He is jealous and diminishes Paolas' and Eugene's input. Initially, he was passive-aggressive, but recently, he has been openly antagonistic. It started to jeopardize the design team. Nico, Julia, and Ana see clearly that the problem is hazardous. Paola and Eugine become increasingly frustrated and talk about leaving the company together and establishing their design studio, selling projects to other factories.

Problems for discussion

1. Name the problem from a) Paola and Eugene perspective; b) from Nico, Julia, and Ana perspectives; and c) from Thomas perspective and, present the summary.
2. Imagine the discussion between all parties involved focused on finding the solution. Prepare the scenario of potential solutions, be careful and respect each party's perspective. Can you see the room for "perfect agreement"?

3. Draw the future scenarios for "My wave" company development if:

    a) Paola and Eugene left.
    b) Thomas left.
    c) No one left, but there is no trust between them anymore.

4. Imagin you are Ana. What would you do? Think critically and strategically. Remember you are responsible for the "My Wave" future.
5. Summarize all the above and formulate:

    a) "lessons learned" and b) best practices.

Additional Questions

1. Regarding KLC, how do you feel about it in a "My Wave" company context? Does it work there? If your answer is "yes," clarify why? If "no," clarify why?
2. What would you propose to strengthen the KLC in "My Wave"?
3. Think about you. How you would cope when one of your workmates one day becomes a master in your expertise. If you have never been in such a situation to "lose a top position," prepare yourself now. How can you save your own enthusiasm and not destroy a "freshly raised star"? How should the organization facilitate such events to keep the team motivated and enthusiastic?

References

Argyris, C., & Schon, D. A. (1978). *Organisational learning*. Addison Wesley.

Dweck, C. S. (2017). *Mindset*. Brown, Little Book Group.

Kargas, A. D., & Varoutas, D. (2015). On the relation between organizational culture and leadership: An empirical analysis. *Cogent Business & Management*, *2*(1), 1055953. https://doi.org/10.1080/23311975.2015.1055953

Kucharska, W. (2017). Relationships between trust and collaborative culture in the context of tacit knowledge sharing. *Journal of Entrepreneurship, Management and Innovation*, *13*(4), 61–78.

Kucharska, W., Balcerowski, T., Kucharski, M., & Jussila, J. (2024a). Who is an agile leader? Technological vs. non-technological mindset employees' views. *20th European Conference on Management, Leadership and Governance*, *20*(1), 397–404. https://doi.org/10.34190/eckm.25.1.2367

Kucharska, W., Balcerowski, T., Kucharski, M., Jussila, J., & Laanti, M. (2024b). Why does the agile leader mindset matter the most? Polish-Finnish, technological and non-technological perspectives on agile and non-agile mindset employees and organizations. *Heliyon*. Available at SSRN: https://ssrn.com/abstract=4988722 or http://dx.doi.org/10.2139/ssrn.4988722

Kucharska, W., & Bedford, D. A. D. (2019). Knowledge sharing and organizational culture dimensions: Does job satisfaction matter? *Electronic Journal of Knowledge Management*, *17*(1), 1–18.

Kucharska, W., & Bedford, D. A. D. (2024). The KLC cultures' synergy power, trust, and tacit knowledge for organizational intelligence. *Electronic Journal of Knowledge Management*, *22*(2), 18–35. https://doi.org/10.34190/ejkm.22.2.3554

Kucharska, W., & Kopytko, A. (2024). Double bias of mistakes: Essence, consequences, and measurement method. *Electronic Journal of Business Research Methods*, *22*(1), 26–42. https://doi.org/10.34190/ejbrm.22.1.3320

Kucharska, W., Kowalczyk, R., & Kucharski, M. (2017). *Trust, tacit knowledge sharing, project performance, and their managerial implications*. Proceedings of the 18th European Conference on Knowledge Management, Vol. 1, pp. 532–539, September 7-8, Barcelona, Spain. ACPI.

Moonen, P. (2017). The impact of culture on the innovative strength of nations: A comprehensive review of the theories of Hofstede, Schwartz, Boisot and Cameron and Quinn. *Journal of Organizational Change Management*, *30*(7), 1149–1183. https://doi.org/10.1108/JOCM-08-2017-0311

Tosey, P., Visser, M., & Saunders, M. N. (2012). The origins and conceptualizations of 'triple-loop' learning: A critical review. *Management Learning*, *43*(3), 291–307.

9 Market culture

9.1 Key challenges in the KLC-approach implementation in market culture organizations

Market culture organizations are strongly motivated internally (shareholders, leaders, employees) and externally (market orientation, stakeholders' pressure with temperate moral obligation) to smoothly implement changes and build the collective intelligence in organization. They have a strong focus on knowledge, learning, and collaboration. Markets expose higher natural predispositions to collective learning, including mistakes as a source. However this motivation is not as high as observed for adhocracies or clans.

Characteristics: A market culture focuses on productivity, competitiveness, and market superiority. So, it strongly encourages market orientation development and consequently it is oriented to sustainable customer value delivery, which is possible thanks to innovations. So, strongly market-oriented organizations are consequently strongly motivated to adapt smoothly to market changes and develop agility. Market culture supports a results-driven organization focused on effects. Therefore, market culture organizations with strong market orientation are strongly motivated to develop collective intelligence that facilitates the overall performance, innovations, market advantage and long-run competitiveness.

Leaders: Market culture organizations' leaders love play and win, so they are demanding, hard-driving, and extremely productive. Often a fixed mindset that might dominate their short-term perspective (the success demand: here and now). However, more experienced long-distance players can also lead markets. Growth-mindset market leaders are those who will superficially clearly understand the organizational intelligence building in the long run. Those will reflect and support the KLC. However, the market orientation will make them less empathetic or understanding than leaders we can meet in adhocracies. Market leaders are winners and will eliminate those who will not support their winning (Gao, 2017; Kargas & Varoutas, 2015; Klein et al., 2013). So, they extremely strongly affect organization (Kargas & Varoutas, 2015), however

DOI: 10.4324/9781003485230-12

they are not the only pressure source motivating to change as it is observed in clans or hierarchies.

Employees: Employees are competent, motivated, and goal orientated. Their internal emphasis is on winning the market, and it unites members. They know they need each other, because market games are impossible to win alone. But they very selectively create alliances. The best wants to play with the best to win all.

Size: medium, middle, often big organizations.

Structure: flat hierarchy works the best for market organizations, especially if they are big and complex.

Strategy-Culture-Structure alignment criterion: Strategy always requires a long-run perspective. So, the KLC-approach implementation serves the organizational intelligence building in the long run. Since market culture organizations are market-oriented then this purpose is clear and easy to accept for all company members. Knowledge management systems supporting the smooth flow from data through information, knowledge, and wisdom to intelligence are key points of market knowledge management strategy. The KLC approach is a perfect tool supporting the transformation of tacit knowledge into explicit form in market culture conditions. The structure that best supports this transformation in market culture conditions (especially if markets are complex) is flat hierarchy.

Critical asset: Relationships (social capital), trust; intellectual capital is critical but market culture organizations usually have it.

Key Challenge: Silo building tendency. Markets similarly to hierarchies need to develop collaborative and learning cultures to gain collective intelligence. Collaboration acts as an exchange of favors in market culture, but entire KLC implemented at all levels can efficiently balance the "silo" building tendency that is an unwelcomed result of a constant acting based on favors exchange—it is why the implementation of the KLC, if successful, is so efficient.

Building silos occur when a specific departments or divisions managers deliberately blocks all collaboration and knowledge sharing that is not supervised by him (he/she feels the need to control everything to secure own supremacy and benefits). In such a case, collaboration is inefficient; departments and teams exist as independent silos instead of as a functional part of the whole. Such a situation jeopardizes the efficiency of the entire business and discourages the achievement of long-term goals, the achievement of which is breakneck in such conditions.

Remedy: Since the market organization focuses on value gaining, to implement KLC approach in the market organization is exposing that KLC approach pays to all. So, the enhancing statement for market culture to implement the KLC approach can be: "Knowledge is a base for development, but can't be static so we need to learn constantly, we avoid mistakes but if they happen it means we omitted something and we need to learn from the case, therefore we do not stigmatize people who fail; we encourage them to share their experience and we learn from the case together; only those who fail constantly and do not take lessons from their experiences and do not share their experiences should be excluded. Generally, inclusion is the way we act. When we collaborate—we can create and disseminate knowledge better and faster. When we do it together, we growth together and organizational intelligence growth this way. When we learn alone, we growth alone. But none of us can win market alone. It is why we need the KLC approach." Markets change adaptability, and internal innovations without the KLC will be rather reactive and incremental, but the KLC approach can make markets (market culture dominated organizations) very proactive.

Priority actions (regarding the KLC): Market intelligence building depends mostly on the learning and collaboration culture developed at the team and division levels. However, the division level is critical to balance markets eventual tendency to build organizational silos. So, organizations must put pressure on cooperation among divisions. Market culture organization must act as an efficient adaptability system to win the market. So, collective organizational intelligence is a "must have" capability to achieve this.

Final advice for market leaders: Since market organizations' members are very competitive it is a temptation to build a motivational system based on competitiveness to enhance productivity. And in the short term, it works perfectly. But it precisely leads to silo building to secure "territory" and control it for best competitiveness benefits. In contrast, motivating by cooperation is not as efficient in a short time as through competitiveness, but it pays back in the long run, and the "silo world" has no chance of occurring. Again, fixed mindset leaders—will select competitiveness as a motivator. Growth-mindset leaders will motivate through cooperation. So, if you are a short-contract leader (2–3 years), obviously you will select motivating through competitiveness to increase productivity and how shareholders or owners have a quick effect. But leaders responsible for long-run perspective probably would prefer to build an organization as an efficient adaptability system with higher-level organizational intelligence. So, for those leaders the KLC cultures rooted in solid cooperation among division would be the most beneficial. Market culture organization must act as an efficient adaptability system to win the market.

9.2 KLC implementation plan in market culture organizations

The implementation of the KLC approach should start as proposed in Section 8.2 regarding adhocracies and follow steps given in this chapter. However, knowing that for markets the critical is overstep the "silo building tendency," the KLC implementation should precisely focused on the collectivism at managerial level. It is critical for gaining synergy from knowledge sharing and learning from all organizational experiences to create a smoothly adapting entity open to new insights regarding clients, competitors, and new trends in the market. Market organizations operate usually in hyper conditions reality. So, they must be intellectually agile, innovative, and sustainable to gain competitiveness in the long run.

So, collective organizational intelligence is a "must have" skill to achieve this. This way, the KLC culture's behaviors must be habitual. So, all the golden rules of the KLC approach presented in the previous chapter should be respected:

1. Leaders golden rule: Leaders create company culture. Organizations interested in collective company intelligence building should employ only those leaders who reflect (expose) the KLC approach: seek and share knowledge, learn constantly (including learning from mistakes) and support others (act inclusively instead exclusively)—those who act oppositely to the KLC (knowledge-learning and collaboration cultures) should not be leaders at any level in organizations interested in collective intelligence building.
2. Knowledge culture golden rule: make decisions based on knowledge (explicit and tacit) use the best knowledge you have; ask for knowledge you need; organize the knowledge needed that is missing in organization; be open to new knowledge, avoid intellectual laziness. Remember, making decisions in uncertainty conditions will force you to decide based mostly on your tacit knowledge that is unusual. In a highly dynamic and competitive markets your company must act based on their best explicit knowledge but mostly using intuitive, tacit knowledge. To develop tacit knowledge, your organization members must learn from from changing contexts through "learning by doing" and through "social interactions" (Kucharska and Erickson, 2023). So, as a leader, be brave to do this. New situations, new problems require new methods of action. What worked yesterday can be irrelevant today. So, there is no one knowledge that works perfectly in each context and forever. So, make your team open to seeking for relevant knowledge. Do not let your organization be a group of slaves of old methods, traditions, and way of thinking or solving problems—be open-minded and enhance employees to stay open—be intellectually agile—learn.
3. Learning culture golden rule: learn constantly from all experiences: good and bad—from successes and failures: "the mistake is a failure if there is no lesson taken from it."

   Enhance others around you to be mindful: "the day without a new learning is a day lost." Learn from others, especially from those who perform exceptionally well. Organize learning sessions when all can learn about the best collective practices of best teams as well as from those individuals who are experts. Make a habit asking for opinion and, make a habit a giving it. Make accepted the fact that opinions differ and that it is very good. Such a situation gives a broader view and deeper understanding that leads to better decisions but only if people listen one another with open minds. Feedback is a special form of giving opinions. Negative feedback is usually the most problematic—equally in giving as taking—but its value is tremendous. If workmates feel its positive intention, it supports their personal development. Collective development concerns the improvement of the group performance, but it starts form personal level. So, it is vital to create the personal and collective positive attitudes toward constant improvement through practicing critical thinking and constant improvement of technology support, management methods and social relations.

It is how collective learning happens in organizations: people think critically, talk about problems openly without blaming others, and give and listen opinions with open minds. So, stimulate employees cooperative learning by giving challenging tasks that require critical thinking and cooperation to be succeeded. Always celebrate the successes and formulate "lessons learned" from successes. Do it equally diligently for failures experience. Mistakes if happen should be used as a source of learning. Reward teams for all initiatives oriented to improvements: technological solutions, managerial methods or social relations—all of them matters for market competitive advantage building (Samhan et al., 2023a, 2023b).

4. Collective culture golden rules: support cooperation between employees, teams, and divisions. Do not build employees' motivation to increase performance through internal competitiveness: competitors are outside the organization, never inside. Let people feel proud of being an integral part of the special whole. Create engagement through trust. Create commitment through empathy and inclusion. Make asking for help and support an organizational habit.

9.3 Case study

Aqua Sprint

Aqua Sprint is a company operating in the FMCG sector, which produces highly alkaline water in Poland. Their weight distribution level is perfect (98%), and they employ 650 people. The competition in the sector is quite high but the "alkaline water" sub-category is dominated by Aqua Sprint, which first noticed this market niche, which is promising and still growing. It is because many positive health claims about alkaline water have made this category of water extremely popular recently. Some say it can help regulate the body's pH level, slow the aging process, and prevent cancer. However, alkaline water remains somewhat controversial. Many health professionals say there isn't enough research to support many of the most popular health claims made by users and sellers. But the group of loyal users is constantly growing.

The company structure is a typical functional flat hierarchy where each division is responsible for the function being a part of the linear delivery process from the production (water bottling plant) through R&D laboratory, warehouses, logistics, sale, and marketing to the final consumer. The most impactful, critical divisions regarding current market drivers (ecology & health) for the company's success is R&D laboratory and marketing. This is because to sell water in plastic bottles successfully today; you must convince the market that your water is exceptional, and their health benefits are much higher than the costs and risks regarding their plastic bottle form of delivery. It is a challenge to win this benefit/guilt game, for the entire beverage market, because a plastic bottle is a symbol of guilt for more and more ecologically oriented consumers.

So, the problem which Aqua Sprint faced recently is a "blame game" between Marketing and R&D divisions. Consumers want both: having healthy products and act ecologically, but they are not ready to pay for the alkaline water more than 20% above market. So, the company is in the moment where they can't grow anymore without reducing the price, which cannot happen without losing the margin that Aqua Sprint can't afford to it. Expansion to other countries is unlikely due to long channel distribution costs and competition with strongly positioned domestic producers.

So, instead of cooperation, there is competition and a "blame game"—both divisions turned into closed silo towers, their employees are in an open distrust, and their bosses barely speak to one another apart of the official meetings where they try to expose the incompetency of the other party. The CEO at the begging has seen this as advantage—each division escalated other party mistakes. So, both divisions became extremely careful to avoid any. Today, they both do not more above the required minimum to be "perfect." But in fact, the company is stepping back into the market. The "required minimum" is not enough to win a bottled water market today.

So, the situation jeopardizes the company's future.

Problems for discussion

1. Prepare three potential scenarios about Aqua Sprint's future if nothing change and select the one you consider the most probable. Justify your choice.
2. Critically assess these scenarios from the following:

   a) the Marketing Division perspective. Propose a solution.
   b) the R&D Division perspective. Propose a solution.
   c) the CEO perspective (include CEO role in problem creation). Propose a solution.
   d) the shareholders perspective. Propose a solution.

3. How would you cope with this being: a) Head of Marketing; b) Head of R&D; c) CEO; and d) shareholder. Changing perspectives when searching for the best solution is a perfect exercise for your brain.
4. Summarize all the above and formulate:

   a) "lessons learned" and b) best practices.

Additional Questions

1. Is "Aqua Sprint" a collectively intelligent organization?
2. Regarding KLC, how do you feel about it in the "Aqua Sprint" company context? Does it work there? Which of the KLC components do you see as the stronger, and which as the weaker? Clarify "why?"
3. What would you propose to strengthen the KLC in "Aqua Sprint"?

References

Gao, Y. (2017). Business leaders' personal values, organisational culture and market orientation. *Journal of Strategic Marketing*, *25*(1), 49–64.

Kargas, A. D., & Varoutas, D. (2015). On the relation between organizational culture and leadership: An empirical analysis. *Cogent Business & Management*, *2*(1), 1055953. https://doi.org/10.1080/23311975.2015.1055953

Klein, A. S., Wallis, J., & Cooke, R. A. (2013). The impact of leadership styles on organizational culture and firm effectiveness: An empirical study. *Journal of Management & Organization*, *19*(3), 241–254.

Kucharska, W., & Erickson, G. S. (2023). Tacit knowledge acquisition & sharing, and its influence on innovations: A Polish/US cross-country study. *International Journal of Information Management*, *71*, 102647.

Samhan, N., Treur, J., Kucharska, W., & Wiewiora, A. (2023a). An adaptive network model simulating the effects of different culture types and leader qualities on mistake handling and organisational learning. In H. Cherifi, R. N. Mantegna, L. M. Rocha, C. Cherifi, & S. Miccichè (Eds.), *Complex networks and their applications. Studies in computational intelligence* (Vol. 1077). Springer. https://doi.org/10.1007/978-3-031-21127-0_19

Samhan, N., Treur, J., Kucharska, W., & Wiewiora, A. (2023b). Computational simulation of the effects of different culture types and leader qualities on mistake handling and organisational learning. In *Computational modeling of multilevel organisational learning and its control using self-modeling network models* (pp. 363–408). Springer International Publishing.

10 Clan culture

10.1 Key challenges in the KLC-approach implementation in clans

Clans' motivation to build organizational intelligence is more internal than external. It does not come from employees' internal motivation to grow or change, but it is strongly moderated by the leaders' attitude. Regarding market pressure, the clans' focus on it is relatively moderate or even nonexistent. Stakeholder pressure is only conditionally motivating to change power. It is if it refers to moral obligation, license to operate, or clan reputation. A motivation for any change comes from the leader who is fully trusted. Clan members believe in their traditional existence "purpose" sometimes very unquestioningly; they are unconditionally loyal to this purpose, the other members, and the leader.

Characteristics: Clan culture supports an open and friendly place to work where people share a lot of themselves. Group loyalty and a sense of tradition are strong. There is an emphasis on long-term benefits of development and great importance is given to group cohesion. There is a strong concern for people and the organization places a premium on teamwork, participation, and consensus (Gao, 2017).

Leaders: Clans' leaders expose strong self-transcendence values, which consist of universalism and benevolence value types tend to emphasize acceptance of others as equals and concern for their welfare, clans' leaders' behaviors are very inclusive toward their exclusive organization members (Gao, 2017; Klein et al., 2013). They impact organization stronger than the organization impacts them (Kargas & Varoutas, 2015), but their impact is not as strong as observed in adhocracies or markets and, in contrary to these cultures' leaders are the main driving force of motivation to implement changes in clans. So, it is critical to select in clan organizations leaders with growth, instead of fixed mindsets (Dweck, 2017; Samhan et al., 2023a, 2023b).

Employees: They are like family to one another: engagement, commitment, and higher-level loyalty characterize clans' members. They feel good working together and doing their jobs. They highly value good relations among people,

DOI: 10.4324/9781003485230-13

so they rarely initiate changes that could make someone feel uncomfortable. So, they learn but this process is controlled. So, their "safety zone" is strictly secured. If they decide to cross it, it happens for "better good," and this way they accept it. They value the "common good" over a good of the individual.

Size: Usually small or medium organization in European conditions, but in Asia clan structure is the most popular and concerns such a giant as Toyota, Honda or Suzuki.

Structure: Hierarchy.

Strategy-Culture-Structure alignment criterion: Strategy always requires a long-run perspective. For clans such a perspective depends on the leader's vision. Regarding knowledge management strategy, clans are based on both explicit and tacit knowledge (but not as passionately as adhocracies), and they believe in the "clan wisdom" built over time. So, the new knowledge and new learnings are acquired but more as a duty than passion. They focus on improvement but rather incremental than radical and only if the risk of change is worth all the efforts. They are not dynamic by nature but can be whatever is necessary—if only the leaders ask for it. The structure that best supports the "clan's wisdom" distribution across the organization is hierarchy.

Critical asset: intellectual capital, (trust is generally critical but clans usually have it).

Key Challenge: based on the given in Part I study findings (Polish context), clans do not care of static organizational knowledge as much as for organizational learning which in broaden context is very good. But without respect to solid knowledge the quality of the tacit can be not optimal. So, clans need to put a special attention to a solid knowledge base for smooth collective learning across divisions and teams.

Remedy: Clans naturally act collectively; therefore, to build organizational IQ, clan leaders can base their strong relations among company members on the characteristic for clans and enhance their collective learning and intelligence building for "organizational growth" and "better good." Moreover, to develop the learning culture fully, they need to care about the learning climate component, because it is powerful enough to overcome the double bias of mistakes in clans.

Priority actions: learning climate (shared motivation to learn) development, clearly presenting the vision of the particular clan future where learning matters in the fast-changing business context. Clan's have the tendency to ignore the external context, therefore such a focus development, it is a real priority to explain the KLC implementation purpose.

Final advice for clans' leaders: the KLC-approach implementation in clans depends the most on learning climate that next fosters learning from all organizational sources, including mistakes. So, to enhance such motivation for collective learning is the clear vision of the future that requires such an approach. So, clans must remain open-minded. They cannot ignore the external power of business context, if they want to survive. So, if you are the clan organization leader, start from the clear vision of the company future where knowledge is a base, learning is a tool and collaboration is an engine for organizational intelligence building, that is critical for the company's future. Create this vision, translate it to benefits of this future and make it attractive for all members.

10.2 KLC implementation plan in clans

The implementation of the KLC approach should start as proposed in Section 8.2 regarding adhocracies and follow steps given in this chapter with the special attention to KLC implementation golden rules given in Section 9.2. However, knowing that for clans the critical is overstep the "strong internal orientation" to create the motivation to the organizational intelligence building through, the KLC implementation should precisely focused on the learning climate (shared motivation to learn) development to understand changes in the external reality. It is critical for the enhancement for deep learning from all the sources internal and external (including mistakes). Former studies showed that growth-mindset leader is potentially the most influential power enabling implementation of any changes in clan culture organizations (Kargas & Varoutas, 2015; Samhan et al., 2023a, 2023b). Therefore, the proposed steps below are strongly connected with the clan leader's positive attitude toward collective intelligence building. If clan leaders do not have such motivation, there is no chance for the KLC implementation in clans.

A set of good practices for leaders to implement the KLC approach in clans:

1. Create a clear vision of your company's future bearing in mind the hyperdynamic of the business environment that affects all market players: environment, consumers, and entities including yours.
   a. Assess the distance between your current position and your vision.
   b. Prepare a plan of what you must to change in your employees behavior and organization best practices to make your vision come true.
   c. Regarding the knowledge management system that should support your new strategy formulation and implementation—name the knowledge gaps you see and find the way to fulfill them (for more, see Section 7.2).
   d. Since the environment, consumers, and market drivers change fast, consequently entities too. So, think if you see the room in your organization, where collective intelligence can help you to be agile and adapt to market changes to leverage your organization position. Can you share your intellectual privilege to think critically, decide, and take actions with company members? If yest, good. If no—think "why?" Is the reason for the knowledge gap between you and your clan members? If so, level up the knowledge between members and create repetitive and mindfulness-oriented

behaviors to embed the knowledge as a basis for each decision. Create a chronic need to base decisions on expertise.

e. If your company members are not skilled enough but expose potential—enhance them to learn together. If they do not reveal their learning potential, find them a place in your organization where they can contribute with their strengths; if not, let them go. Remember, the fact that some of your company members can't or do not want to learn and grow cannot be the reason why your company stops trying to grow, only to make them feel comfortable. Even charity organizations to serve a particular purpose inevitably must adapt methods of its accomplishment and evolve in time to follow the reality changes (market drivers, trends, and your target groups changing attitudes and behaviors, e.g., habits). Think about it. Identify your organizational learnings needs and create the climate to do it together for common purpose of "safe future" of the company.
f. Relations (collective culture) are solid in your organization and are of immense, remarkable value. Still, this value cannot be more important in securing good relations with the market players (your external environment). To follow up on the market, your company today must be intelligent in identifying opportunities and threats and dealing with them to secure your people's jobs and their families' peaceful existence.

2. Translate your vision to strategy and make it clear for all employees. Precisely, next to "big aims" you need to present what change is expected for each division, team, and person by name. Create KPIs, measure, support, and manage your change (Section 8.2).

The KLC implementation is powerful enough to support your Strategy-Culture-Structure alignment that is critical for any organization success. Regarding the structure, clans hierarchical relations supported strongly by KLC cultures synergy have a chance to evolve to networks which thanks to remarkable strong relations can make them exceptionally efficient.

10.3 Case study

Sweet Business

Thomas's grandfather established the chocolate factory at the beginning of the previous century. So, his family has a long tradition of producing chocolate products. The majority of employees work there almost their entire lives across generations; they know each other and their families very well, like each other, support each other, often organize "family picnics," and spend time together also after work. This company has always existed this way. Thomas's grandfather's core idea was that it is a "sweet business," so it must be sweet to the bones. Tomas's father followed this line. But Thomas sees it as sweet enough to make you sick. So, what is "wrong" with Thomas's perception?

Thomas noticed that all these good relations among employees are more important than anything in the company. Precisely this company does not exist to make profit, or make customers happy when eating chocolate but to make their employees happy that they have a perfect community where they feel safe and this makes Thomas crazy. The issue is not because he does not care about people, but the essence of his attitude is that the chocolate business itself is not as sweet as it seems. It is harsh.

At first glance, you might think that a chocolate factory has nothing in common with a knowledge-driven organization, but the truth is that the chocolate market is strongly dependent on the cocoa market, which is dependent on the weather and other environmental conditions challenged recently by climate changes. Furthermore, there is a huge drop in milk chocolate products consumption because of the sugar ingredient called officially a "white dead." Dark chocolate has its own loyal group, but it is comparably small and very sophisticated in tasty selection. So, if someone wants to satisfy this group then he must have a very creative R&D team supported by the newest technology to make new products tasty, healthy, in price and extremely sophisticated in taste, shape, and look. There is no place for the typical chocolate bar. If anyone decides to eat the dark chocolate today then they expect something special, tasty, and healthy.

The milk chocolate market is bigger and much more competitive, and it is going constantly down year by year. It is a mass, multisegmented market, where gender, age, place of living, work, social status matters—there is no chance to win this market without a detailed market and customer knowledge. So, Thomas knows that this "sweet businesses" of his grandpa must be today strongly supported by data, information, knowledge, wisdom, and finally intelligence.

So, Thomas's key problem at this moment is that no one—except him—in the company understands it. His succession was sudden; his father died, and now Thomas is responsible for the entire business built by his family over two generations. His vision of this business is totally different that his ancestors. Employees are simply devastated by the changes he proposes and expectations he formulate toward them. On the one hand, they want to be loyal toward the family one the other they are terrified, because this company is not the same any longer. All miss his father, compare him to his father and express their disappointment.

Problems for discussion

1. Name the problem from a) Thomas's perspective and b) employees' perspective
2. Propose the potential three solutions (course of action options) from a) Thomas's perspective and b) employees' perspective
3. Compare these scenarios and check if there is a chance for "common ground." Justify your opinion.
4. If you were Thomas, what would you do?
5. If you were one of the employees, what would you do?

Additional Tasks:

1. Imagine Thomas decides to build organizational intelligence in "Sweet Business," prepare a plan for him (Sections 7.2, 8.2, 9.2, 10.1, and 10.2 can be helpful).
2. Assess the risks of this plan and prepare mitigation options.

References

Dweck, C. S. (2017). *Mindset*. Brown, Little Book Group.

Gao, Y. (2017). Business leaders' personal values, organisational culture and market orientation. *Journal of Strategic Marketing*, *25*(1), 49–64.

Kargas, A. D., & Varoutas, D. (2015). On the relation between organizational culture and leadership: An empirical analysis. *Cogent Business & Management*, *2*(1), 1055953. https://doi.org/10.1080/23311975.2015.1055953

Klein, A. S., Wallis, J., & Cooke, R. A. (2013). The impact of leadership styles on organizational culture and firm effectiveness: An empirical study. *Journal of Management & Organization*, *19*(3), 241–254.

Samhan, N., Treur, J., Kucharska, W., & Wiewiora, A. (2023a). An adaptive network model simulating the effects of different culture types and leader qualities on mistake handling and organisational learning. In H. Cherifi, R. N. Mantegna, L. M. Rocha, C. Cherifi, & S. Miccichè (Eds.), *Complex networks and their applications. Studies in computational intelligence* (Vol. 1077). Springer. https://doi.org/10.1007/978-3-031-21127-0_19

Samhan, N., Treur, J., Kucharska, W., & Wiewiora, A. (2023b). Computational simulation of the effects of different culture types and leader qualities on mistake handling and organisational learning. In *Computational modeling of multilevel organisational learning and its control using self-modeling network models* (pp. 363–408). Springer International Publishing.

11 Hierarchy culture

11.1 Key challenges in the KLC-approach implementation in hierarchies

Hierarchies' natural motivation to implement organizational intelligence is weak or nonexistent. Hierarchies' attention to external powers potentially motivates hierarchies to adapt to the business environment, such as market pressure or stakeholders' expectations hierarchies, is limited mostly to "license to operate" issues (legal conditions fulfillment) or reputation issues (image security). Regarding internal powers, potentially motivating hierarchies to adapt to the business environment, the most substantial impact belongs to the leader. However, employees' pressure due to their mass hierarchies usually represents big and very big organizations, which can be efficient. Still, if employees use such pressure, it is mainly concerned with working conditions, rarely or never the pressure on the company's development.

Characteristics: Hierarchy and clan cultures were both found to be negatively related to market orientation (Appiah-Adu & Blankson, 1998). Hierarchy culture supports a highly structured and formal place to work managed by control. Rules and procedures strictly govern behavior. Leaders strive to be good coordinators and organizers who are efficiency minded. Stability, high-level performance, and efficient operations are the long-term goals. Success is often seen by the prism of efficient efficacy achievement. However, companies operating for a significantly long period of time (mature entities) are based more on their structured rules, norms, and trends than on their leaders. Probably, it is the reason why, in mature hierarchies, structured rules, norms, and trends often overrule leaders. Hierarchies' maturity paradox essence is that the more mature the hierarchy is the less capable of change and development; it is why hierarchy culture observed often in mature and big organizations a natural motivation to implement organizational intelligence is weak or nonexistent (Kucharska, 2021). Hierarchies are slaves of own rules, procedures, and structures. Therefore, regarding the reality of organizational intelligence

DOI: 10.4324/9781003485230-14

building hierarchy culture, it is the most challenging to consider all the culture types discussed in this book.

Leaders: Leaders with dominant conservation values create and develop a hierarchy culture (Gao, 2017). They impact organization stronger than the organization impacts them (Kargas & Varoutas, 2015), but their impact is not as strong as observed in adhocracies or markets or clans. This situation is the most challenging that in contrary to adhocracies and markets leaders whose impact on the organization is much more impactful than clans' and hierarchies' leaders, leaders of clans and hierarchies are the main and often only driving force of motivation to implement changes. Clans' leaders' can rely on strong collectivism supporting leader's efforts, in contrary to them—hierarchy leader is often alone and only power driving change. And all the power the hierarchy leader has to implement changes is existing policies, rules, and procedures and own persuasive skills. So, hierarchical organizations leaders often behave like politicians to win coalition supporting hierarchical leaders' strategies. So, on the one hand, it is critical to select leaders with growth instead of fixed mindsets (Dweck, 2017; Samhan et al., 2023a, 2023b). On the other hand, the collision of leader-followers mindsets can hinder the organizational cohesion. However, apart from the growth mindset, leaders aiming to enhance the intelligence of hierarchies need to expose strong transformational personalities, and, even so, there is a huge risk of mental collision that can occur and totally paralyze the hierarchical organization. Dynamic, intelligent, smoothly learning agile mindsets of transformational leaders are not compatible with non-agile mindsets seeking stability (Kucharska et al., 2024). So, it can be very challenging to lead to change in people who want to secure the existing "status quo" for any price. So, a leader, by definition, is a person who has a personality, all the skills, and competencies to lead and transform the world. However, the leader is still a human whose abilities are also affected by the environment, for example, follower's mental models. So, mental collision in hierarchies is much more often observed than in other organization types.

Employees: They search for safety and uncertainty avoidance.

Size: Usually big and very big organizations.

Structure: Hierarchies' troubles with learning and adaptability suggest the evolution of hierarchies to a hybrid culture (mixed) to secure organizational IQ building. However, it will cause a problem of constant cultures collision (mental misfit).

Strategy-Culture-Structure alignment criterion: this criterion causes the biggest challenge for hierarchical organizations from the perspective of the organizational intelligence building. Intelligence building requires dynamic, smooth collective, regular actions optimized constantly thanks to collective critical thinking none of this fit to hierarchical organizations. Below, the two scenarios are proposed (scenario "hybrid" and scenario "perfect machine") that can act as remedy for hierarchies with ambition to be intelligent.

Critical asset: Intellectual capital, social capital, trust.

Key Challenges: Next to the weak motivation of hierarchical organization to develop the organizational intelligence, a leader-organization mental collision and cultural collision between organization, division, and team cultures is the second, very often observed in hierarchical organizations problem, due to the fact that their size and multifunctionality make them multicultural organizations (Table 3.3a, b). Regarding the identified this book research (Part I), cultural conflict consequences in a decrease in the intelligence of nonhierarchical teams when operating in hierarchical divisions, and at the organizational level the practical implication is to dedicate less hierarchical, even autonomous divisions to teams that collective work requires creativity, out-of-the-box thinking, effects are not repeatable and predictable (high-risk), for example, R&D teams. The worst course of action is to force such teams dedicated to organizational development to hierarchical and bureaucratic structures—as it is visualized in Figures 4.2a, b the intelligence of such teams is going down when forced to fit themselves to hierarchical realities. Tacit knowledge is a root of the competitive advantage through to its significant contribution to organizational creativity and innovation, and, it requires freedom and smooth collaboration to be created, realized, shared, and transformed to its explicit form (Kucharska & Erickson, 2023). Therefore, forcing creative people to be creative accordingly to procedures, and policies in fact kills their creativity leading in its worst scenario to the total lack of any invention in the hierarchical companies. It is an effect of cause the mental collision. Isn't it absurd to even try to control the aptness of the way creative minds work? In hierarchical organizations with obsessive control and lack of trust is very difficult to invent and implement any change, including solutions that enable hierarchical organizations to grow. This is why the evolution from the pure hierarchy to a hybrid organization with an autonomous division dedicated to creative tasks is proposed. The problem with collective learning should be facilitated by collaboration—as described.

Remedy: Hierarchies' troubles with learning and adaptability suggest the evolution of hierarchies to a hybrid culture (mixed) to secure organizational IQ building. But the challenge hierarchies must overcome to make such a transition is a mental models collision. Hierarchies naturally support knowledge culture because it helps hierarchies avoid uncertainties and control the status quo—that gives hierarchies a sense of safety. But critical for their intelligence development are collaborative culture, which in hierarchies acts as a power that shortens the distance between coworkers. If collaboration is developed only at the team level it is not efficient for organizational intelligence building. Collaboration culture developed at the division level is critical for hierarchies' intelligence building, it is a base for learning. There is no option to develop collective intelligence without collective, also informal learning.

If we want to avoid such a collision and build organizational intelligence in hierarchical organizations there are two the most promising scenarios:

1. Scenario "hybrid." Accept the fact that some functions in your hierarchical organization, dedicated to creative and dynamic actions, to be efficient cannot work in the hierarchy culture and structure. So separate these divisions or teams and give them autonomy if necessary, to make their existence purpose achievable.
2. Scenario "perfect machine." Constantly adapt policies, rules, and procedures to constantly changing realities to secure organizational efficacy. Hierarchy must exist as a "perfectly adaptive, efficient and agile system." So, an "intellectual laziness" cannot be tolerated. Employ transformational leaders with agile mindset to lead the hierarchy. To make transformational leader's mission successfully accomplished hierarchy must work as "perfect machine," for example, military organizations.

Priority actions for intelligence building:

a) For scenario: "hybrid," the priority is not forcing hierarchy structure and culture to teams and divisions dedicated to functions where other cultures will work better (e.g., adhocracy is perfect for the R&D). It is critical to give such a teams and divisions autonomy but at the same time to secure a perfect collaboration.
b) For the "perfect machine" scenario, collaboration and learning cultures are crucial; the required changes must first be identified accurately to be adapted to them smoothly. Therefore, the constant collective learning must be a priority. To do so, teams' and divisions' leaders must expose the KLC approach—it is critical.

Final advice for hierarchies' leaders:

a) Select a "hybrid" scenario if your company's success requires a higher level of innovativeness of your employees.
b) Select a "perfect machine" scenario if your organization operates in a "public service" sector.
c) Select a mix (both of the above) if your company operates in a highly competitive market.

11.2 KLC implementation plan in hierarchies

The implementation of the KLC approach should start as proposed in Section 8.2 regarding adhocracies and follow the steps given in this chapter with special attention to KLC implementation golden rules given in Section 9.2 about markets and, with a full understanding of a set of good practices for leaders to implement the KLC approach in clans (Section 10.2)—they all can be helpful. However, knowing that for the KLC implementation in hierarchies, it is critical to overstep the following challenges:

1. The employees lack motivation to be an "intelligent organization," particularly visible in organizations that are far away from market orientation and market pressure.
2. There is a potential mindset collision between the minority who want to build organizational intelligence in a hierarchical organization and the majority who do not have such an intention. Transformational leaders' dynamic, intelligent, smoothly learning agile mindsets are not compatible with non-agile mindsets seeking stability (Kucharska et al., 2024).

The following steps of KLC implementation plans are proposed regarding the selected scenario ("hybrid," "perfect machine," and "mix: hybrid perfect machine") in the hierarchy reality.

a) "Hybrid scenario"—best if your company's success requires a higher level of innovativeness of your employees. The critical challenge observed for this scenario is a "mindset collision" as a remedy. Autonomy was proposed for teams and divisions responsible for dynamic, creative, innovative, and agile actions where the collective intelligence of such a team or division is critical—having autonomy such units can act as adhocracies when implementing the KLC (Section 8.2). The critical points in such a scenario will be the touching points when the Adhocracy Unit depends on the Hierarchy Master Organization. Some tensions can occur. So, the leaders of the Adhocracy autonomous units and the leader of the Hierarchy Master Organization must be fully aware of these tensions' risks and roots. Both must be very mindful. This scenario can succeed if leaders are mature enough to mitigate tensions caused by mindset collisions. The lack of such competencies to reduce tensions that will naturally occur between these units will turn autonomous units into silos (Sections 10.1 and 10.2). So, the critical factor in this scenario is a mature, higher-level servant leadership quality oriented to cooperation and inclusion with a high level of acceptance for diversity exposed by the Hierarchy Master Organization leader. The adhocracy unit leader must be a transformational agile mindset shark with an extreme growth mindset to be ready to serve as a leading agent for implementing and executing the KLC approach in this unit and as the KLC ambassador in Hierarchy Master Organization.
b) The "Perfect machine" scenario is best if your organization operates in a "public service" sector. The critical challenge to this scenario's success is the mental model of team employees. That critical point is full obedience, loyalty, and dynamic, immediate, higher-level response to any request, according

to the responsibilities and position held. So, clan mentality development in teams is a key to success for hierarchical organizations that want to deliver a higher level of public service. The critical point is the development of the learning climate (shared motivation to learn, Section 10.2), clearly presenting the vision of the particular clan's future where learning matters in the fast-changing business context. Clans tend to ignore the external context and be just perfect in doing something they used to do (the first loop of learning). With such a focus on development, explaining the KLC implementation in a "perfect machine" scenario is a real priority. Still, contrary to typical clans, the division level is equally critical here. However, teams are the first line of public service, but those are dependent on divisions' support. The "perfect machine" must be perfect at each level to secure single- and double-loop learning (Argyris & Schon, 1978). So, the KLC exposing leaders should respect knowledge, focus on learning, and prioritize teamwork, and constantly expose what employees can achieve together that would never be possible to achieve alone (Section 10.2).

c) Mix (both of the above) if your company operates in a highly competitive market. For this scenario, the best plan is to first give autonomy to units responsible for innovativeness (breaking conventions, searching for novelty, experimenting, and so on). Second, make leaders only those who strictly expose the KLC cultures. This rule concerns all leaders at all management levels. Third, making these leaders a clan will secure both the innovativeness and dynamic efficacy of the entire organization.

As was claimed earlier, hierarchies are not naturally disposed by stakeholders or market pressure to build collective intelligence. Therefore, the proposed KLC-approach implementation ideas are embedded in the scenarios that support the motivation for organizational intelligence building (without the motivation for IQ, the KLC-approach implementation is out of interest, Chapter 7).

11.3 Case study

Cultural Collision at the University

Huge public universities are usually strongly hierarchical and bureaucratic. Paradoxically, universities are expected to be leaders in the generation of new ideas, the invention of technologies, the promotion of critical thinking, the development of individual and collective intelligence, and the promotion of innovations across businesses, industries, and society. So, the question arises of how such a hierarchical entity can deliver to society values characteristically delivered by adhocracies. This is a question that Helen asked herself when colleagues encouraged her to become their candidate for the next rector position. This question was relevant because a lot has been done before by external stakeholders and government institutions, such as the European Commission or the Ministry of Higher Education, to encourage universities to participate more intensively in society's development. So, many initiatives were taken to support the cooperation between universities and practices that were implemented at Julia's Alma Mater. However, there are still no visible effects that would satisfy all parties.

The previous provost saw the problem, and as a solution, he established a dedicated unit to commercialize scientists' inventions and organize cooperation with businesses. Eight years have passed, and the unit today is three times bigger than eight years ago, but no successes have been noted. After the thorough analysis and deep interviewing of all employees involved Helena discovered that it is precisely the company culture collision problem.

Specifically, the previous provost started to implement the "hybrid scenario." However, the commercialization unit did not have enough autonomy. The Hierarchy Master Organization, step by step, day by day, imposed its old, well-worn methods of operation on the new entity, specifically, the same hierarchical-bureaucratic methods that had made universities inert over the last decades. "No matter what you do, if you ignore the company culture as a key driving force in organizations—your ideas, the new strategy will fail"—Helen concluded.

In line with this, she started thinking about scientific teams and quickly realized they suffer from the same pain. Scientific teams sometimes act as clans and sometimes as adhocracies—both when having agile mindsets teams led by agile mindset leaders can achieve "everything," but even the most skilled, motivated, and engaged teams cannot survive the collision with Hierarchy Master Organization rules, procedures, policies, and every step overcontrols, cross-controls and double controls and . . . any possible kind of other controls that makes university personnel extremely, constantly "busy," but do not bring the value at the level expected by university stakeholders.

In line with this, she started thinking about the teaching process. Teaching-learning effects depend on the intellectual efforts of all parties involved. However, these efforts' impact on efficacy is moderated by creativity, efficient communication, and good relations between all parties involved. So,

So, what my university needs is a massive cultural revolution—Helen summarized.

Problems for discussion

1. Based on what this book has proposed so far for hierarchies, the clan of the KLC leaders at all management levels is the best method for implementing a "cultural revolution" focused on motivation to building collective intelligence. How do you feel what kind of challenges these KLC leaders can face in the old, hierarchical, intensely bureaucratic organization as typical public European university is?
2. From the student's perspective, identify the most urgent cultural collision between the university and students to overstep. Propose the idea "How?"
3. From the administrative staff perspective, identify the most critical cultural collision between the new idea of "agile and collective learning" university and the current state. How to mitigate it?—propose a solution.
4. From the scientific staff perspective, identify the most critical cultural collision between the new idea of "agile and collective learning" university and the current state. How to mitigate it?—propose a solution.

Additional Tasks:

1. Imagine Helen decides to conduct the "cultural revolution" at her uni; prepare a plan for her (Sections 7.2, 8.2, 9.2, 10.1, 10.2, and 11.2 can be helpful).
2. Assess the risks of your plan and prepare mitigation options.

References

Appiah-Adu, K., & Blankson, C. (1998). Business strategy, organizational culture, and market orientation. *Thunderbird International Business Review, 40*, 235–256.

Argyris, C., & Schon, D. A. (1978). *Organisational learning*. Addison Wesley.

Dweck, C. S. (2017). *Mindset*. Brown, Little Book Group.

Gao, Y. (2017). Business leaders' personal values, organizational culture, and market orientation. *Journal of Strategic Marketing, 25*(1), 49–64.

Kargas, A. D., & Varoutas, D. (2015). On the relation between organizational culture and leadership: An empirical analysis. *Cogent Business & Management, 2*(1), 1055953. https://doi.org/10.1080/23311975.2015.1055953

Kucharska, W. (2021). Wisdom from experience paradox: Organizational learning, mistakes, hierarchy and maturity issues. *Electronic Journal of Knowledge Management, 19*(2), 105–117.

Kucharska, W., Balcerowski, T., Kucharski, M., Jussila, J., & Laanti, M. (2024). Why does the Agile leader mindset matter the most? Polish-Finnish, technological and non-technological perspectives on agile and non-agile mindset employees and organizations. *Heliyon*. https://ssrn.com/abstract=4988722

Kucharska, W., & Erickson, G. S. (2023). Tacit knowledge acquisition & sharing, and its influence on innovations: A Polish/US cross-country study. *International Journal of Information Management, 71*, 102647.

Samhan, N., Treur, J., Kucharska, W., & Wiewiora, A. (2023a). An adaptive network model simulating the effects of different culture types and leader qualities on mistake handling and organisational learning. In H. Cherifi, R. N. Mantegna, L. M.

Rocha, C. Cherifi, & S. Miccichè (Eds.), *Complex networks and their applications. Studies in computational intelligence* (Vol. 1077). Springer. https://doi.org/10.1007/978-3-031-21127-0_19

Samhan, N., Treur, J., Kucharska, W., & Wiewiora, A. (2023b). Computational simulation of the effects of different culture types and leader qualities on mistake handling and organisational learning. In *Computational modeling of multilevel organisational learning and its control using self-modeling network models* (pp. 363–408). Springer International Publishing.

Part III

Organizational intelligence

Collective human versus artificial?

Motivation to develop organizational intelligence (OI) varies between company culture types, and consequently, it determines the implementation of the KLC approach. So, to have a full picture of this phenomenon, it is necessary to consider the development of organizational intelligence in the context of AI's rapid growth. Moreover, such trends as algorithmic management (that can be powered by AI but does not have to) and more and more popular remote work provoke a set of questions: Does company culture still serve as a critical resource supporting organizational strategies in such conditions? How should we create a company culture remotely? Which culture type serves best in AI reality to support organizational growth in virtual reality? How do we shape human relations in a working environment dominated by algorithms? Summing up, Part III discusses the KLC impact on the organizations' propensity to adapt to new algorithmic reality per culture type.

DOI: 10.4324/9781003485230-15

12 What culture, such algorithms—algorithmic management and company culture type

12.1 What culture, such algorithms—because company culture shapes the way work is designed

"Agorithmic management" or "management-by-algorithm" is seen as the delegation of managerial functions to algorithms (Lee, 2018; Noponen et al., 2024). It is a sociotechnical process emerging from the continuous interaction of organizational members and algorithms. Algorithms—basic and advanced—are a base for building artificial intelligence (AI) systems, which role is to support collective human intelligence (CHI) in organizations and impact organizational intelligence (OI). Figure 12.1 visualizes the frame of this relation.

Humans, as algorithm creators, have the power to design and optimize algorithms, so the moderation is mutual. Algorithms design moderates the relation between algorithmic management idea and work design (organization design algorithms according to their own purpose to shape the work accordingly to this purpose), and work design moderates the relation between algorithmic management and algorithms design (algorithmic management idea gives a technological opportunity to improve and re-design work and this way creates a demand to a specific algorithm design). A sociotechnical perspective argues that social actors play an active role in shaping and appropriating technological systems. In other words, workers and managers are not passive recipients of algorithmic results; they can design a role and an understanding of algorithmic systems, create trust toward their outputs, and constantly align the algorithmic management system to companies and their leader's needs and interests (Jarrahi et al., 2021; Jarrahi & Sutherland, 2019). Indeed, in the case of the pre-programmed (PP) algorithms, they can design, re-design, and optimize the entire workflow with confidence. However, regarding machine learning algorithms, human supervision is limited, and those algorithm types are the most controversial. All the transparency and objectivity benefits do not apply since the machine trains itself—the only way how humans impact this training is through the training data set selection. So, technical opacity regarding algorithms is rooted in the specifics of algorithm features and the design of emerging algorithmic systems, causing algorithm aversion due to limited machine learning (ML) algorithms training and output

DOI: 10.4324/9781003485230-16

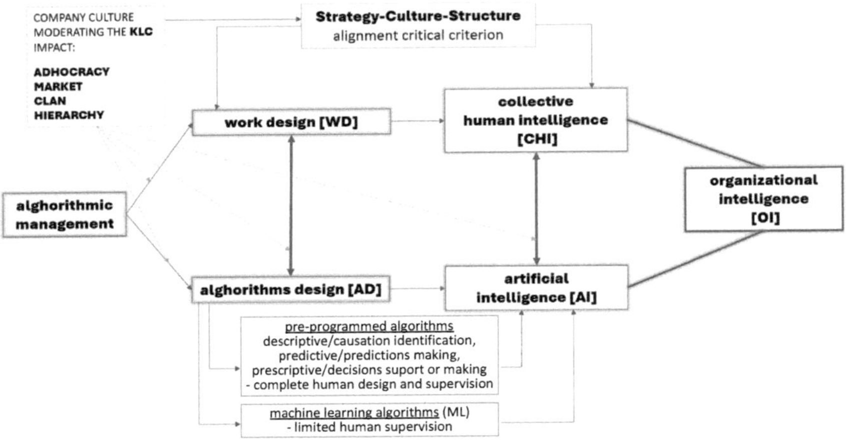

Figure 12.1 Algorithmic management and company's culture type impact on OI

control. Something that cannot be controlled cannot be managed. Responsible managers and workers demand explanations of ML algorithms logic in actual use settings that sometimes are very vague and, therefore, are usually not trusted (Gilpin et al., 2019, 2022). Responsible managers never accept tools designed in a way that cannot be controlled.

On the contrary, due to mental shortcuts, some enthusiasts of AI used to imply that interactions with machines (as opposed to other human beings) can be more trustworthy, unbiased, or altruistic (Sundar & Kim, 2019). Algorithms rely on logic and apply the same logic to all, so they are just and more trustworthy than biased, emotional people, which can be very true. However, such cognitive complacency may manifest itself when human decision-makers do not inquire into the factors driving inferences made by algorithms (Newell & Marabelli, 2015). So, the same logic applies to all, but this logic can be very vague if it is out of control. This is why pre-programmed algorithms are more trusted than those led by ML. Pre-programmed algorithms require intellectual agility to be constantly improved. ML algorithms learn themselves, so they do not require constant human input. Intellectual agility forces PP solutions, and intellectual laziness promotes ML solutions. So, such intellectual laziness can be risky and lead to organizational opacity. If there is a one logic it gives the illusion that the solution is just and free from bias, but if this logic is vague—it entails how algorithms reinforce the opacity of broader organizational choices (Jarrahi et al., 2021). Since algorithmic management involves a complicated network of people, data, and computational systems, the ability to understand, manipulate, and address the algorithmic systems on both a technical and organizational level will determine an individual's agency and power at work (Grønsund & Aanestad,

2020). Therefore, algorithmic management should be implemented with all the diligence securing the company's intelligent growth in the long-run perspective. It is possible if collective human intelligence (CHI) and artificial (AI) are both developed (Figure 12.1).

Algorithmic management, especially advanced by AI solutions, is a significant driver in transforming work, labor norms, and job design today. Recently, almost everything in organizations seems to be driven or drives algorithm design. Algorithms also shape organizational activity through semi- or fully automating workforce management, coordination, and administration (Crowston & Bolici, 2019). This means that while algorithms have a central bearing on how work is managed, their outcomes in transforming management and relationships between workers and managers are socially constructed (Jarrahi et al., 2021). On the one hand, the rapid development of machine learning algorithms, the basis of artificial intelligence systems, has created new opportunities for automation and optimization of work processes and replacing human input in some analytical management functions, for example, monitoring, goal setting, performance management, scheduling, compensation, job termination (Parent-Rocheleau & Parker, 2022). This idea, at its early stage, sounded highly controversial. Considering the potential impact of algorithmic management on building organizational intelligence, on the one hand, it will be a technological advance in reducing tedious, repetitive tasks that often frustrate knowledge workers today. So such boring tasks replacement can, in fact, increase knowledge workers' productivity—they can engage alternatively in more complex, enhancing the development of their minds—challenging tasks. So, from this perspective, we can compare algorithms "revolution" to the industrial revolution humanity faced in the XIX century.

On the other hand, this revolution is much more controversial when advanced algorithms manage people. There is a huge mental barrier for most employees who perceive machines as those who should serve people. So, they do not feel safe being in the organizational hierarchy lower than machines, which are receiving too much power over them. Machines cannot understand a broader context to be objective and transparent based on a defined set of factors determining KPIs, but what if these factors cannot be easily defined? What if they change constantly? So, suppose that the particular job is mostly based on explicit knowledge. In that case, it is quite easy to define KPI and describe and measure all inputs and outputs. Basic analytical algorithms will significantly support this job flow, its assessment, optimization, and decision-making regarding the processes involved. However, what if the particular job is complex and its purpose mostly relates to creating and transforming tacit knowledge? In such a case, algorithms can be helpful but only in limited functions. The higher-level, strongly contextual, consciously vague knowledge conversion processes are exclusively reserved for the agile mindsets of the most intelligent individuals (Kucharska et al., 2024a, 2024b, 2024c). So, agile organizations today are still people, however strongly supported by technology. It might be that the agile organizations of the future will employ algorithms, and people-only roles will supervise them. If so, regarding work, jobs, and competencies design, the question arises of what kind of human mindsets can create, design, control, develop (re-design), and supervise algorithms smoothly to maintain humans' supreme position—those mindsets are agile mindsets (Kucharska et al., 2024a, 2024b, 2024c).

So, going back to Chapter 7, when we discussed the particular culture-type motivation to create organizational intelligence, this motivation also impacts the mental readiness and clarity of purpose to which areas the particular organization wants and can employ algorithms. A particular organizational culture type's attitude toward organizational intelligence building determines its attitude toward its artificial form.

So, from one particular culture's perspective, algorithmic management means technological advancement as it facilitates workflow. But from a sociocultural perspective, it is a potential threat of losing power or position or both for some. Whereas for others, it is a big chance for fair treatment. That is why all the questions regarding the company culture's impact on these processes are fully justified.

Deep down, AI interferes with the existing sources of power in organizations and thus reframes the old order and destroys the sense of security of the currently existing social structures searching for stability. However, at the same time, it brings an opportunity to work in transparent, just, and objective conditions. So, how individuals and organizations perceive AI depends on their culture and individual and collective intelligence drivers. The company culture, which may be oriented to challenge and growth or to stability and survival moderate it.

Depending on the level of advancement of the implemented algorithms, the degree to which they relieve the areas of management functions previously undertaken by people, and the particular organizational culture type and its motivation to constantly develop organizational intelligence, the existing organizational culture can undergo either minor adaptation or revolutionary transformation. Such a new situation can shake the existing organizational strategies, cultures, and structures. How intensively this shake is might be mediated by the tech and non-tech mindset.

Besides, Kucharska and Kucharski (2023) compared the adaptability to remote work between tech and non-tech mindsets employees. They discovered that, before COVID-19, high intensity of contacts via technology-supported change adaptability was significant only for the IT industry. However, non-tech mindsets having troubles with adaptability to technological environment adapted perfectly to any changes that were required in their casual work environment. So, it means that people adapt smoothly if their mindset and working environment align. The results obtained for the same group two and three years later (during and after COVID) revealed that interactions via technology also increased change adaptability in sectors other than IT. This study showed that the technological environment can change the employee mindset. Nevertheless, at the same time, authors noted that the adaptability process from a non-technological to a technological environment could be prolonged and complex even for highly educated knowledge workers' groups. Since there is no development without technology today—patience and long-term perspective thinking are recommended to achieve such transformational success in the long run. It is critical. Adaptation to technology-dominated virtual workspaces or algorithm-supported workplaces must continue, even if this is problematic for non-technological mindsets; abandoning this idea will only make the inevitable transformation longer and more challenging. Knowledge, learning, and collaboration synergy of functional cultures (KLC approach) can help with such adaptability. Knowledge culture brings a habit of searching for understanding. Learning culture motivates employee to leave their comfort zone. Collective culture impacts collective intelligence creation, which requires inclusion and patience instead of exclusion of those who face problems or abandonment of change when facing implementation problems rooted in mindsets. A shared mindset is the essence of the company culture.

So, regarding the algorithms in which technological advancement is much higher than only adaptability to digital workspace, this adaptability-transformational process will also be prolonged, and the company culture precisely determines if those who face troubles with algorithms acceptance and usage will be patiently trained or excluded. The aggressive techno culture makes "algorithms as gods," which is a vast misunderstanding without human feedback and input of contextual tacit knowledge coming from expertise and experience even the most advanced ML algorithms are blind and can do more damage than support (more about human IQ rooted in tacit knowledge creation power over AI in Chapter 14).

Intelligent systems are transforming our understanding of work, knowledge, and organizational structures. Self-learning algorithms challenge traditional ideas about work, as they enable a new division of labor where machines handle mundane, data-driven tasks while humans engage in activities requiring social intelligence and creative problem-solving. This shift will redefine managerial roles to focus more on strategic thinking rather than just coordination (Jarrahi et al., 2021). While concerns about job displacement by machines are valid, it is also crucial to prepare human minds to be agile and capable of outperforming these intelligent systems.

In summary, the company's strategy-culture-structure triangle shapes the purpose to which algorithms serve. The culture will determine their design and usage intentions. Everything we create (including algorithms) can serve for good or for evil. Company culture determines it.

Hierarchies oriented to uncertainty avoidance and control will probably create pre-programmed algorithms supporting control and decision-making, which have the great potential to support the hierarchy's growth scenario named in Chapter 11, the "perfect machine" scenario.

Clans can see the value of descriptive and predictive algorithms but will implement them in a way that secures employees' safety and well-being. Markets and adhocracies will be open to any AI application that advances their intelligence abilities over competitors. So, what culture, such as an algorithm's design mode (control/support) and attitudes toward it (opportunity/threat)—because strategy-culture-structure alignment is the principal criterion shaping how work is designed—consequently determines how algorithms are designed and, consequently, how algorithms are applied and perceived by their users (active and passive).

Figure 12.1 visualizes the general idea of how organizational intelligence happens in organizations supported by algorithmic management.

So, answering the first of the research questions dedicated to this section (Part III): Does, in algorithmic reality, the company culture still serve as a critical resource supporting organizational strategies in such conditions? The answer is YES. Company culture: first, it determines the motivation to build organizational intelligence; second, it determines the role of AI and CHI in this process, which impacts how intention algorithms are designed and used—to support or oppress people. Finally, company culture defines a particular team, division, organization, and society's rules of behavior. Since AI's impact on humanity is vast, the cultural impact on how organizations and societies adapt to it is critical.

The KLC's role in this process is discussed separately below for each culture type.

12.2 Adhocracy—KLC and algorithmic management

Based on everything written so far in this book about adhocracies, it is easy to predict that adhocracies and markets will be the most enthusiastic cultures about AI solutions adaptation since they are the best disposed to build organizational intelligence. They will be internally and externally motivated to organize themselves in a way that enables them to take the most prominent advantage of AI solutions, seeing them as opportunities to grow that technology brings. So, the synergy of knowledge, learning, and collaboration will strongly increase the motivation of adhocracies to utilize AI fully for their developmental purposes.

Adhocracies employees have agile mindsets, so they need to understand business, people, context, and technology; they want to be a subject, not an object, of the change that inevitably is coming. Therefore, ML algorithmic solutions can meet limited acceptance for these reasons, but PP solutions will be developed enthusiastically. So, adhocracies members will actively participate in designing and using AI solutions that best serve their organization and employees' growth; do not mislead this focus with well-being characteristics for clans. Adhocracy members want to grow, and they are ready to leave their comfort zones to do so. Regarding intelligence building, they see the human factor, CHI, as superior to AI. Adhocracies members aim to design and manage algorithm(s) themselves to ensure the best use of them to lead people and improve business performance. They constantly think critically and constantly improve the AI tools to perform better and better.

As it was pointed out in Chapter 8 of Part II, apart from AI solutions, the biggest threat to organizational intelligence building in adhocracies is the risk of putting the particular individual ambition over the collective good, and as a remedy, the collective culture should be strengthened in adhocracies to gain the full advantage of the KLC approach and develop the CHI. In the reality of AI, there is another significant risk. The risk of unequal distribution of power precisely resulting from unequal competencies of employees and the emergence of new employee castes is a result of the division between those employees who can create and manage algorithms and those who cannot do so. The same concerns organizations, for example, IT competencies often differ across sectors (Kucharska & Erickson, 2020, 2023). It is important to highlight and clarify that the most powerful are not algorithms engineers but agile mindset experts (tacit knowledge acquisition and usage masters) who accumulate business, people, and technology knowledge and can use it in changing contexts. So, the remedy here is again the KLC approach. Knowledge, learning, and collaboration can facilitate the discrepancy between employees that inevitably will occur. So, mental agility training to increase the intellectual agility of all adhocracy members can facilitate and diminish the inevitable discrepancy. The agile mindset leader will enhance the CHI through AI and the opposite.

As CHI impacts AI, the same AI impacts CHI, and the KLC facilitates the OI creation by Chi AND AI in both mutual impact directions (Figure 12.1). So, how KLC impacts organizational intelligence was discussed. However, some comments are needed regarding the AI impact on OI through CHI from the perspective of the KLC approach implemented in adhocracy organizations. In such a case, AI will drive the spread of learning culture. Technology is a strong mindset stimulus. Besides, the enthusiasm for organizational intelligence development will drive human and artificial intelligence growth in adhocracies. Thus, the KLC synergy will constantly facilitate knowledge conversion in adhocracies.

Thanks to employees' agile mindsets and technology support, this conversion will be smooth (agile). This is why constant agility mental training was suggested as a remedy to avoid potential intellectual discrepancies in an agile adhocracy organization where all members are intelligent, agile-minded, and internally motivated to learn. So, the leader's role is to sustain it. Mental agile training is one method.

Figure 12.2a summarizes all the above.

ALGORITHMIC MANAGEMENT SUPPORT							**KLC**'s impact on motivation to implement AI	AI's impact on **KLC** (predition)	**STRUCTURE CHANGE** CONSEQUENCES (prediction)
social processes		technological processes **(AI solutions)**							
		pre-programmed (PP)		machine learning (ML)					
individual level	POTENTIAL TENSIONS	algorithms design (tech)	algorithms optimizing	algorithms design	algorithm s training	POTENTIAL SCENARIO (prediction)			
active (managers, specialists) - Individuals define and optimize algorithms to secure its output: business performance and social benefits passive -It is designed (usually bought as a ready software) once as a 'facilitating tool' to eliminate tedious tasks, tracks, set goals, assess performance, make decisions - Algorithm output determines work design **active** (managers, specialists) - Human is a superior. Humans manage algorithm(s) and use them to lead people and manage business performance better. Humans constantly think critically and constantly improve the AI tools to perform better. passive (serial employees) - Algorithm manages humans (tracks, sets goals, assesses performance, makes decisions)	Unequal distribution of power risk resulting from unequal competencies of employees, **the emergence of new employee castes** as a result of the division between those employees who can create and manage algorithms and those who cannot do so. ATTENTION! The most powerful are not algorithms engineers but **agile mindset experts** who cumulate business, people, and technology knowledge and can use it in changing contexts - **tacit knowledge acquisition & usage masters**	**yes**	**yes**	yes/**no**	yes/**no**	Adhocracies employees are agile mindset, so they need to understand business, people, context, and technology; they want to be a subject not object; ML solutions can meet limited acceptance for these reasons, but PP solutions will be developed enthusiastically	**HIGH** **KNOWLEDGE LEARNING** COLLABORATION synergy	**AI will drive the spread of learning culture. Technology is a strong mindset stimulus.** Besides, the enthusiasm for organizational intelligence development will drive growth in both human and artificial intelligence in adhocracies. Thus, the KLC synergy will constantly facilitate knowledge conversion in adhocracies. Thanks to employees' agile mindsets and technology support, this conversion will be smooth (agile).	network remains a favorable structure for adhocracy

Figure 12.2a Adhocracy—KLC and algorithmic management—summary

12.3 Markets—KLC and algorithmic management

Markets next to adhocracies are expected to be very enthusiastic about AI solutions since they can significantly support organizational intelligence. Markets are internally and externally motivated to re-organize themselves in a way that enables them to take the most prominent advantage of AI development opportunities that technology brings. All that was written above about adhocracies applies to market cultures, but there are some minor differences regarding the attitudes toward AI that require attention.

Since market culture organizations usually are bigger and operate on more complex and competitive markets than adhocracies, apart from the PP algorithms, ML algorithms can also be very attractive options for them. So, VUCA reality (volatility, uncertainty, complexity, and ambiguity) significantly affects markets where the time of the reaction is as important as its promptness—for markets, ML solutions can be very attractive to leverage organizational intelligence. Some market process interdependencies are very complex and constantly change because new factors occur that might determine business success. ML AI can help to identify them faster; however, ML AI, apart from the initial training (initial data set) and the constant human feedback, is out of human control. In other words, we cannot control the way the ML AI learns in its third loop; it is out of control due to its complexity (VUCA).

Regarding the KLC approach, it will work in favor of the OI increase through AI, and analyzing the opposite impact, the AI will drive the spread of learning and collaboration culture. Technology is a strong mindset stimulus. New insights will inspire new actions, which is why, next to learning, AI will stimulate cooperation. That may cause a little pressure to adjust the company structure to new realities of market culture organizations. The existing hierarchy will become flat, and it will be mixed with networks in teams responsible for innovations.

Figure 12.2b summarizes all the above.

12.4 Clans—KLC and algorithmic management

Clans are focused on their collective efficacy, so they will work with ready IT solutions rather than adapting them to their own purposes and paying close attention to employees' training and support. Big clans can see ML solutions as attractive for the same reasons as markets operating in competitive sectors. But clans will always search for a good balance between technology usage and employees' well-being.

Clans will try to adapt to new realities simultaneously by gaining the best AI solutions to support organizational development in a way that secures employees' well-being. For clans, their own people always come first. Clans would not try to tailor AI solutions to their own purposes by designing, re-designing, and constantly optimizing them as adhocracies do. They would rather buy a ready solution designed by external engineers and adapt it to their own purposes.

ALGORITHMIC MANAGEMENT SUPPORT							KLC's impact on motivation to implement AI	AI's impact on KLC (predition)	STRUCTURE CHANGE CONSEQUENCES (prediction)
social processes		technological processes (AI solutions)							
individual level	POTENTIAL TENSIONS	pre-programmed (PP)		machine learning (ML)		POTENTIAL SCENARIO (prediction)			
		algorithms design (tech)	algorithms optimizing	algorithms design	algorithm s training				
active (managers, specialists) - Individuals define and optimize algorithms to secure its output: business performance and social benefits **passive** -It is designed (usually bought as a ready software) once as a 'facilitating tool' to eliminate tedious tasks, tracks, set goals, assess performance, make decisions - Algorithm output determines work design **active** (managers, specialists) - Human is a superior. Humans manage algorithm(s) and use them to manage people and business performance better. Human constantly think critically and constantly improve the AI tools to perform better. **passive** (serial employees) - Algorithm manages humans (tracks, sets goals, assesses performance, makes decisions)	Unequal distribution of power risk resulting from unequal competencies of employees, **the emergence of new employee castes** as a result of the division between those employees who can create and manage algorithms and those who cannot do so. ATTENTION! The most powerful are not algorithms engineers but **agile mindset experts** who cumulate business, people, and technology knowledge and can use it in changing contexts - **tacit knowledge acquisition & usage masters**	**yes**	**yes**	yes/**no**	**yes**/no	As above but with one key difference - market organizations are bigger and operate on more complex and often very competitive markets where the time of the reaction is as important as its promptness - for markets, ML solutions can be very attractive tool to leverage organizational intelligence	**HIGH** **KNOWLEDGE LEARNING COLLABORATION** synergy	AI will drive the spread of learning and collaboration culture. Technology is a strong mindset stimulus. New insights will inspire new actions, which is why, next to learning, AI will stimulate cooperation.	flat hierarchy with networks in teams responsible for innovations

Figure 12.2b Market culture—KLC and algorithmic management—summary

Through the limited trust in ML, they will put effort into its training. Still, their skeptical attitudes will not let them trust such solutions fully—they would prefer to rely on their internal agile mindset experts (tacit knowledge acquisition and usage masters) who accumulate business, people, and technology knowledge and can use it in changing contexts. That kind of people will become clan culture leaders of knowledge-driven organizations in AI reality. If not, and, for example, an organization will apply ML blindly, there is a huge risk to it.

The key risk connected with the AI solution implementation in clans blindly is an "unconscious digital slavery risk." It may occur if the ML algorithm is treated as an incomprehensible and almighty entity as God is, an omnipresent tracking system that decides about everyone and everything. AI has unlimited trust. (It is objective and logical). However, no one in the organization understands this logic, and all members blindly follow it. There is no motivation to understand it; there is motivation to follow it and feel safe thanks to doing this perfectly—the illusion of perfection due to intellectual laziness.

So, the key source of knowledge will become the agile mindset leader. AI solutions will drive the spread of learning and collaboration culture. Technology is a strong mindset stimulus. Clans will adapt to new realities collectively—the more changes AI enhances, the more vital learning and collectivism in clans. This collectivism is also a source of safety feeling. The agile mindset leader will enhance the CHI through AI and the opposite in the best way to be accepted by the organization's members to secure their well-being. Regarding company structure, the existing hierarchy will become flat, and it will be mixed with networks in teams responsible for innovations.

Figure 12.2c summarizes all the above.

12.5 Hierarchies—KLC and algorithmic management

Hierarchies will face more trouble with AI implementation than any other culture type. Apart from all the risks described for clans, they apply to hierarchies too; there is an additional one—a risk that they will transfer the same bureaucratic complexity processes from the paper form to digital form, which will not make them more efficient at all; it will only make the entire bureaucratic process faster by human factor elimination. The best scenario would be to optimize some complex processes thanks to AI solutions to increase efficiency. The worst scenario would be simply transferring the same routines from people to machines due to intellectual laziness. Hierarchies are usually big and extremely bureaucratic, and AI seems to be a truly saving solution for organizations that enable the automation of complex processes whose logic is unknown but rooted in tradition (perfectly repeated without critical thinking). But digitalizing everything 1:1 without any necessary correction, especially with ML tempting solutions that would limit human involvement to a minimum would lead hierarchies to total digital slavery. Some knowledge-driven organizations can lose their purpose in this way.

ALGORITHMIC MANAGEMENT SUPPORT							KLC's impact on motivation to implement AI	AI's impact on KLC (predition)	STRUCTURE CHANGE CONSEQUENCES (prediction)
social processes		technological processes (AI solutions)							
		pre-programmed (PP)		machine learning (ML)					
individual level	POTENTIAL TENSIONS	algorithms design (tech)	algorithms optimizing	algorithms design	algorithm s training	POTENTIAL SCENARIO (prediction)			
active (managers, specialists) - Individuals define and optimize algorithms to secure its output: business performance and social benefits **passive** -It is designed (usually bought as a ready software) once as a 'facilitating tool' to eliminate tedious tasks, tracks, set goals, assess performance, make decisions - Algorithm output determines work design active (managers, specialists) - Human is a superior. Humans manage algorithm(s) and use them to manage people and business performance better. Human constantly think critically and constantly improve the AI tools to perform better. **passive** (serial employees) - Algorithm manages humans (tracks, sets goals, assesses performance, makes decisions)	**unconscious digital slavery risk** The algorithm is as incomprehensible and almighty as God, an omnipresent tracking system that decides about everyone and everything. AI has unlimited trust. (It is objective and logical). However, no one in the organization understands this logic, and all members blindly follow it. There is no motivation to understand it; there is motivation to follow it and feel safe thanks to doing this perfectly. **illusion of perfection** **intellectual laziness**	buy ready solution	yes/**no**	buy ready solution	yes	Clans are focused on their collective efficacy, so they will work with ready IT solutions rather than adapting them to their own purposes and paying close attention to employees' training and support. Big clans can see ML solutions attractive for the same reasons as markets operating in competitive sectors. But clans will always search for a good balance between the technoogy usage and employees well-being.	**MODERATE** KNOWLEDGE **LEARNING** **COLLABORATION** synergy	AI will drive the spread of learning and collaboration culture. Technology is a strong mindset stimulus. Clans will adapt to new realities collectively—the more changes AI enhances, the more vital learning and collectivism in clans. This collectivism is also a source of safety feeling.	flat hierarchy with networks in teams responsible for innovations

Figure 12.2c Clan culture—KLC and algorithmic management—summary

ALGORITHMIC MANAGEMENT SUPPORT							KLC's impact on motivation to implement AI	AI's impact on KLC (predition)	STRUCTURE CHANGE CONSEQUENCES (prediction)
social processes		technological processes (AI solutions)							
		pre-programmed (PP)		machine learning (ML)					
individual level	POTENTIAL TENSIONS	algorithms design (tech)	algorithms optimizing	algorithms design	algorithms training	POTENTIAL SCENARIO (prediction)			
active (managers, specialists) - Individuals define and optimize algorithms to secure its output: business performance and social benefits	**unconscious digital slavery risk** The algorithm is as incomprehensible and almighty as God, an omnipresent tracking system that decides about everyone and everything. AI has unlimited trust. (It is objective and logical). However, no one in the organization understands this logic, and all members blindly follow it. There is no motivation to understand it; there is motivation to follow it and feel safe thanks to doing this perfectly. **perfect illusion of excellence intellectual laziness**	buy ready solution	yes/**no**	buy ready solution	yes	Hierarchies are big and bureaucratic, and AI is a saving solution that enables the automation of complex processes whose logic is unknown but rooted in tradition (perfectly repeated without critical thinking). But digitalizing everything 1:1 without any necessary correction, especially with ML temptating solutions that would limit human involvement to minimum would lead hierarchies to total digital slavery. Some of organizations can loose this way they purpose.	**WEAK** **KNOWLEDGE** LEARNING COLLABORATION synergy	In extreme cases (ML system) AI can totally kill the KLC in organizations	hierarchy with autonomous divisions dedicated to innovations & change adaptability
passive -It is designed (usually bought as a ready software) once as a 'facilitating tool' to eliminate tedious tasks, tracks, set goals, assess performance, make decisions - Algorithm output determines work design									
active (managers, specialists) - Human is a superior. Humans manage algorithm(s) and use them to manage people and business performance better. Human constantly think critically and constantly improve the AI tools to perform better.									
passive (serial employees) - Algorithm manages humans (tracks, sets goals, assesses performance, makes decisions)									

Figure 12.2d Hierarchy culture—KLC and algorithmic management—summary

So, the risk of "unconscious digital slavery" described for clans applies to hierarchies, too. This impact is weak regarding the impact of KLC on motivation to implement AI solutions. In extreme cases (the ML system) leads precisely to "unconscious digital slavery." It may occur if the ML algorithm is treated as an incomprehensible and almighty entity as God is, an omnipresent tracking system that decides about everyone and everything. AI has unlimited trust. (It is objective and logical). However, no one in the organization understands this logic, and all members blindly follow it. There is no motivation to understand it; there is motivation to follow it and feel safe thanks to doing this perfectly. The illusion of perfection due to intellectual laziness of blindly following the ML algorithms can totally kill such a poor CHI-building motivation and, consequently, the need for the KLC to be sustained in organizations.

So, hierarchies must be very careful when implementing the ML-based AI system.

Figure 12.2d summarizes all the above.

12.6 Case study

AI at the Public University

Jonathan was the PM responsible for migrating all bureaucratic processes from reality to digital form at a Public University. Thanks to this project, "Virtual Guide," all administrative staff employment should be reduced to 25% from the current level (due to the complexity of the entire bureaucracy, there are five times more administrative staff than scientific and teaching staff together). The project lasted 24 months, and the budget was 4.5 million €.

Jonathan accomplished the project on time and within scope and achieved the critical KPI of staff reduction. The provost was happy. Jonathan received his reward and closed another project successfully.

After one year of usage, the "Virtual Guide" received two times more negative reviews than the entire administrative staff in the same period long before the migration. What happened?

Jonathan, after the lecture about all the negative feedback "Virtual Guide" received after almost each "Virtual Visit," realized that the entire issue comes from the fact that Virtual Guide (VG) was trained by administrative staff who precisely did it from their perspective—they teach VG to mirror them. So, VG was trained to follow all existing procedures to secure their perfect (strict) control. The user perspective was totally ignored. So, the same disappointment caused by many unlogic and annoying activities bringing no value that existed before remains alive, but they start their new life in a virtual world. However, unfortunately, the AI thought to control these procedures strictly ignored users' feedback.

As a result, students, teachers, and scientists stopped undertaking activities beyond the standard to avoid contact with VG, which was very problematic in case of any actions above standards. So, all creative, innovative initiatives were stopped.

So, the question arises: What is the purpose of a "standardized university" existence?

Problems for discussion:

1. What is the purpose of the existence of a "standardized university"?
2. Prepare three potential scenarios about this university's future with VG in its current shape, and next select the one you see fits best to particular group interests; before, name (assume) the interest of each group first: a) provost perspective, b) Jonathan's perspective, c) administrative staff perspective, d) teaching staff perspective, e) scientists, and f) students. Is it the same scenario? If yes—why? If not—why?
3. Prepare three potential scenarios about your dream university's future. Look at this task from each of the stakeholder's perspectives. To do so properly, you need to find out (assume) what is in the best interest of each group. Next, choose which scenario is the best for the particular group's interests: a) provost's perspective, b) Jonathan's perspective, c) administrative staff perspective, d) teaching staff perspective, e) scientists, f) students, and g) society. Is it the same scenario? If yes—why? If not—why?

Additional tasks:

1. If you were Jonathan, what would you do if you could start this project again?
2. What would you do if you were provost and could not spend another 4.5 million € and wait another two years for the VG improvement?

References

Crowston, K., & Bolici, F. (2019). *Impacts of machine learning on work*. Proceedings of the 52nd Hawaii International Conference on System Sciences, Hawaii, USA.

Gilpin, L. H., Paley, A. R., Alam, M. A., Spurlock, S., & Hammond, K. J. (2022). "Explanation" is not a technical term: The problem of ambiguity in XAI. *arXiv preprint*. arXiv:2207.00007

Gilpin, L. H., Testart, C., Fruchter, N., & Adebayo, J. (2019). Explaining explanations to society. *arXiv preprint*. arXiv:1901.06560

Grønsund, T., & Aanestad, M. (2020). Augmenting the algorithm: Emerging human-in-the-loop work configurations. *The Journal of Strategic Information Systems, 29*(2), 101614.

Jarrahi, M. H., Newlands, G., Lee, M. K., Wolf, C. T., Kinder, E., & Sutherland, W. (2021). Algorithmic management in a work context. *Big Data & Society, 8*(2). https://doi.org/10.1177/20539517211020332

Jarrahi, M. H., & Sutherland, W. (2019, March 31–April 3). Algorithmic management and algorithmic competencies: Understanding and appropriating algorithms in gig work. In *International conference on information* (pp. 578–589). Springer.

Kucharska, W., Balcerowski, T., Kucharski, M., Jussila, J., & Laanti, M. (2024a). Why does the Agile leader mindset matter the most? Polish-Finnish, technological and non-technological perspectives on agile and non-agile mindset employees and organizations. *Heliyon*. https://ssrn.com/abstract=4988722

Kucharska, W., Balcerowski, T., Kucharski, M., Jussila, J., & Laanti, M. (2024b). *Why does the Agile leader mindset matter the most? (1–)* [Dataset]. Data Bridge Repository. Gdansk University of Technology. https://doi.org/10.34808/b23f-9197

Kucharska, W., Balcerowski, T., Kucharski, M., & Jussila, J. (2024c). Who is an agile leader? Technological vs. non-technological mindset employees' views. *20th European Conference on Management, Leadership and Governance*, *20*(1), 397–404. https://doi.org/10.34190/eckm.25.1.2367

Kucharska, W., & Erickson, G. S. (2020). The influence of IT-competency dimensions on job satisfaction, knowledge sharing and performance across industries. *VINE Journal of Information and Knowledge Management Systems*, *50*(3), 387–407. https://doi.org/10.1108/VJIKMS-06-2019-0098

Kucharska, W., & Erickson, G. S. (2023). A multi-industry and cross-country comparison of technology contribution to formal and informal knowledge sharing processes for innovativeness. *Knowledge and Process Management*, *30*(3), 300–316. https://doi.org/10.1002/kpm.1755

Kucharska, W., & Kucharski, M. (2023). Technological vs. non-technological mindsets: Learning from mistakes, and organizational change adaptability to remote work. *19th European Conference on Management, Leadership and Governance*, *19*(1), 205–214. Academic Conferences and Publishing Limited. https://doi.org/10.34190/ecmlg.19.1.1902

Lee, M. K. (2018). Understanding perception of algorithmic decisions: Fairness, trust, and emotion in response to algorithmic management. *Big Data & Society*, *5*(1). https://doi.org/10.1177/2053951718756684

Newell, S., & Marabelli, M. (2015). Strategic opportunities (and challenges) of algorithmic decision-making: A call for action on the long-term societal effects of 'datification'. *The Journal of Strategic Information Systems*, *24*(1), 3–14.

Noponen, N., Feshchenko, P., Auvinen, T., Luoma-aho, V., & Abrahamsson, P. (2024). Taylorism on steroids or enabling autonomy? A systematic review of algorithmic management. *Management Review Quarterly*, *74*(3), 1695–1721.

Parent-Rocheleau, X., & Parker, S. K. (2022). Algorithms as work designers: How algorithmic management influences the design of jobs. *Human Resource Management Review*, *32*(3), 100838.

Sundar, S. S., & Kim, J. (2019). *Machine heuristic: When we trust computers more than humans with our personal information. Proceedings of the 2019 CHI Conference on Human Factors in Computing Systems*, Paper no. 538, pp. 1–9. https://doi.org/10.1145/3290605.3300768. ACM Digital Library.

13 What culture, such virtual workspace standards

13.1 What culture experienced, such culture learned

Virtual teams are composed of dispersed members and strongly rely on communicative technologies to collaborate (Costa et al., 2021). To be fruitful, such collaboration requires a remarkable work ethos and high-quality leadership to build high motivation and sustain the team remotely to enable higher-level performance. The recent results by Davaei and Gunkel (2024) and, Audrin and Audrin (2024) or Warrier et al. (2024) indicate that cognitive ability, emotional intelligence, and cultural intelligence are critical factors contributing to various virtual work team-related outcomes. So, the efficacy of virtual collaboration depends clearly on collective intelligence. So, the implementation of the KLC approach to the virtual teams' working conditions will definitely pay back in their intelligence increase. Knowledge and learning cultures foster cognitive abilities, whereas collective culture supports emotional and cultural intelligence. Cultural intelligence is understood as the ability to function effectively in culturally diverse settings. We gain this intelligence through cultural knowledge, experience, and practical, smooth application. The question arises: How can the culture be implemented virtually?—similarly to reality: through all experiences employees face at work. Moreover, leaders remain, similarly to on-site working teams, divisions, and organizations, the key source of company culture shaping. The key issue is that remote leaders have limited tools to do so, and almost everything depends on the remote leader's personality and competencies. However, technological tools designed to mediate remote social interactions can be designed to support the company's spirit—mission, vision, values, cognitive ability, emotional intelligence, and cultural intelligence of team members to increase employees' commitment.

Company culture determines employees' attitudinal and behavioral norms. Employees' attitudes and behaviors are learned from experiences, not from official statements, and company culture is this way more tacitly than explicitly acquired. Precisely, it is important to set up norms and make them "official," but even more important is to follow them and make them live. And the more frequent problem with company culture implementation is that the desired culture usually exists only

DOI: 10.4324/9781003485230-17

in the explicit "paper" form ("dummy culture"). What makes it alive is practice. Leaders are those who are responsible for the design, implementation, and exposition by their own example and the execution of company culture. The truth is that our experiences with leaders who represent the company shape the company's culture of understanding the most. So, regarding the virtual space or traditional space—leaders are equally responsible for all the relational experiences employees gain and, this way, experience the company culture. Regarding the virtual or really shaping culture, the key issue is that doing it efficiently is a leader's mindset alignment with the working environment. In other words, the leader who does not feel at ease in virtual reality will not be able to shape the culture there, and reversely, the leader whose working environment is digital may not feel comfortable in on-site working conditions. Work environment consistency: Culture can be shaped in an environment where the manager feels confident and at ease—and it doesn't matter whether it's the virtual or real world; it simply has to be "his/her world" (Kucharska & Kucharski, 2023). Technology is just a tool; at most, we have to learn how to communicate in the new reality. The biggest mistake is to assume that "if I can't shape the culture the way I have been doing it so far, I cannot do it at all"—that is a mistake. We need to learn to think "in" and "out" of the box simultaneously to solve the new virtual reality challenges. An agile mindset leader adapts to reality by thinking creatively (Kucharska et al., 2024a, 2024b). So, the leader's mindset and self-confidence matter to make the desired standard of human relations quality sharply clear and inevitable.

Besides solid agile leadership and its mindset-environment alignment criterion, virtual teams face another challenge: a limited opportunity to experience the culture, which is even more critical for multicultural teams. This obstacle is challenging even for powerful leaders; weak leaders cannot overcome it.

To understand this obstacle correctly, we need to recall that we best learn culture tacitly—through experience. To experience any culture, we always use all our senses to support cognitive processes. The active senses during virtual meetings are limited compared to on-site relations options. Sight and hearing dominate and are additionally mediated by technology's ups (dedicated online meetings software with graphics that create impressions supporting the desired company culture) and downs (disruptions).

So, in the extreme case, if the particular worker has a minimal opportunity to experience company culture due to being assigned to tasks that can be accomplished independently, the number of contacts with the parent company is rare, then such a worker has a limited chance to learn company culture. Additionally, suppose the contact person and leader do not expose company culture clearly and sharply, and the supporting contacts software is not designed to support company culture through graphics, emoticons, and so on. In that case, the worker has no chance to learn the company culture deeply. Additionally, let us imagine that this particular company member has many contacts with his family, friends, and society of his own country—then—company culture as a "dummy culture" has no chance to exist in this particular worker's consciousness. A culture is a dummy if it cannot be experienced (it is not alive—it does not exist in practice). Therefore, it is vital to organize virtual team meetings also in the "on-site" form; from time to time, such a meeting should include a "culture training," but in fact, the more thorough experience, the better. Such a form is a great opportunity to shape organizational culture intensely, enhancing company culture experiences through all senses and positive emotions that help employees learn faster and remember the cultural pattern better (Tyng et al., 2017).

Moreover, regarding the "everyday" virtual workspace, it would be very helpful if this space were designed to expose company culture. The graphics of software supporting virtual meetings, which present and perpetuate company values, and the gamification of this cooperation form would be beneficial tools for enhancing communication quality, desired attitudes, and behaviors. Gamification of virtual working space is probably one of the best methods to create a company's internal world, which naturally has its own culture that can be naturally learned by experience.

Grover et al. (2022) proposed transitioning all four culture types to digital reality through overarching toolkits for using digital resources to compete effectively in the adhocracy, market, clan, or hierarchy culture. However, following Kane et al.'s (2016) view, created based on more than 4,300 managers, executives, and analysts, traditional cultures need to transition to digital (virtual today) reality by changing shared mindsets and becoming more flexible. According to them, the virtual workplace requires constant development to increase its own efficacy and deliver better services. Therefore, virtual cultures must be open to experimentation and risk-taking. Experimentation and iteration are vital ways companies respond to digital and virtual reality changes—so they constantly learn, unlearn, and re-learn formally and informally. Kane and colleagues stressed that companies should take lessons from those experiments — successes and failures — to drive change across the organization, precisely as the learning culture constituting the KLC approach proposed in this book. Moreover, Kane and colleagues stressed that the new company culture must prepare the organization to accept ambiguity as a new normal, deal with ambiguity caused by constant change, and be open to constant (right) technology adoption and development. So, comparing their findings to the agile organization and agile mindset of employees and leaders view given recently by Kucharska et al. (2024a-c), it is clear that these new types of company cultures support company's growth in the digital era for virtuality and AI expansion should be agile, and undoubtedly the KLC approach supports agility.

Another issue brought up by Kane et al. (2016) regarding the digitalized world is a urgent need for a new quality of leadership. Regarding them, efficient digital leadership's key traits enable the organization to provide vision and purpose, create conditions for experimentation, empower people to think differently and get them to collaborate across boundaries. Once again, this description aligns with Kucharska and Kucharski's (2023) findings and aligns with the empirical evidence of agile mindset leaders dominating role in driving organizations in the virtual world delivered recently by Kucharska et al. (2024a). These authors proved that agile organizations' critical driving power is agile mindset leaders, who empower agile mindsets and non-agile mindsets employees. However, employees with non-agile and agile mindsets are incompatible, and their cooperation cannot exist without friction. So, concluding from this picture—the agile culture requires agile mindset leaders to be implemented. The KLC approach proposed in this book is the bridge to transforming the traditional adhocracy, market, clan, and hierarchy culture into the best possible agile forms. Agile mindset leaders can successfully lead agile organizations that often are increasingly dispersedly located and work in virtual teams.

Figure 13.1 visualizes the general summary and guidelines for company cultures' transition from traditional to agile forms thanks to the KLC approach.

The above summary and guidelines are based on the following literature: Aghimien et al. (2024); Driskell et al. (2024); Gardner et al. (2024); Gilson et al. (2015, 2021); Grover (2022); Horwitz et al. (2006); Hardin et al. (2024), Kane et al. (2016); Kanse et al. (2024); Kucharska et al. (2024a, 2024b, 2024c); Lizares and Cuyegkeng (2024); Mumtaz and Nadeem (2024); Murphy (2024); Pereira et al. (2024).

Below, the guidelines (Figure 13.1) for company cultures' transition from traditional to agile forms, thanks to the KLC approach, are discussed in more depth.

13.2 What a leader, such a culture experienced

Company culture must be first experienced to be learned, as Section 13.1 states. Leaders shape the company culture through their own everyday behavior examples and deliver these experiences. Therefore, all the experiences employees have with their leaders (at the team, division, or central level) are those experiences that shape the company's culture perception the most. Consequently, these experiences impact most employees' conscious and unconscious cultural learning. Therefore, leaders must act as "model roles" for cultures they want to see among their employees. So, regarding virtual reality, where the opportunities for interaction are limited and virtually specific, the experiences employees have with their leaders must be very diligent and consciously designed. The worst possible option is a leader who does not control the impact he or she has on the people.

A virtually working organization requires leaders to expose the following behaviors:

- exposes by own behaviors knowledge-learning-collaboration (KLC) approach perfectly;
- exposes extreme efficacy, professionalism, courage, commitment, authenticity;
- exposes a positive attitude toward constant learning, unlearning and relearning;
- breaks schemes of thinking and acting;

- exposes agile thinking and acting and executes it to make it a shared habit;
- exposes a positive attitude toward challenges;
- motivates and implements changes for growth;
- creates a shared vision: clear communication and advocating changes for organizational growth;
- empowers best contributors to collective intelligence-building knowledge-learning-collaboration (KLC);
- search for cooperators/contributors intellectually equal to or better than him/herself;
- exposes openness and transparency; openly communicates;
- engages through responsibility sharing with the team: asks for opinions and ideas—gives people a voice;
- embraces diverse perspectives and reframes problems;
- shares leadership: problem-solving and decision-making delegates;
- gives people respect, safety feeling, and acceptance—exposes inclusive behaviors;
- is not blindly consequent, if necessary—changes the mind, claims mistakes, and learns constantly;
- inspires, motivates, and supports—cares about "team spirit";
- gives autonomy (trust)/minimum control;
- gives people stability and challenge at the same time;
- enforce a higher level of intellectual-technological-social performance;
- systematically controls changing business context to, if necessary, initiate change;
- deals smoothly with complexity, diversity, and uncertainty;
- takes advantage of technology to support organizational growth.

Leaders of virtually working organizations should sustain integrity between tech-professional and social skills. Therefore, tech-agile mindset leaders (Kucharska & Kucharski, 2023; Kucharska et al., 2024a, 2024b, 2024c) seem to be quite capable of leading people virtually. This matters because apart from the agile mindset skills, they must feel very comfortable in a virtual space to play a "model role" convincingly. This is especially true since the opportunities to shape company culture are specific and limited. The vital specificity is for virtual workspace a technology-mediated communication, which puts technology, next to leadership, as a critical factor determining cooperation quality. Therefore, leaders and employees of agile adhocracies, markets, clans, and hierarchies should characterize tech-agile mindsets and expose as many of the above behaviors as possible. It is easy to imagine a typical adhocracy, market, and clan leaders focusing on these behaviors. It is not to do so for a typical hierarchical leader to maintain social distance and order and focus on control. Therefore, hierarchy culture and virtual space seem to be incompatible in the context of collective intellectual agility building to keep organizational efficacy in a constantly evolving virtual space.

KNOWLEDGE-LEARNING-COLLABORATION KLC approach for agility				virtual workspace characteristics				
agile adhocracy	agile market	agile clan	agile hierarchy					
strong **collaborative culture** facilitates resource smooth sharing to a reasonable limit	strong **collaborative culture** facilitates resource smooth sharing to a reasonable limit	strong **collaborative culture** facilitates resource sharing	**collaborative culture** facilitates resource-sharing at minimum required level (control need makes resources sharing problematic for hierarchies)	shared (conflict risk, but it is a cheaper option)	resources assignment	quality of team composition	agile management quality critical impact	**agile mindset**
				dedicated (no conflicts risks - more expensive)				
knowledge culture secures the need to seek the best-qualified people	**knowledge culture** secures the need to seek the best-qualified people	**knowledge culture** secures the need to seek the best-qualified people whose personality & values fits to the clan	**knowledge culture** secures the need to seek the best-qualified people	team unreliable (do not expect a high level of performance employing cheaper but unqualified people)	appointing sufficient qualified people			
				team reliability (performance) depends on each member professional and social skills (both matters equally)				
collaborative culture is critical	**collaborative culture** is critical	**collaborative culture** is critical	**collaborative culture** is critical	focal ingredient of CHI building; give people voice & responsibilities	critical, collective thinking execution			
collaborative & knowledge cultures secure the best aims for decomposition & execution for 'breakthrough' achievement	**collaborative & knowledge cultures** secure the the best aims decomposition & execution for 'winning market together'	**collaborative & knowledge cultures** secures the the best aims decomposition & execution for 'common good' achievement	**knowledge culture** secures the need of control	vague (vague goals, vague effects)	goals precise assignment & execution			
				clear (precise goals, precise effects e.g., SMART method)				
collaborative & knowledge cultures secures the the best roles & responsibilities assignment & execution for 'breakthrough'	**collaborative & knowledge cultures** secures the the best roles & responsibilities assignment & execution for 'winning market together'	**collaborative & knowledge cultures** secures the the best roles & responsibilities assignment & execution for 'common good'	**knowledge culture** secures the need of control	vague (vague roles & responsibilities, no effects)	roles & responsibilities assignment & execution			
				clear (precise roles & responsibilities, precise effects)				
collaborative and learning culture are critical	**collaborative and learning culture** are critical	**collaborative and learning culture** are critical	**collaborative and learning culture** are critical	on time (immediate) for best performance and learning effects	constructive feedback giving & taking			
				belated - no learning, weak performance				
				recognition - let's outstanding performers be noticed				
collaborative culture is critical	**collaborative culture** is critical	**collaborative culture** is critical	**collaborative culture** is critical	cognitive (coming from personal reliability & performance, e.g., 'good job'; open, frequent & transparent communication)	trust & commitment building (constant process)			
				affective (coming from good relationships at work; open, frequent & transparent communication)				
				shifted (prior cooperation experience)				
knowledge culture	**knowledge culture** secures logic of	**knowledge culture** secures logic of	**knowledge culture** secures logic of	spatial distance (organizing teams around the same time zone)	geographical location			

Figure 13.1 Company's cultures' guidelines transition from traditional to agile forms through the KLC-approach support

Note: The strongest expected effects determined by the culture type are shadowed.

leadership							
		(manage it)	cultural distance (organizing teams around similar cultural values)	spatial design of the team	spatial design of the team	spatial design of the team	secures logic of spatial design of the team
	human dynamics	team phase (take it into account when team design; foster phases transition or avoid 'fluid' teams)	forming	**collaborative culture** is critical	**collaborative culture** is critical	**collaborative culture** is critical	**collaborative culture** is critical
			storming				
			norming				
			performing				
		conflict management - critical	advanced (methodical, fast and constructive)	**collaborative and learning culture** are critical	**collaborative and learning culture** are critical	**collaborative and learning culture** are critical	**collaborative and learning culture** are critical
		cultural intelligence level - critical	cultural knowledge, cultural training, cultural experiences, cultural mastery				
		emotional intelligence	emotions as social information (emotions recognition, roots understanding, and their regulation - managing skills)				
		social skills - critical	communication, empathy, respect, inclusion, bonding, social interactions and cohesion support				
		work ethos	shared values and work ethics - we all care about our team performance	**collaborative & knowledge cultures**	**collaborative & knowledge cultures**	**collaborative & knowledge cultures**	**collaborative & knowledge cultures**
	processes interdence & project design	task characteristics and their correct assignement	highly idenpendent (perfect for remote job)	**collaborative & knowledge cultures** secure the logic of task assignment	**collaborative & knowledge cultures** secure the logic of task assignment	**collaborative & knowledge cultures** secure the logic of task assignment	**collaborative & knowledge cultures** secure the logic of task assignment
			highly dependent - require intensive, in real time cooperation (not recommended for remote jobs; keep it on-site)				
			creative & challenging (assign to best performers)				
			repetitive & boring (assign to AI)				
technological support critical impact	availabilty of algorithmic management tools (AI support)	workflow facilitating software (collaborative technologies) - critical	explicit knowledge management support (acquisition, storage, security, distribution accordingly to authorizations)	**smooth agile learning culture** is critical, working with AI tools requires constant innovative and critical thinking and optimizing; there is no end of AI tools improvements	**smooth agile learning culture** is critical, working with AI tools requires constant innovative and critical thinking and optimizing; there is no end of AI tools improvements	**smooth agile learning culture** is critical, working with AI tools requires constant innovative and critical thinking and optimizing; there is no end of AI tools improvements	**smooth agile learning culture** is critical, working with AI tools requires constant innovative and critical thinking and optimizing; there is no end of AI tools improvements
			tacit knowledge acquisition (semantic analysis tools support)				
			communication tools (managing meetings)				
			individuals job tracking & optimizing tools				
			decision supporting tools				
			goal setting supporting tools (KPI design & assignement)				
			correlation & anomalies detection (work flow monitoring)				
			team performance tracking & optimizing				
			team well-being tracking & optimizing				
			scheduling				
			compensation				
			observability and monitoring tools				
			workflow automation tools				
			task automation tools				
			working tools & infrastructure secured				

Elaborating more in-depth on the guidelines given for agile adhocracies' transitions (Figure 13.1) through the KLC approach, it is worth highlighting that the most critical for their success are regarding human factors: *appointing sufficient qualified people* and *critical, collective thinking execution*, determined by the collective culture implementation and execution. Regarding technological skills critical for *smooth workflow facilitating software (collaborative technologies) usage and development, a smooth, agile learning culture development* is critical. The skills required to work with AI tools require constant innovation, critical thinking, and optimization; there is no "end" of AI tool improvements. The same factors are important for markets. However, through their nature, markets are not as well disposed to virtual reality as adhocracies or clans are. Clan cultures perfectly secure human-related factors critical for successful virtual cooperation. Based on the Figure 13.1 summary, clan culture seems to be best disposed to build a thriving virtual cooperation thanks to perfect *resource assignment, constructive feedback giving and taking, efficient trust and commitment building, geographical location managing, team phases development, perfect managing (take it into account when team design; foster phases transition or avoid "fluid" teams, manage crisis, supports cultural and emotional intelligence, social skills are in a high priority*. What makes clans less efficient than adhocracies in the virtual space is a limited focus on technology. Summing up, the mix of these two cultures would probably serve the best to smooth, virtual cooperation of brilliant minds. These findings align with the conclusions of Goncalves et al. (2020), who see the mix of clans and adhocracies as an agile culture. Section 14.4 more profoundly discusses an agile culture's idea that seems to be more complex.

Hierarchy culture is a fascinating case in the context of virtual workplaces. On the one hand—the natural order and control make them easy to manage with AI support; on the other hand, their formal human relations and a lack of disposition to constant contextual learning, optimizing, and change implementation make them totally unagile. Unagile organizations cannot be efficient in virtual reality in the long-run perspective. Therefore, hierarchies should probably evolve into structurally and culturally hybrid organizations if they want to incorporate virtual space into their business strategies.

Answering the question set up in the introduction to this section: Which culture type serves best in AI reality to support organizational growth in virtual reality?—The answer is: *Adhocracies and clans are the best disposed of. However, the mix of these two would bring the best effects because adhocracy culture facilitates the need for constant growth and development, whereas a spatial distance requires mitigation by high-quality human interactions offered by clans*. Therefore, thanks to adhocracy and clan cultures mix tech-agile mindsets, employees' cooperation in the virtual space has a chance to go the most smoothly.

13.3 Case study

Let us all go back to office work!

George was always a very successful manager, leading the Department of Software Development of Virtual Retail Network. When COVID-19 pushed everyone to virtual space, it was precisely the moment when Georges' managerial problems began. Besides, its roots were not in George's technological skills—he was obviously always a tech-minded shark. The issue was that he could not find himself comfortably in the virtual environment. He loved meeting people and working on-site. Working virtually—everything was artificial to him. New tools and working methods were unnatural to him and made him stressed. It is quite paradoxical, since his department develops software, designs, and services customer automation, advanced ML AL solutions, and so on. However, so far, his department has worked together in one big open space where they constantly interacted, searching for new solutions and optimizing existing algorithms and where George could control everything how he used to. He had a lot of fun working on-site together with his team. This fun—disappeared.

George attended many training courses dedicated to working and managing people in a virtual space, frequently organized by his company, and always passed the control test with good scores. Nevertheless, he was working without a characteristic for him, a positive energy flow. His department's performance started going down, which could not be explained by the sector condition that went well (IT & retail). It was a signal to the management board that something was wrong. George explained that the issue is precisely in people, their increased performance because of the lack of live human contacts and George's constant support and control, easy to provide on-site. Nevertheless, when he proposed that the entire department would work again on-site after the lockdown, his teams were not so happy with this. No one except George wanted this. The management board was not happy either, since they had reduced office space rental costs. Young parents did not want to go back to offices and were happy to work from home, which allowed them to save much time when not standing in traffic jams, and they could combine better home duties with work and maintain a work balance. However, George tried to force his idea to make his department return to on-site work and started searching for the "rationale." As a result, the management board, to make everything transparent, asked for installing to all employees a tracking-work system that shows that no one cheats and all are doing their jobs; that precisely should be better managed by George, who could not find himself in a new situation.

ML AI tools analyzed the entire structure of his team's daily tasks. He split them into tasks with higher interdependence and tasks that can be performed alone by someone and do not require any immediate responses from George or any intensive collaboration with colleagues in real-time and assigned those who prefer to work from home to tasks that do not require cooperation. Those who prefer to work in an office were assigned tasks with a high level of dependence on the work of others. Some people decided to work in a hybrid form, and finally, all were happy except George -again.

Why?—65% of employees preferred to work online, which aligned with the structure of tasks (65% independent tasks); 20% selected hybrid work, and only 15%, responsible for highly interdependent tasks, consequently returned to the daily office work. So, this small optimization did improve the workflow. However, it does not change anything about George's feeling of "self" at work. He noticed that this entire situation affected his clan and department performance results. So, George's adaptability problems become increasingly apparent to him. It was his moment of truth. The entire issue with department performance was caused by his misfit in managing people remotely.

Problems for discussion:

1. Here, we have a situation where employees adapt to new conditions better than their boss. How might this affect the alignment of the "company culture," "strategy," and "structure" golden criterion?
2. How does George's idea of forcing people to go back to offices because of his personal problems with managing people in new conditions look from the employee's perspective?

Additional tasks:

1. If you were George, what would you do? Prepare three scenarios and select the one you think is the best—justify your choice.
2. If you were George's boss, what would you do?

Simon

Simon—data analyst—loved his job in office as long as his boss was Angelina. Angelina did great, the team spirit was fantastic—work was perfectly organized, and it was simply pleasure to face challenges together with such a fantastic team of the most clever guys—as Simon said, and make money and have a fun at work at the same time—sounds as impossible for many of Simon's colleagues working in other teams. Angelina's team was awarded for a third year in a row as the best. So, the entire team was highly motivated and do everything to never lose this honorable title.

But everything changed when Angelina was promoted, and Jim took her place, who, as team named him, was a total "jerk," and meeting him every day took entire joy from Simon and his colleagues. So, when the HR officer asked who wanted to work online, Simon and entire team went online. Their relations were strong enough to make them feel a "flow" even remotely. Jim was naturally not a part of the clan. Jim was just an external satellite. About team performance—it remained "the best." The truth is that mostly because Adam became an "informal leader," his positive energy remained the team integrity.

Problems for discussion:

1. How do you think, how often is a "remote work" a form of runaway from "bad bosses" or poor company culture? Justify your point.
2. What would have happened with the team if Adam had not informally taken Angelina's position?
3. Why do you think, why did the team not complain about Jim to Angelina or to HR?
4. Should a company track more deeply the motives of the "remote work" of their employees? If yes, why; if no, why?

Additional tasks:

1. If you were a part of this team, what would you do?

References

Aghimien, D., Aghimien, L., Aigbavboa, C., & Dhladhla, S. (2024). Too far apart! An evaluation of the challenges impeding virtual teams' success. *International Journal of Business Governance and Ethics*, *18*(2), 136–153.

Audrin, C., & Audrin, B. (2024). Emotional intelligence in digital interactions–a call for renewed assessments. *Personality and Individual Differences*, *223*, 112613.

Costa, P. L., Handke, L., & O'Neill, T. A. (2021). Are all lockdown teams created equally? Work characteristics and team perceived virtuality. *Small Group Research*, *52*(5), 600–628. https://doi.org/10.1177/1046496421997897

Davaei, M., & Gunkel, M. (2024). The role of intelligences in teams: A systematic literature review. *Review of Managerial Science*, *18*(1), 259–297.

Driskell, T., Funke, G., Tolston, M., Capiola, A., & Driskell, J. E. (2024). Fluid and virtual teams. *Small Group Research*, *55*(5), 680–705.

Gardner, R., Blomme, R. J., Kil, A., & van Dam, N. (2024). Cultural influences on early trust development in virtual teams. *Management Research Review*, *47*(6), 861–882.

Gilson, L. L., Costa, P., O'Neill, T. A., & Maynard, M. T. (2021). Putting the "TEAM" back into virtual teams. *Organizational Dynamics*, *50*(1), 1–10. https://doi.org/10.1016/j.orgdyn.2021.100847

Gilson, L. L., Maynard, M. T., Jones Young, N. C., Vartiainen, M., & Hakonen, M. (2015). Virtual teams research: 10 years, 10 themes, and 10 opportunities. *Journal of Management*, *41*(5), 1313–1337. https://doi.org/10.1177/0149206314559946

Goncalves, D., Bergquist, M., Bunk, R., & Alänge, S. (2020). Cultural aspects of organizational agility affecting digital innovation. *Journal of Entrepreneurship, Management and Innovation*, *16*(4), 13–46. https://doi.org/10.7341/20201641

Grover, V. (2022). Digital agility: Responding to digital opportunities. *European Journal of Information Systems*, *31*(6), 709–715. https://doi.org/10.1080/0960085X.2022.2096492

Grover, V., Tseng, S. L., & Pu, W. (2022). A theoretical perspective on organizational culture and digitalization. *Information & Management*, *59*(4), 103639. https://doi.org/10.1016/j.im.2022.103639

Hardin, A., Davison, R. M., Schneider, C., Looney, C. A., & Sarker, S. (2024). Contextualising collective efficacy in virtual team research: The essential role of collaborative technologies in the virtual team efficacy conceptual framework. *Information Systems Journal*, *34*(2), 469–498.

Horwitz, F. M., Bravington, D., & Silvis, U. (2006). The promise of virtual teams: Identifying key factors in effectiveness and failure. *Journal of European Industrial Training*, *30*(6), 472–494.

Kane, G. C., Palmer, D., Phillips, A. N., Kiron, D., & Buckley, N. (2016). Aligning the organization for its digital future. *MIT Sloan Management Review*, 1–27.

Kanse, L., Stephenson, E. K., Klonek, F. E., & Wee, S. (2024). Interdependence in virtual teams—a double-edged sword? *Small Group Research*, *55*(5), 729–762.

Kucharska, W., Balcerowski, T., Kucharski, M., Jussila, J., & Laanti, M. (2024a). Why does the Agile leader mindset matter the most? Polish-Finnish, technological and non-technological perspectives on agile and non-agile mindset employees and organizations. *Heliyon*. https://ssrn.com/abstract=4988722

Kucharska, W., Balcerowski, T., Kucharski, M., Jussila, J., & Laanti, M. (2024b). *Why does the Agile leader mindset matter the most? (1–)* [Dataset]. Data Bridge Repository. Gdansk University of Technology. https://doi.org/10.34808/b23f-9197

Kucharska, W., Balcerowski, T., Kucharski, M., & Jussila, J. (2024c). Who is an agile leader? Technological vs. non-technological mindset employees' views. *20th European Conference on Management, Leadership and Governance*, *20*(1), 397–404. https://doi.org/10.34190/eckm.25.1.2367

Kucharska, W., & Kucharski, M. (2023). Technological vs. non-technological mindsets: Learning from mistakes, and organizational change adaptability to remote work. *19th European Conference on Management, Leadership and Governance*, *19*(1), 205–214. Academic Conferences and Publishing Limited. https://doi.org/10.34190/ecmlg.19.1.1902

Lizares, R. E. J. R., & Cuyegkeng, M. A. C. (2024). Building sustainable organizations online: How leaders embed sustainability into organizational culture in virtual contexts. *Sustainable Development*, *32*(6), 6434–6448. https://doi.org/10.1002/sd.3036

Mumtaz, S., & Nadeem, S. (2024). How far can I trust you? Understanding the social identity perspective of trust development in global virtual teams. *Cross Cultural & Strategic Management*, *31*(4), 659–684. https://doi.org/10.1108/CCSM-05-2024-0102

Murphy, L. (2024). Wellbeing in the age of virtual teams and workplace automation–a systematic review and future research agenda. *International Journal of Organizational Analysis*. https://doi.org/10.1108/IJOA-08-2023-3938
Pereira, L., Jerónimo, C., Simões, F., Dias, Á., Costa, R. L. D., & Gonçalves, R. (2024). Project virtual teams: Systematic literature review. *International Journal of Agile Systems and Management*, *17*(1), 15–45.
Tyng, C. M., Amin, H. U., Saad, M. N., & Malik, A. S. (2017). The influences of emotion on learning and memory. *Frontiers in Psychology*, *8*, 235933.
Warrier, U., Shankar, A., & Belal, H. M. (2024). Examining the role of emotional intelligence as a moderator for virtual communication and decision making effectiveness during the COVID-19 crisis: Revisiting task technology fit theory. *Annals of Operations Research*, *335*(3), 1519–1535.

14 Agile mindset leader's era—new leadership quality to support organizational intelligence in AI-supported workplaces

14.1 Agile mindset leader impact on intellectual agility in knowledge-driven organizations today

Cameron and Quinn (2006, p. 1)—two decades ago, said that "*we are in one of those great historical periods that occur every 200 or 300 years when people do not understand the world anymore, and the past is not sufficient to explain the future.*" It looks like all the recent changes, including the rapid AI expansion, have made us come to the same conclusion today. Even the most advanced ML algorithms are always trained based on old data sets and cannot predict the future. In conclusion from the recent studies by Kucharska et al. (2024a, 2024b, 2024c), agile mindset leaders are probably those who can. They are seen as those who mix analytical solid skills with higher-level learning skills reflecting in constant, contextual tacit knowledge acquisition and transformation into explicit form, which lets them understand more and predict the consequences of complex events better than anyone else.

An agile mindset leader (AM-L) is defined by Kucharska et al. (2024a) as a "hybrid mindset" mastering ambidexterity. According to these authors, an agile mindset leader characterizes the person who mixes usually separated focuses and competencies such as stability and agility, experimentation and exploitation, flexibility and control, scheme following, and rules breaking, exposing simultaneously "in" and "out of the box" thinking. Therefore, AM-L perfectly aligns with management style and perfectly manages tensions and paradoxes in response to constantly changing business contexts. AM-L is efficient, makes good decisions on time, exposes a remarkable mix of professional and social skills, and exposes expertise-based intuition gained thanks to constant contextual learning, unlearning, and relearning. AM-L mind constantly analyzes options, predicts impact, and optimizes solutions. AM-L is entrepreneurially oriented (sees opportunities everywhere) and selects those that most empower the organization and employees in the long run (perfect risk manager). AM-L cares about agile and non-agile people, keeps promises, and, therefore, is rewarded in trust. AM-L uses his agile mindset skills to embrace change through primary control skills and smoothly share

DOI: 10.4324/9781003485230-18

knowledge and collaborate; inspire, motivate, and support others to share her/his vision of prospective changes as opportunities to generate collectively new value, gain new benefits, and collectively win the market; and use technology to support efficacy. Summing up, agile mindset leaders expose the new standard of leadership that responds to challenges of the current VUCA reality.

Agile leaders adapt to rapid changes, implement innovation, take risks, and act with foresight in unpredictable, fast-changing reality (Denning, 2016; Medinilla, 2012). They focus on continuous learning, development, technology application, and innovativeness (Hayward, 2018). Agile leaders are then transformational. So, transformational leaders identify, adapt to external, and implement internal and external changes. Regarding agile leaders' characteristics, Denning (2018) identified such vital agile CEO qualities as a customer-first mindset, a company vision for the future, and the ability to continuously create new business models that match employees' skills and create multiple paths to the same aim (scenarios creation) and are ready to take risks and acquire new institutional skills to develop new paths. According to Sanatigar et al. (2017), agile leaders foster a culture that promotes collaboration and nurturance, accepting diversity, competency, innovation, creativity, transparency, and trust. Kergel et al. (2022) summarized that the power of agile leadership is its exemplary commitment to inspiring the group to pursue intrinsic values and the skill created by agile cognition to envision how these values can be made factually possible. It is because, according to the authors, leading by instrumental values does not align with the agile perspective. The power of agile leadership is its status as an inspiring exemplar and a role model loved by the group and admired for the success its team creates. It serves intrinsic values and nourishes the development of agile cognition, creative relations, and community. Kergel et al. (2022) emphasize that agile leadership does not need harmful and threatening techniques to control people.

Agile leaders are those leaders who support employees' growth, are wisely dynamic (respond to changes quickly and accurately), are open-minded; reflect, revise, and re-frame strategies and plans smoothly; learn from experiences; love changes and prefer them over repetitive actions therefore enthusiastically adapt to changes; are highly self-aware, empathetic, respectful, and inclusive; integrate people and technology; observe and analyze business context changes; smoothly operates on paradoxes (Kucharska et al., 2024a, b). However, according to Kucharska et al. (2024c), there is a difference between technological and non-technological mindset views on agile mindset characteristics. So far, agility has been seen as an IT domain. The COVID-19 pandemic has changed it. After-COVID-19, agility has been lifted to the position of the most desired and highly valued organizational competency, not only in the IT sector (Stei et al., 2024). Changes in the business context create the need to adjust organizational knowledge to the new contexts for all knowledge-driven organizations. Without it, the organizational agile responses can be problematic or impossible. Cegarra-Navarro and Martelo-Landroguez (2020) claimed that efficient knowledge management supports agility, significantly increasing organizational performance. So, since leaders create standards in organizations, it is important to understand who an agile mindset leader is.

Consequently, there is a simple conclusion regarding identified key behaviors: the technological mindset perception notices technology usage, development, and risk management (non-technological mindsets ignore these behaviors), whereas the non-technological mindset focuses on employee growth support and dynamic acting. Regarding features, the technological mindset stands out in market orientation importance, multitasking, critical thinking, knowledge sharing, efficiency, and efficacy. In contrast, the non-technological mindset view stands out in perfect operation on managerial paradoxes and creativity. Regarding attitudes, technological mindsets highlight personal growth needs and responsibility, whereas non-technical mindsets strongly highlight inclusion as vital for successful agile leader status. Regarding personality, non-technological mindsets identify more themes than technological ones: self-confidence and empathy. In contrast, technological mindsets dominated specialists focused uniquely on analytical skills and technology support. What is common—both mindsets highlight a positive attitude toward challenges, an open-minded personality visible in a sequential habit of revisions, reflection, and re-framing, learning from experience, smooth and accurate actions (wise dynamic), perfect change implementation skills, and change adaptability skills. It leads us to conclude that, generally, both mindsets see agile leaders quite similarly. However, the roots of agility—technological mindsets are seen in analytical skills and technology support. In contrast, non-technological mindsets next to the dynamism and adaptability skills highlight socially oriented skills (employee support, inclusion, creativity) as vital to leading organizations' agility. Studies by Kucharska et al. (2024a, 2024b) confirmed these findings.

14.2 Is an agile mindset leader made or born?

Today's increasingly complex socio-information-techno systems require a flexible mindset to survive, operate, thrive, and contribute to society's well-being (Atkinson et al., 2012). Agile mindsets seem to be a result of intellectual evolution responding to current challenges. So, the question arises: *Are people with an agile mindset made or born?*

Mindset is the cognitive framework used to understand an event (French, 2016). Generally, psychology literature defines mindset as a set of cognitive procedures (e.g., being open-minded, reflective, critical, skeptical, or foresighted) constituting habits of mind formed by previous experiences (Gollwitzer & Keller, 2016). Ormrod (2017) argued that emotions, beliefs, attitudes, motives, and intentions constitute a mindset. These habitual, dominant, and characteristic mental processes determine how we interpret (effect of emotions, beliefs, attitudes, motives, and intentions) and respond to situations (how we interpret effects resulting in our or someone else's behaviors). The fact that this process is habitual suggests that agility is acquired rather than given. However, the fact that agile mindset people are rather in the minority than the majority suggests that the intellectual capacity of particular individuals can determine this process.

Agility means being quick, smart, and clever and having a resourceful and adaptable character (Merriam-Webster Dictionary, 2017). Social science expanded this concept to responsiveness, speed, flexibility, and customer centricity (Nagel, 1991). In IT (Beck et al., 2001), agility is a set of four principles: (1) individuals and interactions over processes and tools, (2) utility over comprehensive documentation, (3) collaboration over negotiation, and (4) responding to change over following a plan. Agile leadership drives agile organizations (Denning, 2018). At its core, agility is a framework for decision-making and a decision implementation-oriented management approach to align with the current fast-changing business context so a company can quickly adapt and reposition itself (Hayward, 2018; Salvetti & Bertagni, 2020). Leaders today are confronted with a constantly changing, complex, and challenging business environment. So, agile leadership's essence is leading effectively and efficiently when rapid change and uncertainty occur, and success is determined by strong analytical skills and smoothly processing multiple options, views, and priorities (Joiner & Wise, 2009; Lundqvist et al., 2023). To cope with such challenges, agile leaders usually build their leading paths on multiple management styles that involve guidance rather than command and collaboration rather than hierarchical control (Kumar & Ray, 2023; Lundqvist et al., 2023). These skill combinations are distinct; agile leadership excellence results from a combination of practice and talent (Mensvoort & Mesa, 2023). According to these points, it can be concluded that an agile leader mindset is partially a gift of fate and partially the effect of life experiences and conscious personal training. This suggests that an agile mindset should be trained to reach its full potential. To determine how to train an agile mindset, it is good to rely on mindset theories. *Theory of action* (Gollwitzer, 1990, 2012) and Dweck's (1999) *Theory of mindset* provide a foundation for a deeper understanding of how the agile mindset happens.

The mindset theory of action states that different and unique cognitive procedures are activated in the human mind when people tackle setting goals, which are different from those applied in task contractors' minds (Gollwitzer, 1990, 2012). These unique cognitive procedures of those who can establish goals characterize the deliberative mindset and include identifying opportunities and deliberating on the feasibility and desirability of the particular opportunity. Such procedures characterize the other mindset—termed an implemental mindset—as planning when, where, and how to act to gain the best advantage: the issue is how to act to benefit best. Moreover, the aspect of this theory most pertinent to the current study is that some people's mindsets develop stronger *deliberative* cognitive processes—open-minded processing in and out of the box; whereas others develop *implemental* processes—focusing strictly on the particular task, which leads to closed-mindedness when it comes to processing new information (Gollwitzer & Keller, 2016). Discussing a broader implemental mindset—the dominant, habitual, limited focus on easily solvable or mundane problems—gives this group illusory feelings of control and safety (Gollwitzer & Kinney, 1989). Notably, being dominated to feel safe and in control is critical for this group. Thus, a deliberative mindset deals better with setting goals in unpredictable, dynamic conditions, which is close to an agile mindset. However, implementation is necessary to achieve your goal and win identified opportunities for agility. Combining aim-setting and aim-striving skills seems to be the most beneficial. Those who developed all cognitive processes constituting deliberative, implementing, and evaluative mindsets (a minority of the population) are arguably the most intelligent group (and can quickly adapt). They represent the highest potential to achieve success. Theoretically, their mindsets are closest to our phenomenon of interest: agile mindset leaders. Overall, this theory supports the findings of Ambituuni et al. (2021) that inspired the formulation of the current study's research problem; that is, the lack of understanding of how agility happens in organizations if most employees have a non-agile mindset. As stated in the chapter's introduction, this lack of knowledge is an issue of agile leadership—to lead with agility despite most employees not having an agile mindset. The next theory partially supports this suspicion.

A fundamental assumption in Dweck's (1999) theory of mindset, also called the theory of success, is that how we see our potential determines its utilization. Those who believe intelligence and other traits are relatively stable have a "fixed mindset" that is close to the "entity theory" of intelligence. Conversely, those who believe that abilities are changeable with effort have a "growth mindset" that is close to the "incremental theory" of intelligence (Dweck & Bempechat, 1983). According to Dweck (2006), having a growth mindset is much more beneficial. Individuals with growth mindsets are likelier to exert effort to overcome a challenge, leading to more outstanding achievements (e.g., Dweck, 2006; Dweck & Yeager, 2019; Zingoni & Corey, 2016). In contrast, individuals with fixed mindsets are more likely to avoid challenges and fear failure, which kills their self-confidence and motivation to take risky actions. As a result of their conformity, they do not achieve anything spectacular but do their best to expose themselves as successful. The visibility of their success, rather than real growth, fuels their motivation. Mindsets are assumed to develop from the type of praise a child receives from teachers and parents; for example, children who receive "process praise"—praise for effort and perseverance—will develop growth mindsets. Conversely, children who receive praise for their intelligence and abilities will develop fixed mindsets (Dweck, 2006). Further, those with growth mindsets are happier, more intelligent, and more successful in the longer term (Macnamara & Rupani, 2017). The "growth-mindset" theory is a foundation for the agile leader mindset to construct deeper development.

Summing up, both of these theories expose that human minds consolidate specific cognitive processes during life experiences that determine how people respond to new situations, tasks, and other challenges that can bring success or failure. Dominating habitual cognitive processes constitute a state of mind that determines emotions, attitudes, beliefs, and motivations, which ultimately shape behaviors. This finding confirms that an agile mindset can be trained, although a person's intelligence level can determine the efficiency of agility training.

14.3 Collective intellectual agility—how does it happen?

The rapid development of machine learning algorithms, the basis of artificial intelligence systems, has created new opportunities for automation and optimization of work processes and replacing human input in most management functions. So, the most extreme scenario of such a reality assumes that human input into such an algorithmically defined working reality will consist of two streams: one stream, the data stream—whatever we do, we leave traces, and these are simply data, and the second stream, the production (creation) of data analytics algorithms and their learning optimization and management. So, the human population, from this perspective, will be divided into those who feed algorithms with data and those who design and manage algorithms. Both groups will follow algorithms, some more, some less consciously. Intellectual agility skills are critical to have a chance to belong to this first group. What is then an intellectual agility?

Intellectual agility in an organizational context is perceived as the speed at which an organization constantly converts its tacit and explicit knowledge. Chapter 2 elaborated on this conversion meaning for organizational intelligence, innovativeness, and sustainability (Kucharska & Karwowska, 2024; Kucharska & Erickson, 2023a). So, in the center of this conversion is intellectual capital, which is precisely a result of such a smooth conversion (Kucharska, 2022). To make this happen, organizations need to care about company culture supporting tacit knowledge acquisition and sharing, which always happens voluntarily (Kucharska & Erickson, 2023a, 2023b), as well as for technology facilitating input regarding explicit knowledge creation, acquisition, storage, security, and distribution accordingly to authorization and utilization (Section 7.2). Intellectual capital quality and creation velocity in organizations result from collective intellectual agility driven by the culture, and the KLC approach fosters it. Precisely collective intellectual agility is critical today in building organizational intelligence in AI growth reality.

The discussion about organizational and collective intelligence today must be given with specific attention to the rapid development and interest in artificial intelligence. How should we understand organizational intelligence in reality, where special attention is put today to develop it artificially? Are organizations still interested in the development of human intelligence? If hierarchies are not as deeply disposed of as adhocracies, markets, and clans in the development of human collective intelligence, are they interested in developing artificial ones?

So, organizations need to know how they want to build organizational intelligence today: through a collective human one, artificial one, or through the synergy of both? Bader and Kaiser (2019) claim that without algorithmic competencies and the active involvement of knowledge workers in creating AI, artificial and human intelligence do not assemble. Figure 14.1 illustrates how artificial intelligence (AI) and collective human intelligence (CHI) impact organizational intelligence (OI) and how impactful an agile mindset leader is in this entire process.

So, it was said in this book that mindsets that can create, optimize, cooperate, and overperform must be agile. How, then, could we develop and sustain a growth agile mindset to create, control, and overperform artificial intelligence? The answer is precisely by securing a tacit knowledge acquisition and sharing in human minds. Intellectual agility is a critical factor that, on the one hand, requires a solid base of explicit knowledge and an intelligent mind stimulated by the smoothly cooperating network of other equally brilliant minds. ML machines can serve as a stimulus to agile mindsets, too; the fact is that tacit knowledge happens in the human mind based precisely on all experiences. Tacit knowledge is contextual and produced over time. Company culture facilitates all the interactions between human-human and human-machine and can support the

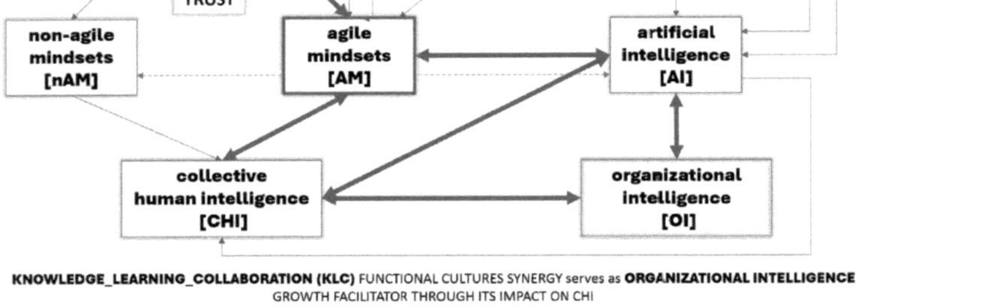

Figure 14.1 The KLC approach as the organizational growth facilitator

occurrence of tacit knowledge and smooth transition. As it was said, intellectual agility in an organizational context is perceived as the speed at which an organization constantly converts its tacit and explicit knowledge. So, organizations interested in keeping the superior human position over machines should employ and train agile mindsets employees.

The question arises of *How we can train agile mindsets*? A solid set of research should precede the precise, detailed answer, but the general idea is to find a way to train the human mind to adapt. However, Ambituuni et al. (2021) observed that the critical problem with agile organization building is that, generally, some people have an agile mindset by nature. In contrast, others have not and probably never will. So, finding the way the human mind should be trained to smooth adaptability is a challenge. However, the basis for the creation of such training is adaptability practice in safe cultural conditions, and undoubtedly, the agile adhocracy or agile clan and KLC approach can serve perfectly for this purpose.

Kucharska et al. (2024a) examined the impact of the agile mindset leader on the agile organization and revealed that agile organizations cannot thrive without an agile-minded leader. Their findings also revealed that employees with agile and non-agile mindsets are fundamentally incompatible. This incompatibility negatively impacts the effectiveness of team cooperation and raises questions about the feasibility of creating mixed (agile with non-agile mindsets) teams, which inherently face mental friction. The implications of these findings are profound, calling for a reevaluation of organizational structures and leadership practices to empower agile-minded staff. Company culture is critical in supporting agile mindset leader efforts in agile company building.

14.4 Agility strategies building for adhocracies, markets, clans, and hierarchies

Organizational agility is a learned, permanently available dynamic capability that can be performed to a necessary degree quickly and efficiently and whenever needed to increase business performance in a volatile market environment (Walter, 2021). In today's business environment of extreme change and uncertainty, all businesses need to be more agile. Adopting an agile approach helps organizations develop internal adaptability and organizational learning capabilities, improve their responsiveness (Kettunen et al., 2022), and gain a competitive advantage (Pulakos et al., 2019; Zastempowski & Cyfert, 2023).

Before the COVID-19 era, agility was often seen mainly as the need and domain of the fast-developing IT sector. However, after COVID-19, this perspective has changed. Agility has been recently lifted to the position of the most desired and highly valued organizational competency, not only in the IT sector (Stei et al., 2024). However, agile organizations are often characterized as those that adopt agile management methods referring to project management methodologies (e.g., Scrum and Scaled Agile Framework) rooted in the *Agile Manifesto* (Beck et al., 2001). Rožman et al. (2023) and Zeitoun (2023) stressed that although implementing agile project management methods solves some critical IT project management problems, they also cause others because the essence of agility is not rooted in certified agile management methods but in agile mindsets of employees. Therefore, implementing agile management methodologies does not fully utilize agility principles: (1) individuals and interactions over processes and tools, (2) utility over comprehensive documentation, (3) collaboration over negotiation, and (4) responding to change over following a plan. In light of these principles, it is evident that agility is the issue of perception, which is precisely a mindset. A shared mindset constitutes a culture.

An agile shared mindset (culture) and agile leadership are essential for building an agile organization (Eilers et al., 2022; Kucharska et al., 2024a; Payol, 2022; Zeitoun, 2023). Payol (2022) described an agile culture as one free from bureaucracy, control, and fear, and an agile leader is characterized by energy, resilience, strong motivation, a growth mindset, courage, and vulnerability.

The agile way of thinking mobilizes the entire staff across an organization. It is considered the essence of a successful agile enterprise that positions customers and societies at the center, supports employees to reach their full potential, and achieves 20%–40% greater productivity because of gained engagement (Rigby et al., 2020). In light of such evidence, implementing agile methods without developing an agile mindset wastes organizational time and effort. So, today's company culture that supports agile, dynamic capability is critical to all knowledge-driven organizations motivated to develop and grow in the AI-dominated digital world.

Regarding strategies of implementation agility capability of agile acting and thinking collectively rooted in collective intellectual agility (the speed at which an organization constantly converts its tacit and explicit knowledge), theoretically, it is possible to shift adhocracies, markets, clans, and hierarchies cultures to their more agile forms (Chapter 13; Figure 13.1). However, the best effects we can expect for adhocracies and clans. Section 13.2 of this book shows that hierarchical cultures and virtual space seem to be incompatible in the context of collective intellectual agility building to maintain organizational efficacy in a constantly evolving virtual space. Hierarchy culture is a fascinating case in the context of virtual workplaces. On the one hand—the natural order and control make them easy to manage with AI support; on the other hand, their formal human relations and a lack of disposition to constant contextual learning, optimizing, and change implementation make them totally unagile. Unagile organizations cannot be efficient in virtual reality in the long-run perspective. Therefore, hierarchies should probably evolve into structurally and culturally hybrid organizations if they want to incorporate virtual space into their business strategies. Market culture's alignment with virtuality is much more promising than hierarchies. However, it is not a perfect match as a mix of clans and adhocracies. The mix of these two would bring the best effects because adhocracy culture secures the constant development call, and clan culture mitigates spatial distance disturbances thanks to securing high-quality human interactions mediated by technology, which puts their high quality in high demand. Therefore, thanks to the adhocracy and clans' cultures mix supported by the KLC-approach tech-agile mindsets, employees' cooperation in the virtual space has a chance to go the most smoothly.

Summing up, bearing in mind the golden rule given in this book of strategy-culture-structure alignment for best organizational performance gaining, thanks to collective intelligence building through the KLC, and accepting the fact that without the agile mindset leader, there is no chance for company culture to shift to its more agile form, and without it, there is consequently no chance to build organizational agility too—the following rethinking-steps are proposed:

1. Are you an agile mindset leader? (Section 14.1)

   YES—perfect, go to STEP 2
   NO—I am afraid your company has no chance for agility without an agile mindset leader. So, train your mind or resign from your position.

2. Verify your long-run strategy against the fast-changing reality we all operate in today. Identify what changes you need to initiate to prepare your organization for the "dynamic future." Think holistically; your strategy, culture, and structure must align if you are seriously interested in agility building.
3. Think about your company culture type, and name it (Part II; Appendix 3). Identify what changes you need to initiate to shift it to its more agile form (Figures 13.1 and 14.2). Prepare a plan and implement it.
4. Remember, a leader must be the perfect example of the change he/she wants to see. So, be self-aware of who you are and what experiences you deliver to your team every day (Section 13.2). Company culture to be learned must be first experienced. It is an intangible asset of your organization. Therefore, there is no better way to learn it than by observation and experience.

Figure 14.2 exposes agile culture characteristics that strongly expose the KLC approach focused on collective change adaptability. These characteristics expose the adhocracy and clan culture mix. However, implementing them, even partially, in markets and hierarchies will foster their shift to agile forms.

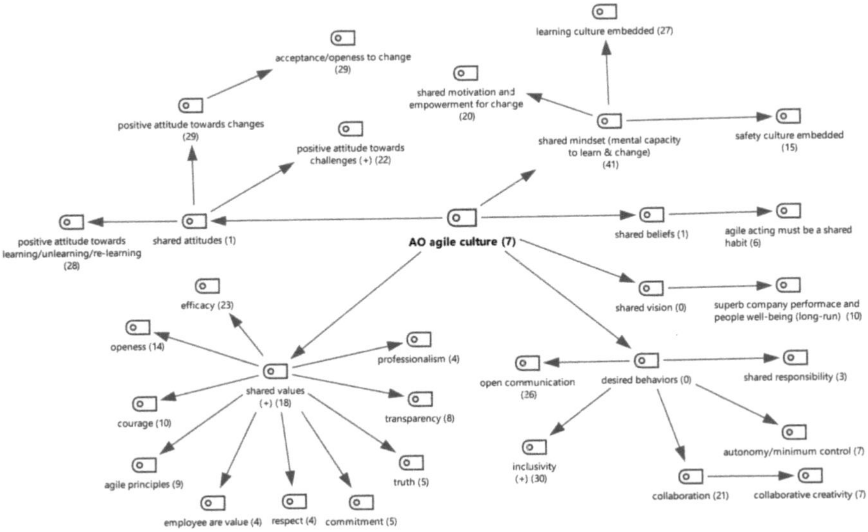

Figure 14.2 The agile culture framework

Source: Kucharska et al. (2024a, 2024b)

Note: Figure drawn using MaxQDA Analytics Pro software.

14.5 Case study

Kathy

Kathy is a leading Credit Division manager at a FutureBank that mainly operates online. The bank's credit services evolve constantly due not only to the macroeconomic situation but also to the changing lifestyles of young clients searching for finances for their new life ideas.

FutureBank is a typical hierarchy dominated by rules, procedures, and controls. So, it is not so easy to propose any changes but being realistic—there is no other choice on such a competitive market. Kathy, being passionate, enthusiastic, and engaged, was a leader of changes implementation. Her division was one of the most innovative. What she always expected from her team was the positive attitude toward changes. To create it among employees she exposed it clearly by own example—she constantly learned, un-learned and re-learned. People saw it clearly when recently their division implemented and optimized AI-based system and Kathy optimized its efficacy through trial-error learning and experimenting but based on the very logical conclusions from the system output. She always took her lessons from mistakes and quickly overperform, she was always searched for the best knowledge and support others in improvements.

Besides, Kathy always communicated changes as opportunities and clarified their positive impact on clients, the bank, the entire division, and even the employees. She was a fantastic visionnaire: Kathy was a perfect analyst. So, she understood interdependences and, therefore, easily predicted the consequences of any change. So, she inspired the entire division. She was trusted, admired, and followed with passion. She always empowered those who brought their own ideas or developed someone's. Everyone who contributed to making division work more accessible, better, and more profitable was recognized. Kathy was a real respectful, inclusive, and transparent team player who respected each member but, at the same time, constantly challenged the team to push them to cooperate and think collectively for the best solutions. In a short time, her division characterized exceptional efficacy, professionalism, commitment, and openness to constant changes. People feel safe together experimenting and breaking a typical thinking convention. They knew that they could rely on one another. They communicated openly and transparently and solved conflicts that occurred occasionally—as it does between people.

As a result, when the entire FutureBank moved to virtual space, only Kathy's division did it without harming their performance or mental condition. Bonding pays—Kathy says, but to make it work, it must be authentic.

Problems for discussion:

1. Which Kathy's actions do you see as critical for her success:
   - from her perspective?
   - from her employees' perspective?
   - from her bosses' perspective?
2. Prepare at least a three possible scenario's on how Kathys career can develop. Choose the most probable one and justify your choice.
3. Imagine Kathy's received a job offer from Future Bank key competitor. If you were Kathy, what would you do?

Additional tasks:

1. Follow the proposed in this chapter four steps to help in shifting the company culture type to its more agile form, based on Kathy's case, and assess their actions.

2. How do you think to which culture type Kathy shifted her division's culture? How do you think it can affect the entire FutureBank culture? Do you predict any possible tensions? List them and propose solutions. If you do not see any tension risks—elaborate on how it was possible to avoid them.

References

Ambituuni, A., Azizsafaei, F., & Keegan, A. (2021). HRM operational models and practices to enable strategic agility in PBOs: Managing paradoxical tensions. *Journal of Business Research*, *133*, 170–182. https://dx.doi.org/10.1016/j.jbusres.2021.04.048

Atkinson, S. R., Goodger, A., Caldwell, N., & Hossain, L. (2012). How lean the machine: How agile the mind? *Learning Organization*, *19*(3), 183–206. https://doi.org/10.1108/09696471211219877

Bader, V., & Kaiser, S. (2019). Algorithmic decision-making? The user interface and its role for human involvement in decisions supported by artificial intelligence. *Organization*, *26*(5), 655–672. https://doi.org/10.1177/1350508419855714

Beck, K., Grenning, J., Martin, R. C., Beedle, M., Highsmith, J., Mellor, S., Bennekum, A., van Hunt, A., Schwaber, K., Cockburn, A., Jeffries, R., Sutherland, J., Cunningham, W., Kern, J., Thomas, D., Fowler, M., & Marick, B. (2001). *Manifesto for agile software development*. Agile Alliance. https://www.agilealliance.org

Cameron, K. S., & Quinn, R. E. (2006). *Diagnosing and changing organizational culture: Based on the competing values framework*. John Wiley & Sons.

Cegarra-Navarro, J.-G., & Martelo-Landroguez, S. (2020). The effect of organizational memory on organizational agility: Testing the role of counter-knowledge and knowledge application. *Journal of Intellectual Capital*, *21*(3), 459–479. https://doi.org/10.1108/JIC-03-2019-0048

Denning, S. (2016). Agile's ten implementation challenges. *Strategy & Leadership*, *44*(5), 15–20.

Denning, S. (2018). The role of the C-suite in agile transformation: The case of Amazon. *Strategy & Leadership*, *46*(6), 14–21. https://doi.org/10.1108/SL-10-2018-0094

Dweck, C. S. (1999). *Self-theories: Their role in motivation, personality, and development*. Psychology Press.

Dweck, C. S. (2006). *Mindset: The new psychology of success*. Random House.

Dweck, C. S., & Bempechat, J. (1983). Children's theories of intelligence: Consequences for learning. In S. Paris, G. Olson, & H. Stevenson (Eds.), *Learning and motivation in the classroom* (pp. 239–256). Erlbaum.

Dweck, C. S., & Yeager, D. S. (2019). Mindsets: A view from two eras. *Perspectives on Psychological Science*, *14*(3), 481–496. https://doi.org/10.1177/1745691618804166

Eilers, K., Peters, C., & Leimeister, J. M. (2022). Why the agile mindset matters? *Technological Forecasting & Social Change*, *179*, Article 121650. https://doi.org/10.1016/j.techfore.2022.121650

French, R. P. (2016). The fuzziness of mindsets. *International Journal of Organizational Analysis*, *24*(4), 673–691. https://doi.org/10.1108/ijoa-09-2014-0797

Gollwitzer, P. M. (1990). Action phases and mind-sets. In E. T. Higgins & R. M. Sorrentino (Eds.), *The handbook of motivation and cognition: Foundations of social behavior* (Vol. 2, pp. 52–92). Guilford Press.

Gollwitzer, P. M. (2012). Mindset theory of action phases. In P. A. M. Van Lange, A. W. Kruglanski, & E. Higgins (Eds.), *Handbook of theories of social psychology* (Vol. 1, pp. 526–545). SAGE.

Gollwitzer, P. M., & Keller, L. (2016). Mindset theory. In V. Zeigler-Hill & T. K. Shackelford (Eds.), *Encyclopedia of personality and individual differences*. Springer. https://doi.org/10.1007/978-3-319-28099-8_1141-1

Gollwitzer, P. M., & Kinney, R. F. (1989). Effects of deliberative and implemental mindsets on illusion of control. *Journal of Personality and Social Psychology, 56*, 531–542.

Hayward, S. (2018). *The agile leader: How to create an agile business in the digital age*. Kogan Page.

Joiner, B., & Wise, C. (2009). *Creating a culture of agile leaders: A developmental approach*. Agile Business Consortium. https://www.agilebusiness.org/resource-report/white-papercreating-a-culture-of-agile-leaders.html

Kergel, D., Heidkamp-Kergel, B., Nørreklit, H., & Paulsen, M. (Eds.). (2022). *Agile learning and management in a digital age: Dialogic leadership*. Taylor & Francis.

Kettunen, P., Gustavsson, T., Laanti, M., Tjernsten, A., Mikkonen, T., & Männistö, T. (2022). *Agile enterprise transformations: Surveying the many facets of agility for the hybrid era*. 2022 48th Euromicro Conference on Software Engineering and Advanced Applications (SEAA), pp. 157–160. https://doi.org/10.1109/SEAA56994.2022.00032

Kucharska, W. (2022). Tacit knowledge influence on intellectual capital and innovativeness in the healthcare sector: A cross-country study of Poland and the US. *Journal of Business Research, 149*, 869–883. https://doi.org/10.1016/j.jbusres.2022.05.059

Kucharska, W., Balcerowski, T., Kucharski, M., Jussila, J., & Laanti, M. (2024a). Why does the Agile leader mindset matter the most? Polish-Finnish, technological and non-technological perspectives on agile and non-agile mindset employees and organizations. *Heliyon*. https://ssrn.com/abstract=4988722

Kucharska, W., Balcerowski, T., Kucharski, M., Jussila, J., & Laanti, M. (2024b). *Why does the Agile leader mindset matter the most? (1–)* [Dataset]. Data Bridge Repository. Gdansk University of Technology. https://doi.org/10.34808/b23f-9197

Kucharska, W., Balcerowski, T., Kucharski, M., & Jussila, J. (2024c). Who is an agile leader? Technological vs. non-technological mindset employees' views. *20th European Conference on Management, Leadership and Governance, 20*(1), 397–404. https://doi.org/10.34190/eckm.25.1.2367

Kucharska, W., & Erickson, G. S. (2023a). Tacit knowledge acquisition & sharing, and its influence on innovations: A Polish/US cross-country study. *International Journal of Information Management, 71*, 102647.

Kucharska, W., & Erickson, G. S. (2023b). A multi-industry and cross-country comparison of technology contribution to formal and informal knowledge sharing processes for innovativeness. *Knowledge and Process Management, 30*(3), 300–316. https://doi.org/10.1002/kpm.1755

Kucharska, W., & Karwowska, E. (2024). Company culture matters! Knowledge-driven companies' way to innovations and sustainability through learning and social interactions. *Social Science and Humanities Open*. https://papers.ssrn.com/sol3/papers.cfm?abstract_id=4780014

Kumar, S., & Ray, S. (2023). Moving towards agile leadership to help organizations succeed. *IUP Journal of Soft Skills, 17*(1), 5–17.

Lundqvist, D., Wallo, A., Coetzer, A., & Kock, H. (2023). Leadership and learning at work: A systematic literature review of learning-oriented leadership. *Journal of Leadership & Organizational Studies, 30*(2), 205–238. https://doi.org/10.1177/15480518221133970

Macnamara, B. N., & Rupani, N. S. (2017). The relationship between intelligence and mindset. *Intelligence, 64*, 52–59. https://doi.org/10.1016/j.intell.2017.07.003

Medinilla, Á. (2012). *Agile management: Leadership in an agile environment* (pp. I–XII). Springer.

Mensvoort, B., & Mesa, M. C. (2023). Lightschools® space and freedom for the co-creation of new possibilities, opportunities, and valuable solutions. In D. Kergel, B. Heidkamp-Kergel, H. Norreklit, & M. Paulsen (Eds.), *Agile learning and management in a digital age* (pp. 146–165). Routledge. https://doi.org/10.4324/9781003188728-11

Merriam-Webster Dictionary. (2017). *Merriam-Webster.com dictionary*. Retrieved July 30, 2024, from https://www.merriam-webster.com/dictionary/dictionary

Nagel, R. N. (1991). *21st century manufacturing enterprise strategy: An industry-led view. Lehigh report*. Lehigh University.

Ormrod, J. E. (2017). *How we think and learn: Theoretical perspectives and practical implications*. Cambridge University Press.

Payol, J. (2022). Agile servant leadership is not fluffy. In B. Underhill, J. Passmore, & M. Goldsmith (Eds.), *Coach me! Your personal board of directors: Leadership advice from the world's greatest coaches* (pp. 114–116). Wiley.

Pulakos, E. D., Kantrowitz, T., & Schneider, B. (2019). What leads to organizational agility: It's not what you think. *Consulting Psychology Journal: Practice and Research, 71*(4), 305–320. https://doi.org/10.1037/cpb0000150

Rigby, D., Elk, S., & Berez, S. (2020). *Doing agile right: Transformation without chaos*. Harvard Business Review Press.

Rožman, M., Tominc, P., & Štrukelj, T. (2023). Competitiveness through development of strategic talent management and agile management ecosystems. *Global Journal of Flexible Systems Management, 24*(3), 373–393. https://doi.org/10.1007/s40171-023-00344-1

Salvetti, F., & Bertagni, B. (2020). Leadership 5.0: An agile mindset for a digital future. *International Journal of Advanced Corporate Learning, 13*(2), 57–66. https://doi.org/10.3991/ijac.v13i2.17033

Sanatigar, H., Hadi Peikani, M., & Gholamzadeh, D. (2017). Identifying organizational agility and leadership dimensions using Delphi technique and factor analysis: An investigation among public sector pension funds (PSPFs) in Iran. *International Journal of Public Leadership, 13*(4), 276–294.

Stei, G., Rossmann, A., & Szász, L. (2024). Leveraging organizational knowledge to develop agility and improve performance: The role of ambidexterity. *International Journal of Operations & Production Management*. https://doi.org/10.1108/IJOPM-04-2023-0274

Walter, A.-T. (2021). Organizational agility: Ill-defined and somewhat confusing? A systematic literature review and conceptualization. *Management Review Quarterly, 71*, 343–391. https://doi.org/10.1007/s11301-020-00186-6

Zastempowski, M., & Cyfert, S. (2023). A new angle on SMEs' competitiveness. How do agility capabilities affect a firm's competitive position? *Journal of Organizational Change Management, 36*(4), 635–662. https://doi.org/10.1108/JOCM-09-2022-0255

Zeitoun, A. (2023). *Program management: Going beyond project management to enable value-driven change*. Wiley.

Zingoni, M., & Corey, C. M. (2016). How mindset matters: The direct and indirect effects of employees' mindsets on job performance. *Journal of Personnel Psychology, 16*(1). https://doi.org/10.1027/1866–5888/a000171

What have we learnt from this book—closing conclusions

This book presented the study, which is the first that shows that the KLC-approach components' impact on intelligence varies depending on company culture type and management level (team, division, and organization) and exposes that implementing this approach requires different methods that significantly affect the organization's change adaptability and intelligence building skills. Moreover, this book demonstrates that organizational culture type (adhocracy, market, clan, and hierarchy) and culture strength and consistency (congruence) across different company levels are critical for benefits to be derived from the KLC approach for company intelligence building.

Based on empirical evidence, this book exposes that company culture matters for a company's achievement of its aims. Moreover, it proves that company culture type and the synergy of functional cultures knowledge-learning-collaboration drive organizational intelligence through human collective intelligence development, which matters the most every day in the era of AI growth. So, organizations need to know how they want to build organizational intelligence today: through human one? Artificial one? Or through the synergy of both? How to do so? How do we develop and sustain a growth agile mindset needed to create, control, and overperform artificial intelligence? This book answers.

Each company culture type can support organizational intelligence through the KLC approach, but achieving it requires different methods. One thing is common: Leaders create company culture. This book content serves as evidence that organizations interested in collective company intelligence building should employ only those leaders who reflect (expose) the KLC approach—those who act oppositely to the KLC (knowledge-learning and collaboration cultures) should not be leaders at any level. Moreover, these leaders should have agile mindsets.

This book showed that the KLC functional cultures synergy approach supports organizational intelligence development and, that the organizational level culture type and its strength and consistency across levels are critical for KLC efficiency. Adhocracy and market cultures have been confirmed to be more than clan and hierarchy cultures that are efficient for KLC implementation to support

DOI: 10.4324/9781003485230-19

organizational intelligence building and internal innovations development in the traditional business environment driven by strong market orientation. In less competitive sectors, clan cultures will probably also work perfectly smoothly. This is because adhocracies and market cultures are more oriented to competitive advantage building than clans, oriented to employee well-being and hierarchies, and oriented to rules, procedures, bureaucracy, and control. However, adhocracies and clans adapt better to the digital reality driven by AI development, thanks to KLC. Virtual teams are efficient thanks to the collective focus on growth and strong team integrity secured by agile mindset leaders. The mix of adhocracy (innovation focus) and clan (social relations focus) cultures best facilitates the smooth cooperation of brilliant agile mindset networks operating remotely. Being naturally oriented to solid social relations, clans are the most efficient in compensating for all disadvantages related to remote work. Therefore, clans mixed with growth-oriented adhocracies support virtual teams' performance the most efficiently.

Finally, this book details the practical implications of the presented research, making the delivered science useful for business practice. Moreover, the included case studies not only illustrate research results and their practical implications in broader contexts but also make perfect teaching materials that inspire searching for understanding on how to design company culture for the company's best.

Appendix 1

Bibliometric analysis

The bibliometric analysis aimed to verify which contexts of adhocracy, hierarchy, clan, and market cultures have been more frequently researched so far. Besides, all the given visualizations below prove that the study on which this book is based is unique. This analysis was made by putting queries below in the Scopus database (searching: all files till September 2024). Next, the keywords were visualized based on all authors' keyword units of analysis using the fractional counting method using Vosviewer software.

Adhocracy culture

TITLE-ABS-KEY (("adhocracy culture") AND ("innovations" OR "change adaptability" OR "collective intelligence" OR "organizational intelligence")) AND (LIMIT-TO (LANGUAGE, "English")) 39 documents found; 35 articles and four conference papers.

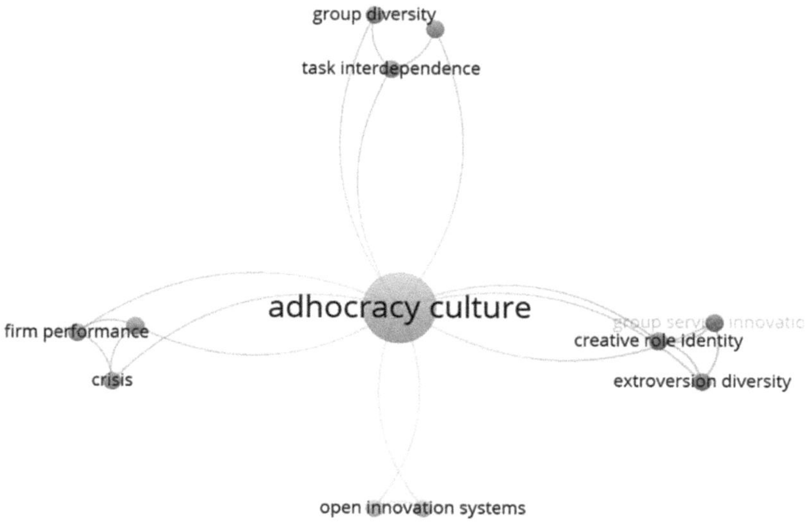

Figure A1.1 Adhocracy culture—bibliometric view

Hierarchy culture

TITLE-ABS-KEY (("hierarchy culture") AND ("innovations" OR "change adaptability" OR "collective intelligence" OR "organizational intelligence")) AND (LIMIT-TO (LANGUAGE, "English")) 24 documents found; 23 articles and 1 conference papers.

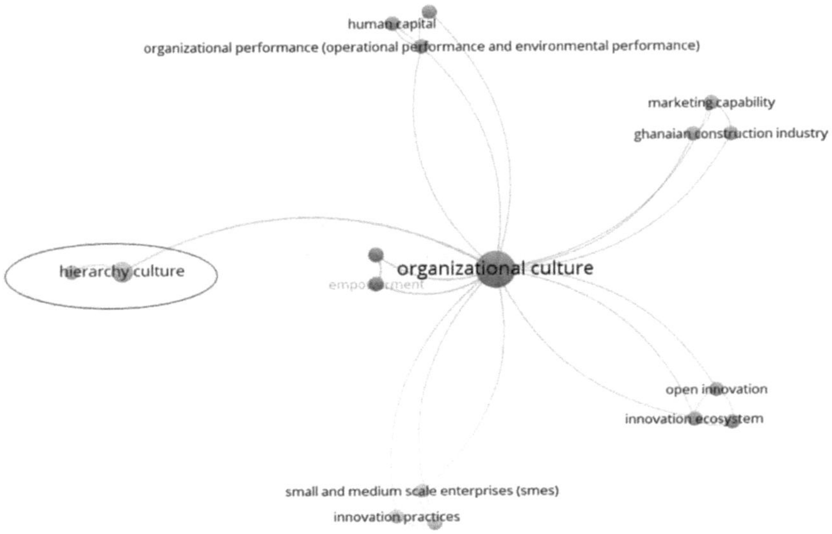

Figure A1.2 Hierarchy culture—bibliometric view

Clan culture

TITLE-ABS-KEY (("clan culture") AND ("innovations" OR "change adaptability" OR "collective intelligence" OR "organizational intelligence")) AND (LIMIT-TO (LANGUAGE, "English")) 30 documents found; 27 articles and 3 conference papers.

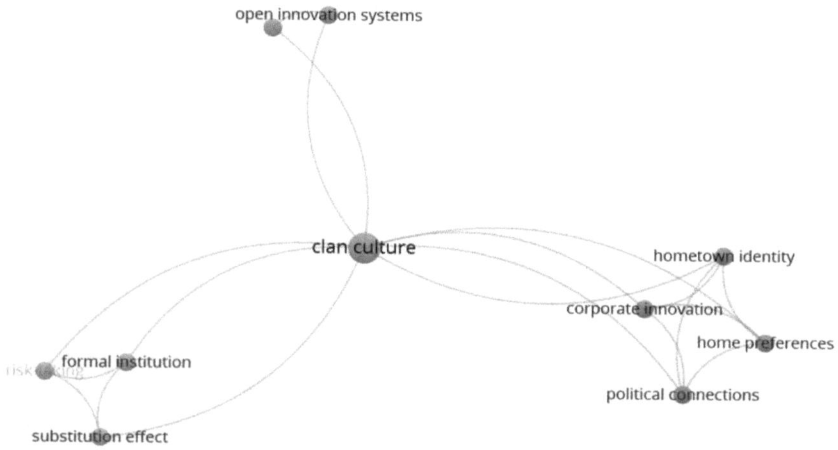

Figure A1.3 Clan culture—bibliometric view

Market culture

TITLE-ABS-KEY (("market culture") AND ("innovations" OR "change adaptability" OR "collective intelligence" OR "organizational intelligence")) AND (LIMIT-TO (LANGUAGE, "English")) 43 documents found; 32 articles and 8 conference papers

In summary, the given bibliometric analysis confirmed the research gap presented in the Introduction and the Literature review sections. None of the studies examining so far company culture type (adhocracy, clan, market, and hierarchy) refers to organizational change adaptability or collective intelligence.

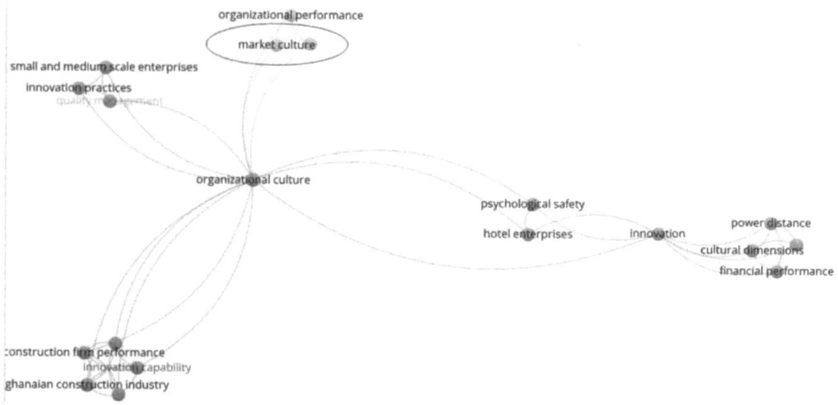

Figure A1.4 Market culture—bibliometric view

Appendix 2

SPSS PROCESS output

Appendix 2a: The functional KLC cultures approach moderated by division and team power influence on organizational change adaptability—SPSS PROCESS output for hierarchy, market, clan, and adhocracy cultures.

Hierarchy culture

a) Knowledge culture (KC)

```
Run MATRIX procedure:
************* PROCESS Procedure for SPSS Version 4.2 *************
         Written by Andrew F. Hayes, Ph.D. www.afhayes.com
 Documentation available in Hayes (2022). www.guilford.com/p/hayes3
******************************************************************
Model : 2
     Y:  IQ    X: KC      W: Team      Z: Div
Sample Size: 185
******************************************************************
OUTCOME VARIABLE: IQ
Model Summary
           R     R-sq     MSE        F        df1       df2        p
       ,6761    ,4571  2,5502   30,1439    5,0000  179,0000    ,0000
Model
              coeff        se         t         p       LLCI      ULCI
constant      ,9605     ,5131    1,8719     ,0629     -,0521    1,9730
KC            ,1899     ,1024    1,8539     ,0654     -,0122     ,3920
Team        -,1430     ,1818    -,7865     ,4326     -,5016     ,2157
Int_1         ,0896     ,0337    2,6558     ,0086      ,0230     ,1561
Div           ,7360     ,1635    4,5013     ,0000      ,4134    1,0587
Int_2       -,0875     ,0318   -2,7489     ,0066     -,1503    -,0247
Product terms key:
  Int_1    :        KC        x       Team
  Int_2    :        KC        x       Div
```

```
Covariance matrix of regression parameter estimates:
Test(s) of highest order unconditional interaction(s):
       R2-chng          F          df1         df2          p
X*W      ,0214     7,0530       1,0000    179,0000       ,0086
X*Z      ,0229     7,5565       1,0000    179,0000       ,0066
BOTH     ,0268     4,4153       2,0000    179,0000       ,0134
------ END MATRIX -----
```

b) Learning culture climate component (LCc)

```
Run MATRIX procedure:
Model : 2
     Y:  IQ    X: LCc      W: Team      Z: Div
Sample Size: 185
*******************************************************************
********
OUTCOME VARIABLE: IQ
Model Summary
           R     R-sq      MSE         F        df1         df2          p
       ,6786    ,4605   2,4411   30,5552     5,0000    179,0000      ,0000
Model
                coeff         se          t          p        LLCI        ULCI
constant       1,3999      ,5180     2,7028      ,0075       ,3778      2,4220
Ba3             ,0896      ,1106      ,8097      ,4192     -,1287       ,3079
Team           -,1296      ,1811     -,7153      ,4754     -,4870       ,2279
Int_1           ,1155      ,0362     3,1915      ,0017       ,0441       ,1870
Div             ,6672      ,1802     3,7037      ,0003       ,3117      1,0228
Int_2          -,0994       ,367    -2,7115,      0074      -,1718      -,0271
Product terms key:
  Int_1    :        LCc       x        Team
  Int_2    :        LCc       x        Div
Test(s) of highest order unconditional interaction(s):
       R2-chng          F          df1         df2          p
X*W      ,0307    10,1859       1,0000    179,0000       ,0017
X*Z      ,0222     7,3523       1,0000    179,0000       ,0074
BOTH     ,0320     5,3009       2,0000    179,0000       ,0058
----------
------ END MATRIX -----
```

c) Learning culture mistake-acceptance component (LCm)

In hierarchy culture, the LCm component moderated by the division level power or by the team level is not significant for organizational change adaptability (IQ).

d) Collaborative culture (CC)

```
Run MATRIX procedure:
Model : 2
     Y:  IQ    X: CC      W: Team      Z: Div
Sample Size: 185
*******************************************************************
```

```
OUTCOME VARIABLE: IQ
Model Summary
          R       R-sq       MSE          F        df1        df2          p
      ,7114      ,5062    2,3199    36,6923     5,0000   179,0000      ,0000
Model
              coeff         se          t          p       LLCI       ULCI
constant      ,1878      ,5082      ,3696      ,7121     -,8150     1,1907
CC            ,5270      ,1233     4,2753      ,0000      ,2837      ,7702
Team          ,8266      ,1739     4,7522      ,0000      ,4834     1,1699
Int_1        -,1240      ,0343    -3,6115      ,0004     -,1917     -,0562
Div          -,0997      ,1863     -,5352      ,5932     -,4673      ,2679
Int_2         ,0722      ,0359     2,0123      ,0457      ,0014      ,1430
Product terms key:
 Int_1   :        CC       x      Team
 Int_2   :        CC       x      Div
Covariance matrix of regression parameter estimates:
            constant         C3       Gaq2      Int_1       Gaq3      Int_2
constant       ,2583     -,0519     -,0268      ,0049     -,0405      ,0074
CC            -,0519      ,0152      ,0049     -,0013      ,0067     -,0017
Team          -,0268      ,0049      ,0303     -,0053     -,0211      ,0038
Int_1          ,0049     -,0013     -,0053      ,0012      ,0039     -,0008
Div           -,0405      ,0067     -,0211      ,0039      ,0347     -,0060
Int_2          ,0074     -,0017      ,0038     -,0008     -,0060      ,0013
Test(s) of highest order unconditional interaction(s):
       R2-chng          F        df1        df2          p
X*W      ,0360    13,0431     1,0000   179,0000      ,0004
X*Z      ,0112     4,0494     1,0000   179,0000      ,0457
BOTH     ,0370     6,7096     2,0000   179,0000      ,0015
****************** ANALYSIS NOTES AND ERRORS ******************
Level of confidence for all confidence intervals in output: 95,0000
W values in conditional tables are the 16th, 50th, and 84th percentiles.
Z values in conditional tables are the 16th, 50th, and 84th percentiles.
------ END MATRIX -----
```

Market culture

a) Knowledge culture (KC)

```
Run MATRIX procedure:
************* PROCESS Procedure for SPSS Version 4.2 *************
Written by Andrew F. Hayes, Ph.D. www.afhayes.com
Documentation available in Hayes (2022). www.guilford.com/p/hayes3
******************************************************************
Model : 2
    Y: IQ    X: KC     W: Team     Z: Div
Sample Size: 210
******************************************************************
```

```
OUTCOME VARIABLE: IQ
Model Summary
          R      R-sq       MSE          F        df1        df2         p
      ,6063     ,3677    1,8484    23,7221     5,0000   204,0000     ,0000
Model
               coeff         se          t          p       LLCI       ULCI
constant      1,0165      ,4635     2,1928      ,0295      ,1025     1,9304
KC             ,0504      ,0937      ,5376      ,5914     -,1344      ,2352
Team           ,4944      ,1453     3,4013      ,0008      ,2078      ,7809
Int_1         -,0496      ,0259    -1,9152      ,0500     -,1008      ,0015
Div            ,1494      ,1523      ,9815      ,3275     -,1508      ,4496
Int_2          ,0553      ,0282     1,9625      ,0501     -,0003      ,1108
Product terms key:
  Int_1    :         KC         x        Team
  Int_2    :         KC         x        Div
Test(s) of highest order unconditional interaction(s):
        R2-chng          F        df1        df2          p
X*W       ,0114     3,6679     1,0000   204,0000      ,0500
X*Z       ,0119     3,8515     1,0000   204,0000      ,0501
BOTH      ,0157     2,5370     2,0000   204,0000      ,0816
----------
```

b) Learning culture climate component (LCc)

```
********************************************************************
*******
Model : 2
     Y: IQ    X: LCc      W: Team      Z: Div
Sample Size: 210
********************************************************************
*******
OUTCOME VARIABLE: IQ
Model Summary
          R      R-sq       MSE          F        df1        df2         p
      ,6264     ,3923    2,0354    26,3406     5,0000   204,0000     ,0000
Model
                coef         se          t          p       LLCI       ULCI
constant       ,9047      ,4826     1,8748      ,0622     -,0467     1,8561
LCc            ,2253      ,1111     2,0279      ,0439      ,0062      ,4444
Team           ,5392      ,1434     3,7591      ,0002      ,2564      ,8220
Int_1         -,0833      ,0295    -2,8219      ,0052     -,1416     -,0251
Div           -,0209      ,1546     -,1349      ,8928     -,3256      ,2839
Int_2          ,0922      ,0317     2,9051      ,0041      ,0296      ,1548
Product terms key:
  Int_1    :         LCc        x        Team
  Int_2    :         LCc        x        Div
Test(s) of highest order unconditional interaction(s):
        R2-chng          F        df1        df2          p
X*W       ,0237     7,9633     1,0000   204,0000      ,0052
X*Z       ,0251     8,4393     1,0000   204,0000      ,0041
BOTH      ,0325     5,4618     2,0000   204,0000      ,0049
------ END MATRIX -----
```

c) Learning culture mistake-acceptance component (LCm)

```
Run MATRIX procedure:
Model : 2
    Y: IQ   X : LCm     W : Team     Z : Div
Sample Size: 210
*************************************************************
OUTCOME VARIABLE: IQ
Model Summary
          R      R-sq     MSE        F        df1       df2         p
      ,6145   ,3777  2,2093  24,7581   5,0000  204,0000   ,0000
Model
              coeff        se         t          p       LLCI     ULCI
constant    1,3911     ,5554    2,5049     ,0130,      2961   2,4861
LCm         -,0587     ,1578    -,3718     ,7104    -,3698    ,2525
Team        -,0469     ,1489    -,3149     ,7531    -,3406    ,2468
Int_1         ,1260     ,0423    2,9784     ,0032      ,0426    ,2094
Div           ,6181     ,1640    3,7692     ,0002      ,2948    ,9414
Int_2       -,0873     ,0429   -2,0322     ,0434    -,1719   -,0026
Product terms key:
  Int_1   :        LCm      x      Team
  Int_2   :        LCm      x      Div
Test(s) of highest order unconditional interaction(s):
        R2-chng        F        df1       df2          p
X*W     ,0271     8,8706     1,0000   204,0000      ,0032
X*Z     ,0126     4,1299     1,0000   204,0000      ,0434
BOTH    ,0271     4,4404     2,0000   204,0000      ,0130
----------
------ END MATRIX -----
```

d) Collaborative culture (CC)

```
Run MATRIX procedure:
Model : 2
Y : IQ
X : CC
W : Team
Z : Div
Sample Size: 210
OUTCOME VARIABLE: IQ
Model Summary
          R      R-sq     MSE        F        df1       df2         p
      ,6477   ,4195  1,6970  29,4815   5,0000  204,0000   ,0000
Model
            coeff        se          t          p       LLCI     ULCI
constant     ,8976    ,4439     2,0221     ,0445     ,0224   1,7728
CC           ,1486    ,1022     1,4538     ,1475    -,0529    ,3501
Team        -,1165    ,1297     -,8980     ,3702    -,3721    ,1392
Int_1        ,0863    ,0286     3,0152     ,0029     ,0299    ,1428
Div          ,6753    ,1447     4,6677     ,0000     ,3901    ,9606
Int_2       -,0747    ,0312    -2,3926     ,0176    -,1363   -,0131
```

```
Product terms key:
 Int_1    :        CC       x      Team
 Int_2    :        CC       x      Div
Test(s) of highest order unconditional interaction(s):
       R2-chng         F        df1        df2         p
X*W     ,0259    9,0914     1,0000   204,0000      ,0029
X*Z     ,0163    5,7245     1,0000   204,0000      ,0176
BOTH    ,0277    4,8643     2,0000   204,0000      ,0086
----------
****************** ANALYSIS NOTES AND ERRORS *******************
Level of confidence for all confidence intervals in output: 95,0000
W values in conditional tables are the 16th, 50th, and 84th percentiles.
Z values in conditional tables are the 16th, 50th, and 84th percentiles.
------ END MATRIX -----
```

Clan culture

a) Knowledge culture (KC)

In clan culture, the KC moderated by the division level or by the team level power is not significant for organizational change adaptability (IQ).

b) Learning culture climate component (LCc)

```
Run MATRIX procedure:
Model : 2
    Y: IQ    X: LCc      W: Team      Z: Div
Sample Size: 151
*****************************************************************
*******
OUTCOME VARIABLE: IQ
Model Summary
          R      R-sq      MSE          F       df1        df2         p
      ,6936     ,4810   1,6693    26,8791    5,0000   145,0000     ,0000
Model
              coeff        se          t          p        LLCI       ULCI
constant      ,8784     ,5042    1,7421,      0836     -,1182     1,8749
LCc           ,0681     ,1103     ,6177      ,5378     -,1498      ,2860
Team          ,7023     ,1850    3,7961      ,0002      ,3366     1,0680
Int_1        -,1158     ,0348   -3,3311      ,0011     -,1845     -,0471
Div          -,0428     ,2024    -,2116      ,8327     -,4428      ,3572
Int_2         ,1153     ,0376    3,0705      ,0026      ,0411      ,1895
Product terms key:
 Int_1    :        LCc      x      Team
 Int_2    :        LCm      x      Div
Test(s) of highest order unconditional interaction(s):
       R2-chng         F        df1        df2         p
X*W     ,0397   11,0961     1,0000   145,0000      ,0011
X*Z     ,0337    9,4282     1,0000   145,0000      ,0026
BOTH    ,0439    6,1328     2,0000   145,0000      ,0028
----------
```

c) Learning culture mistake-acceptance component (LCm)

In clan culture, the LCm moderated by division power is not significant for organizational change adaptability, but it is significant when moderated by the team level. Details below.

```
Run MATRIX procedure:
Model : 1
     Y: IQ    X: LCm     W: Team
Sample Size: 151
******************************************************************
OUTCOME VARIABLE: IQ
Model Summary
          R     R-sq     MSE         F        df1        df2          p
      ,5573   ,3106   2,4622   22,0766   3,0000   147,0000    ,0000
Model
             coeff        se          t          p        LLCI      ULCI
constant    -,2365    ,5746      -,4117      ,6812     -1,3720     ,8990
LCm          ,7931    ,1825      4,3470      ,0000       ,4326    1,1537
Team         ,7686    ,1414      5,4344      ,0000       ,4891    1,0481
Int_1       -,1153    ,0382     -3,0232      ,0030      -,1907    -,0399
Product terms key:
Int_1 : LCm x Team
Test(s) of highest order unconditional interaction(s):
        R2-chng         F         df1         df2          p
X*W     ,0429    9,1395     1,0000    147,0000      ,0030
------ END MATRIX -----
```

d) Collaborative culture (CC)

```
Run MATRIX procedure:
Model : 2
Y: IQ X: CC W: Team Z: Div
Sample Size: 151
******************************************************************
OUTCOME VARIABLE: IQ
          R     R-sq     MSE         F        df1        df2          p
      ,7947   ,6315   1,5896   49,6956   5,0000   145,0000    ,0000
Model
             coeff        se          t          p        LLCI      ULCI
constant   -,4196     ,4796      -,8748      ,3831     -1,3675    ,5283
CC          ,2324     ,1221      1,9033      ,0590      -,0089    ,4737
Team       -,0171     ,1982      -,0865      ,9312      -,4089    ,3746
Int_1       ,1579     ,0546      2,8922      ,0044       ,0500    ,2658
Div 1       ,1557     ,1833      6,3043      ,0000       ,7933   1,5180
Int_2      -,2112     ,0534     -3,9520      ,0001      -,3168   -,1056
Product terms key:
   Int_1 :        CC        x       Team
   Int_2 :        CC        x       Div
```

```
Test(s) of highest order unconditional interaction(s):
       R2-chng         F        df1         df2          p
X*W      ,0213    8,3646     1,0000    145,0000      ,0044
X*Z      ,0397   15,6181     1,0000    145,0000      ,0001
BOTH     ,0420    8,2585     2,0000    145,0000      ,0004
***************** ANALYSIS NOTES AND ERRORS ********************
Level of confidence for all confidence intervals in output: 95,0000
W values in conditional tables are the 16th, 50th, and 84th percentiles.
Z values in conditional tables are the 16th, 50th, and 84th percentiles.
------ END MATRIX -----
```

Adhocracy culture

a) Knowledge culture (KC)

```
Run MATRIX procedure:
************ PROCESS Procedure for SPSS Version 4.2 *************
         Written by Andrew F. Hayes, Ph.D. www.afhayes.com
Documentation available in Hayes (2022). www.guilford.com/p/hayes3
******************************************************************
Model : 2
    Y  : IQ      X  : KC      W  : Team        Z  : Div
Sample Size: 94
******************************************************************
OUTCOME VARIABLE: IQ
Model Summary
         R      R-sq      MSE       F(HC3)    df1       df2        p
     ,7470    ,5580    2,3856    96,9090    5,0000   88,0000     ,0000
Model
             coeff     se(HC3)         t          p        LLCI      ULCI
constant   -,1109      ,6400      -,1733      ,8628     -1,3828    1,1609
KC          ,3274      ,1435      2,2818      ,0249       ,0423     ,6125
Team       -,9299      ,4075     -2,2820      ,0249     -1,7396    -,1201
Int_1       ,1884      ,0679      2,7753      ,0067      , 0535     ,3233
Div 1       ,7094      ,3550      4,8154      ,0000      1,0039    2,4148
Int_2      -,2018      ,0614     -3,2844      ,0015      -,3239    -,0797
Product terms key:
   Int_1 :         KC        x       Team
   Int_2 :         KC        x       Div
Test(s) of highest order unconditional interaction(s):
       R2-chng     F(HC3)       df1         df2          p
X*W      ,0260     7,7021    1,0000     88,0000      ,0067
X*Z      ,0324    10,7871    1,0000     88,0000      ,0015
BOTH     ,0325     5,3939    2,0000     88,0000      ,0062
----------
------ END MATRIX -----
```

b) Learning culture climate component (LCc)

```
Run MATRIX procedure:
Model : 2
    Y  : IQ     X  : LCc     W  : Team     Z : Div
Sample Size: 94
*****************************************************************
OUTCOME VARIABLE: IQ
Model Summary
          R      R-sq      MSE       F(HC3)    df1        df2          p
      ,7955     ,6328   1,7186    102,9070   5,0000    88,0000      ,0000
Model
               coeff      se(HC3)          t          p       LLCI       ULCI
constant     ,1558       ,5386        ,2894      ,7730     -,9144     1,2261
LCc          ,3322       ,2100       1,5819      ,1173     -,0851      ,7496
Team        -,3979       ,2069      -1,9229      ,0577     -,8092      ,0133
Int_1        ,1341       ,0463       2,8995      ,0047      ,0422      ,2261
Div 1        ,2945       ,2457       5,2682      ,0000      ,8062     1,7829
Int_2       -,1682       ,0388      -4,3332      ,0000     -,2453     -,0910
Product terms key:
  Int_1   :        LCc       x       IQ
  Int_2   :        LCc       x       IQ
Test(s) of highest order unconditional interaction(s):
      R2-chng      F(HC3)       df1         df2          p
X*W     ,0294     8,4072      1,0000    88,0000       ,0047
X*Z     ,0400    18,7768      1,0000    88,0000       ,0000
BOTH    ,0405     9,5383      2,0000    88,0000       ,0002
----------
------ END MATRIX -----
```

c) Learning culture mistakes acceptance component (LCm)

```
Run MATRIX procedure:
Model : 2
    Y  : IQ     X  : LCm     W  : Team     Z : Div
Sample Size: 94
*****************************************************************
OUTCOME VARIABLE: IQ
Model Summary
          R      R-sq      MSE       F(HC3)    df1        df2          p
      ,7270     ,5285   2,5451     45,1632   5,0000    88,0000      ,0000
Model
               coeff    se(HC3)           t          p       LLCI       ULCI
constant     ,4099       ,6935        ,5911      ,5560     -,9682     1,7881
LCm          ,3468       ,2831       1,2252      ,2238     -,2157      ,9093
Team 1       ,1042       ,1880       5,8726      ,0000      ,7306     1,4779
Int_1       -,1900      ,0536      -3,5452      ,0006     -,2965     -,0835
Div         -,2112      ,1964      -1,0755      ,2851     -,6014      ,1790
Int_2        ,1456      ,0446       3,2685      ,0015      ,0571      ,2342
```

```
Product terms key:
 Int_1    :        LCm      x       IQ
 Int_2    :        LCm      x       IQ
Test(s) of highest order unconditional interaction(s):
       R2-chng      F(HC3)       df1         df2          p
X*W       ,0540     12,5687     1,0000    88,0000       ,0006
X*Z       ,0285     10,6832     1,0000    88,0000       ,0015
BOTH      ,0542     6,9875      2,0000    88,0000       ,0015
----------
------ END MATRIX -----
```

d) Collaborative culture (CC)

In adhocracy culture conditions, the CC moderated by team power is not significant for the organizational change adaptability, but it is significant when moderated by the division level. Details below.

```
Run MATRIX procedure:
Model : 1
     Y  : IQ     X  : CC     W : Div
Sample Size: 94
*******************************************************************
OUTCOME VARIABLE: IQ
Model Summary
           R     R-sq     MSE        F(HC3)   df1        df2         p
       ,7817   ,6111  2,0526   176,2946  3,0000   90,0000     ,0000
Model
               coeff          se(HC3)       t         p        LLCI      ULCI
constant    -,8052      ,6884       -1,1697    ,2452      -2,1728   ,5624
CC           ,8256      ,1893        4,3618    ,0000       ,4496   1,2016
Div          ,8832      ,2212        3,9931    ,0001       ,4438   1,3227
Int_1       -,0851      ,0373       -2,2834    ,0248      -,1592   -,0111
Product terms key:
 Int_1    :        CC        x       Div
Test(s) of highest order unconditional interaction(s):
       R2-chng      F(HC3)       df1         df2          p
X*W       ,0223     5,2137      1,0000    90,0000       ,0248
****************** ANALYSIS NOTES AND ERRORS *******************
Level of confidence for all confidence intervals in output:
95,0000
Number of bootstrap samples for percentile bootstrap confidence
intervals:
5000
W values in conditional tables are the 16th, 50th, and 84th percentiles.
------ END MATRIX -----
```

Appendix 2b

The Double Bias of Mistakes (DBM) test per culture type

DBM Test—adhocracy culture

There is no significant effect of the DBM on LCc-LCm relation. So, adhocracy culture is free from the DBM.

DBM Test—clan culture

```
Run MATRIX procedure:
************* PROCESS Procedure for SPSS Version 4.2 *************
          Written by Andrew F. Hayes, Ph.D. www.afhayes.com
Documentation available in Hayes (2022). www.guilford.com/p/hayes3
******************************************************************
Model: 1       Y: LCm     X: LCc     W: dbm  Sample Size: 151
******************************************************************
OUTCOME VARIABLE:
LCm
Model Summary
          R      R-sq     MSE          F        df1        df2        p
      ,4776    ,2281   1,7038   14,4773    3,0000   147,0000    ,0000
Model
             coeff        se           t          p       LLCI      ULCI
constant   ,4068      ,9116        ,4462      ,6561   -1,3948    2,2084
LCm        ,8183      ,2294       3,5671      ,0005      ,3649    1,2717
dbm        ,7552      ,5082       1,4860      ,1394    -,2491    1,7595
Int_1     -,2720      ,1277      -2,1309      ,0348    -,5243    -,0197
Product terms key:
  Int_1    :         LCc       x       dbm
Test(s) of highest order unconditional interaction(s):
         R2-chng          F        df1         df2        p
X*W       ,0238    4,5407    1,0000    147,0000   ,0348
----------
       Focal predict: LCc      (X)
             Mod var: dbm      (W)
```

```
Conditional effects of the focal predictor at values of the moderator(s):
       dbm       Effect      se          t       p       LLCI    ULCI
    1,0000       ,5463   ,1100   4,9642  ,0000   ,3288   ,7638
    2,0000       ,2743   ,0647   4,2388  ,0000   ,1464   ,4021
****************** ANALYSIS NOTES AND ERRORS ******************
Level of confidence for all confidence intervals in output: 95,0000
------ END MATRIX -----
```

DBM Test—market culture

```
Run MATRIX procedure:
************* PROCESS Procedure for SPSS Version 4.2 *************
         Written by Andrew F. Hayes, Ph.D. www.afhayes.com
Documentation available in Hayes (2022). www.guilford.com/p/hayes3
******************************************************************
Model: 1        Y: LCm     X: LCc      W: dbm  Sample Size: 210
******************************************************************
OUTCOME VARIABLE: LCm
Model Summary
          R      R-sq     MSE          F          df1         df2        p
       ,4578    ,2096  1,7331    18,2078     3,0000    206,0000     ,0000
Model
              coeff          se            t          p         LLCI        ULCI
constant    ,8021        ,5704        1,4061       ,1612      -,3225     1,9267
LCc         ,5966        ,1396        4,2742       ,0000       ,3214      ,8718
dbm         ,7454        ,4288        1,7382       ,0507      -,1001     1,5908
Int_1      -,2167        ,1051       -2,0606       ,0406      -,4240     -,0094
Product terms key:
  Int_1    :          Ba4       x        db3
Test(s) of highest order unconditional interaction(s):
         R2-chng          F          df1         df2        p
X*W        ,0163    4,2461     1,0000    206,0000     ,0406
----------
      Focal predict: LCc       (X)
            Mod var: dbm       (W)
Conditional effects of the focal predictor at values of the moderator(s):
       dbm       Effect      se          t       p       LLCI    ULCI
    1,0000       ,3799   ,0530   7,1682  ,0000   ,2754   ,4844
    2,0000       ,1633   ,0908   1,7980  ,0536  -,0158  ,3423
Data for visualizing the conditional effect of the focal predictor:
Paste text below into a SPSS syntax window and execute to produce plot.
****************** ANALYSIS NOTES AND ERRORS ******************
Level of confidence for all confidence intervals in output: 95,0000
------ END MATRIX -----
```

DBM Test—hierarchy culture

```
Run MATRIX procedure:
************* PROCESS Procedure for SPSS Version 4.2 *************
        Written by Andrew F. Hayes, Ph.D. www.afhayes.com
Documentation available in Hayes (2022). www.guilford.com/p/hayes3
******************************************************************
Model: 1       Y: LCm     X: LCc     W: dbm  Sample Size: 185
******************************************************************
OUTCOME VARIABLE: LCm
Model Summary
          R     R-sq     MSE          F        df1        df2        p
      ,4088    ,1671  3,2642    12,1083     3,0000   181,0000    ,0000
Model
              coeff         se          t          p       LLCI      ULCI
constant      ,2123       ,9565      ,2220      ,8246   -1,6749    2,0995
LCc           ,6449       ,1760     3,6637      ,0003     ,2976      ,9922
dbm           ,9779       ,5594     1,7482      ,0501    -,1258    2,0816
Int_1        -,2233       ,1045    -2,1369      ,0339    -,4295    -,0171
Product terms key:
 Int_1    :        LCc      x       dbm
Test(s) of highest order unconditional interaction(s):
       R2-chng          F       df1        df2        p
X*W       ,0210    4,5665    1,0000   181,0000    ,0339
----------
Focal predict: LCc (X)
Mod var: dbm (W)
Conditional effects of the focal predictor at values of the moderator(s):
       dbm      Effect     se         t      p      LLCI    ULCI
    1,0000      ,4216   ,0818   5,1551  ,0000    ,2602    ,5830
    2,0000      ,1983   ,0651   3,0473  ,0027    ,0699    ,3266
Data for visualizing the conditional effect of the focal predictor:
Paste text below into a SPSS syntax window and execute to produce plot.
****************** ANALYSIS NOTES AND ERRORS ******************
Level of confidence for all confidence intervals in output: 95,0000
------ END MATRIX -----
```

Appendix 3

Company culture assessment tools

You can gain a high-level description of your company's culture type and the KLC approach by conducting a two-part assessment. The first part concerns the company culture type, the second concerns the KLC cultures approach base.

Regarding the company culture type, the sample survey questionnaire below (Part A), provide a selected set of questions for the four culture types—adhocracy, market, clan, and hierarchy. Respondents (your employees) will record their impressions regarding the culture type in your organization using a 7-point Likert scale, indicating strong agreement or disagreement with the statements given. You can analyze the results obtained comparing the average answers of company members at organizational-division and team level comparing these "average perceptions" with the perception given by their leaders will expose the discrepancy. The discrepancy between leader-entity is a lesson that requires action. Precisely, according to the triple-loop learning level, we need to understand why such a discrepancy happened to make decisions and tailor the actions (required change identification and implementation).

Similarly, for the three KLC-approach cultures, which synergy supports organizational intelligence building—knowledge, learning, and collaboration. Respondents will record their impressions using a 7-point Likert scale, indicating strong agreement or disagreement with describing statements (Part B). Analyzing the results will give you a starting point for understanding your KLC-culture profile. This phase answers the question—"What is the nature of my KLC culture?" Moreover, comparing the average employee answers at organizational-division and team level comparing these "average perceptions" with the perception given by their leaders will expose the discrepancy. The discrepancy between leader-entity is a lesson that requires action. Precisely, according to the triple-loop learning level, we need to understand why such a discrepancy happened to make decisions and tailor the actions (required change identification and implementation).

Moreover, setting up the company culture type or the KLC-approach level desired and comparing this desired (aimed) level with the level obtained from the analysis of the average level of their perceptions by employees will also expose the discrepancy that precisely shows the room for improvements.

Moreover, your analysis will also show you whether any of the three KLC-approach cultures are dominant or nonexistent. You can compare your findings about your culture type with the general KLC implementation framework (Figure 7.1) characteristics that will give you a "big picture" on what you have in your company. It will be a perfect basis for critical thinking and strategizing.

Part A: The company culture type measurement form

SELECT POSITION:	**ADHOCRACY**	**MARKET**	**CLAN**	**HIERARCHY**
CEO Manager Team leader Specialist	informal relations without rigid canons; employees take initiatives; they are engaged, learn, share knowledge and experiences, are creative, innovative, and experiment; the leader is an inspiring one with a vision; people can discuss with him and share new ideas and propositions; he listens	market relations; competition prevails; coalitions are possible if there are mutual benefits; striving to win in every field; employees are creative and innovative; the leader must be clever or the best—otherwise, he will cease to be a leader	relationships resemble a clan; strong bonds between employees; high sense of belonging; employees are engaged; learn, share knowledge and experiences; their leader is always right; loyalty is sometimes more important than common sense	hierarchy, formal relations, rigid canons of behavior; dominant control; task repetition; instead of learning, repeating established patterns; here, the leader "knows better"
Organization Division Team				

Part B: The KLC cultures measurement form

THE KLC APPROACH STRONG	*7 6 5 4 3 2 1*	*THE KLC APPROACH WEAK*
STRONG KNOWLEDGE CULTURE		**WEAK KNOWLEDGE CULTURE**
Based on my experience, in my place of work all of the employees see knowledge as a value		Based on my experience, in my place of work, all of the employees do not see knowledge as a value
We have at work a common language to support knowledge exchange		We don't have a common language to support knowledge exchange
We are encouraged at work to share knowledge, ideas, and thoughts		We are not encouraged at work to share knowledge, ideas, and thoughts. We are expected just to do our jobs
We care about the quality of knowledge that we share		We do not care enough about the quality of knowledge that we share
We care about the quality of knowledge that we use		We do not care enough about the quality of knowledge that we use
STRONG LEARNING CULTURE		**WEAK LEARNING CULTURE**
LEARNING CLIMATE COMPONENT		LEARNING CLIMATE COMPONENT
Based on my experience, in my place of work: all staff demonstrate a high learning disposition		Based on my experience, in my place of work: nobody demonstrates a high learning disposition
We are encouraged to engage in personal development		We are not encouraged to engage in personal development
We are encouraged to implement new ideas every day		We are not encouraged to implement new ideas every day
We are encouraged to engage in new solutions seeking		We are not encouraged to engage in new solutions seeking
MISTAKES ACCEPTANCE (as a source of learning) COMPONENT		MISTAKES ACCEPTANCE (as a source of learning) COMPONENT
Based on my experience in my place of work: we know that mistakes are a learning consequence and tolerate it up to a certain limit		Based on my experience in my place of work: mistakes are not tolerated
Most people freely claim mistakes		Most people hide mistakes

(*continued*)

(Continued)

THE KLC APPROACH STRONG	*7*	*6*	*5*	*4*	*3*	*2*	*1*	*THE KLC APPROACH WEAK*
We discuss problems openly without blaming								Problems are not discussed openly, and blame is behind your back
Mistakes are seen as learning opportunities								Mistakes are seen as negligence indicator
STRONG COOPERATION CULTURE								**WEAK COOPERATION CULTURE**
Based on my experience in my place of work: cooperation between workers is supported								Based on my experience in my place of work: cooperation between workers is not supported
Employees cooperate across duties								Employees DO NOT cooperate across duties
Employees cooperate across teams								Employees DO NOT cooperate across teams
Employees cooperate across departments								Employees DO NOT cooperate across departments
My coworkers volunteer their support even without being asked								My coworkers NEVER volunteer their support without being asked
We support one another								We DO NOT support one another

Index

adaptability: employee vs. leadership 143; organizational 11, 16, 88
adhocracy: AI solutions 122
adhocracy culture 8, 13, 28, 41–43, 72, 82, 83, 162; AI approach 123; best practices 65; change response 71; characteristics 13, 72, 82; collaborative culture effects 175; critical assets 83; DBM resistance 45; division level impact 43; employees 82; innovation focus 162; intelligence building 55; key challenges 83; knowledge culture interaction 173; knowledge culture relationship 42; leaders 82; learning from mistakes 48; research prevalence 163; size and structure 83; trust building 84; values 82; virtual environment benefits 140
agile culture 136, 140, 154
agile culture framework 156
agile leaders: characteristics 147
agile leadership 149; case study 157
agile manifesto 154
agile mindset experts 123, 127
agile mindset leader(s) 127, 136, 146–148, 155, 162; characteristics 146; organizational impact 153
agile mindset leadership 134
agile mindset(s) 119, 120, 122, 149, 151, 154; cognitive foundations 150; training 153
agility 6, 149; as higher-level adaptability skill 6; IT principles 149; mindset dependency 7; organizational 7; skills 63
agility building: implementation steps 155
AI implementation: case study 130–131
AI training: user perspective neglect 130
algorithmic management 115, 117–120; stakeholder perspectives 131
algorithms: machine learning (ML) 117; pre-programmed (PP) 117
AM-L *see* agile mindset leader(s)
artificial intelligence (AI): impact on organizational power structures 120; organizational applications 152; organizational impact 151
autonomy: lack in hierarchical structures 111

bias of mistakes 25, 44
bibliometric analysis 163–165
blame game 97
BM *see* bias of mistakes

Cameron & Quinn framework 9
case studies: adhocracy culture 89; AI implementation 131; Aqua Sprint 98; FutureBank 156; My Wave company 90; Sweet Business 104; virtual work adaptation 143
change adaptability 5, 17, 20, 24, 29, 30, 50, 61, 69, 73; culture moderation 34; internal innovation 17
change agents 71
change communication 157
change motivation sources 71
CHI *see* collective human intelligence
clan culture 8, 13, 28, 99, 127, 162, 171; AI implementation 127; AI implementation approach 127; algorithm implementation 122; bibliometric analysis 164; case study 103; challenges 100; change

implementation 104; change resistance factors 74; characteristics 13, 72, 76, 99; collective action 16; collective learning 102; employee relationships 103; employees 99; implementation challenges 79; intelligence building 53; intelligence development 44; internal orientation 101; knowledge culture effects 40; knowledge culture relationship 171; knowledge management 100; leaders 99; leadership importance 66; learning culture relationship 41; organizational intelligence factors 39; size and structure 100; social relations focus 162; team-level moderation 172; virtual cooperation advantages 140; virtual environment benefits 140
clan mentality 110
clan wisdom 100
cognitive bias of mistakes 47
cognitive double bias of mistakes 61
collaboration: division level 94; lack of 97
collaboration culture(s) 16, 30, 63; division level 107; limitations 51
collaborative culture 24, 31, 170, 175; division-level moderation 175; hierarchy impact 34; impact in clan organizations 41; impact on organizational IQ 39; in market organizations 37; moderation effects 172; organizational level effects 43
collective culture 87; golden rules 96; in hierarchical organizations 35
collective human intelligence 115, 117, 119, 152; relationship with ai 123
collective intellectual agility 151, 154
collective intelligence 1, 3, 5, 6, 8, 11, 12, 16, 17, 19, 61, 64, 69, 72, 79, 82, 92, 101, 133; assessment 98; barriers in adhocracies 84; building motivation 112; building strategies 62, 86; culture type impact 44; development 11; drivers and blockers 85; implementation strategies 66; in hierarchies 67; leadership role 75; prerequisites 107
collective intelligence in adhocracies 83
collective intelligence-building behaviors 51
collective intelligence development 71
collective learning 58, 64, 96
collective organizational intelligence 95
collectivism 65
company culture 1, 9, 12, 21, 63, 65, 134, 135; assessment 179, 180; AI relationship 115; algorithm implementation 121; algorithmic design influence 122; as change driver 5; as change facilitator 8; experiential learning 88, 136; human-machine interactions 152; implementation 86; key driving force 111; as shared mindset 6, 7; as strategic asset 79; as strategic resource 64; as strategic tool 65; strategy alignment 8, 51; as superpower 7; tacit acquisition 133; taxonomy 12; types 1, 3, 5, 165; type measurement 180; virtual implementation 133; virtual implementation 135
competing values framework 12
competitive advantage: building through learning 96
control variables 18
cooperation culture 182; discrepancy identification 85
corporate social responsibility 73; motivating factors 73
COVID-19: impact on organizational agility 147
critical thinking 96
CSR *see* corporate social responsibility
cultural collision 107, 110–112
cultural congruence 35, 38, 39, 41, 44, 62
cultural intelligence 133
cultural revolution 112
culture: consistency 53, 54; experiential learning 134; hybridization 140; perception discrepancies 86
culture-strategy alignment 79
culture type(s) 28, 69; assessment methodology 179; change perception 71; characteristics 180; coexistence 79; company size distribution 28; comparison of learning capabilities 48; competitive advantage orientation 162; congruency 60; consistency 26, 27, 50, 52, 60, 62; DBM effects 45; digital transition 135; employee behavior 76; hierarchy 61; leadership influence 75; managerial levels 17; mistake

acceptance comparison 47; moderation effects 32; organizational levels 18; organizational shifts 158; sustainability focus 73; virtual compatibility 137; virtual space compatibility 155

DBM *see* double bias of mistakes
DBM Test 177
deliberative mindset 150
digital leadership 135
digital reality adaptation 162
digital slavery, unconscious 130
discrepancy analysis: leader-entity perception 179
double bias of mistakes 25, 45, 46, 48, 56–58, 176, 178; culture type analysis 46, 176; effects on leaders 57; impact on organizational learning 56; impact on organizational learning 58; *see also* cognitive double bias of mistakes
dummy culture 134

empirical evidence 29
employees: change agents 76

fixed mindset 150
flat organizational structures 77

gamification: virtual workspace 135
growth mindset 150
growth-mindset leader(s) 92, 101

hierarchical-bureaucratic methods 111
hierarchical culture 67; challenges 67; change implementation 156
hierarchical organizations 54; consistency requirements 54; intelligence building scenarios 108; intelligence sources 54; learning limitations 36; public universities 110
hierarchies: AI implementation challenges 127; algorithm implementation 121; KLC and algorithmic management 0; leadership challenges 75, 80; learning climate requirements 47
hierarchies' maturity paradox 105
hierarchy culture 8, 12, 28, 34–36, 66, 105, 106, 166; AI implementation 127, 130; bibliometric analysis 164; change adaptability 53; change response 71; characteristics 72, 105; consistency across levels 35; DBM test 178; hybrid evolution 106, 107; hybrid forms 60; implementation challenges 79, 109; key challenges 107; KLC-approach implementation challenges 105; knowledge culture dominance 36; leaders 106; leadership impact 36; learning barriers 45; learning barriers 66; learning climate 45–46; learning from mistakes 48; limitations 77; virtual space incompatibility 137; virtual workplace compatibility 140; virtual workplace compatibility 154
Hierarchy Master Organization 109, 111
hybrid culture 67
hybrid scenario 109, 111
hybrid work model 142

implemental mindset 150
individual ambition: team conflict 89
innovation: AI implementation barriers 130
innovativeness 31
intellectual agility 118, 146, 152, 153
intellectual capital 151
intellectual laziness 52, 127, 130
intelligence building pillars 78
intelligence-driven organizations 11
intelligent organizations: characteristics 52
intelligent systems: work transformation 121
internal pressure: leadership 75

key performance indicators 88
KLC: organizational assessment 98
KLC and algorithmic management 125, 127
KLC approach 1–3, 6, 8, 12, 14, 16, 19, 23, 24, 29–31, 36, 52, 60, 61, 69, 78, 90, 94, 115, 133, 135, 152, 153, 155; adaptability support 121; application in adhocracies 123; assessment tools 182; components 19; cultural transformation 136; culture type compatibility 43; culture type implementation 55; culture-specific implementation 122; golden rules 95; impact on AI implementation 130; implementation 63–65, 180; implementation in clans 100; implementation in market

culture 93; implementation methods 56; implementation scenarios 110; implementation strategies 44, 61; intellectual agility 151; knowledge culture requirements 73; leadership implementation 136; market culture application 125; organizational culture compatibility 54; synergic influence 30
KLC approach assessment 179
KLC approach implementation 79
KLC components 33
KLC culture(s) 50, 51; approach 166; impact on organizational intelligence 50; measurement form 181; relationship with organizational intelligence 32; simultaneous implementation 51; synergy 64; synergy approach 26
KLC functional culture synergy 11
KLC implementation 87, 88, 94; in clan culture 102; clan organizations 101; engagement strategies 87; framework 80; hierarchies 108; in hierarchies 109; plan 84, 101; project management 88; stakeholder pressure 74
KLC leaders 112
KLC-approach assessment tool 84
KLC-approach implementation 82, 92, 99
Knowledge culture 14, 15, 24, 29–31, 87, 166; assessment criteria 181; clan culture interactions 40; discrepancy assessment 84; hierarchy impact 34; implementation 87; in hierarchical organizations 35; in market organizations 37; limitations 15, 30, 51
knowledge culture golden rule 95
knowledge-driven organization(s) 1, 23, 103; culture 78; structure 77
knowledge economy 1
knowledge management: long-run perspective 63
knowledge management processes 77
knowledge management system(s) 77, 93
knowledge workers 23; polish 26; productivity 119
KPIs *see* key performance indicators

LCc *see* learning culture climate component
leaders: culture shaping 134; role in learning culture 57
leader self-awareness 86
leaders golden rule 95
leadership 75; adaptability challenges 142; in adhocracy culture 13; behavioral modeling 64; change implementation 156; as change motivator 75; clan culture 99; in clan culture 13; in clan organizations 102; cultural modeling 136; culture creation 44; KLC implementation role 88; market culture 14; organizational culture influence 76; remote 133; role in culture formation 65
leadership challenges: creative teams 89
learning climate 54, 100, 101, 110
learning climate component 181
learning culture 15, 16, 24, 30, 31, 87; assessment criteria 37; climate component 16, 58, 171; components 34, 57, 84; fear and shame as blockers 85; hierarchy impact 24; implementation 87; learning climate component 51; limitations 15; mistake acceptance 24; mistake tolerance vs. learning 47; mistake-acceptance component 25, 45, 58; mistake-acceptance component 36, 37, 170, 172, 174; mistakes acceptance component (LCm) 182; motivational climate component 45
learning culture climate component 174; mistakes as opportunities 169
learning culture golden rule 95
lessons learned 96

machine learning 127, 130
management levels 60; risks in hierarchies 1, 3
managerial levels 18, 32
market culture 8, 13, 14, 28, 37, 38, 66, 92, 125, 165; adaptability 14; AI adaptation 125; AI adoption 94; best practices 65; characteristics 38, 92; collaborative culture relationship 66; collectivism challenges 93; employees 95; intellectual agility 55; intelligence building 97; interdivisional competition 38; knowledge culture relationship 92; knowledge management 53; leaders 94; leadership approaches 38; learning

culture relationship 39; organizational intelligence relationship 125; organizational structure 93
market orientation: structure 71, 72
mediation effects 32
mental agility training 123
mental collision 106, 107
mindset collision 109
mindset compatibility 153
mindset theory 150
mindset theory of action 149
mindset(s); compatibility 136; definition 148; technological vs. non-technological 120, 121
mistake-acceptance component 26, 39, 43, 47
mistakes 57; acceptance as learning source 56, 85
mistakes acceptance component: as learning source 181
ML *see* machine learning
ML algorithms 118, 125
models 29
motivation: for change 71; theoretical 81
motivational climate for collective learning 48
multilevel analysis 18

network structure 78
non-technological mindset: characteristics 148

OI *see* organizational intelligence
organizational agility 1, 3, 5, 153; culture requirements 155
organizational change 103; resistance 72
organizational change adaptability 33; moderating factors 172; resistance in hierarchies 166, 171
organizational collective intelligence 63
organizational culture(s) 175; agile forms 154; attitude toward AI 120; congruence 2, 26; congruency 56; knowledge transformation 77; moderating factors 52; strength 2; transition to agile forms 136
organizational culture type(s) 23, 33, 163
organizational discrepancy analysis 180
organizational innovativeness 24, 30
organizational intelligence 1, 3, 20, 21, 24, 29–31, 33, 50, 52, 58, 69, 76, 94, 99, 104, 115, 117, 143, 152; activation 42; artificial vs. human 40; clan culture factors 34; culture type impact 8, 43; development factors 105; in hierarchical organizations 45–46; hierarchical resistance 35; mistake bias impact 108
organizational intelligence for change adaptability 158
organizational intelligence quotient 174
organizational IQ 60
organizational IQ building 54
organizational learning 102
organizational levels 27; in clan culture 9
organizational silos 66, 97
organizational structure: alignment with strategy 78
organizational sustainability 6

perfect machine scenario 109, 110
perspective-taking 98
power distribution 123
pre-programmed algorithms 118
public organizations: in AI environments 74; change motivation 142

remote work 143
research gap: team dynamics 165
research methodology 163
reward systems: collective vs. individual 83

scenario ‘hybrid’ 108
scenario ‘perfect machine’ 108
shame 58
shareholders value orientation 74
silo building 94
silo building tendency 93
single and double-loop learning 110
situational learning 15
sociotechnical perspective 117
statistical analysis 173; PROCESS procedure 169
status quo security: organizational intelligence predictors 72
strategic transformation 8
strategy-culture alignment 7
strategy-Culture-Structure alignment 76, 78, 83, 93, 100, 102, 106, 155
strategy-culture-structure triangle 121

sustainability 74; culture-specific approaches 74
SVO *see* shareholders value orientation

tacit knowledge 11, 12, 30, 57, 77, 95, 107, 119; acquisition and sharing 152; conversion 151; flow 78; sharing 73, 146
task interdependence: transformation to explicit form 142
team-division alignment: leadership impact 42
team influence 170
team-level influence: adhocracy culture 173
team performance: on learning culture 143
tech-agile mindset leaders 137
technological mindset: characteristics 148
theoretical framework 19
theoretical models: comparison 18
transformational leadership 75, 147
triple-loop learning 86, 179
trust 64, 90
trust building 83

unconscious digital slavery risk 127

VG *see* Virtual Guide
Virtual Guide (AI system) 130, 131
virtual leadership 136
virtual organizations 136
virtual reality: leadership behaviors 140
virtual teams 2; cultural challenges 134; leadership 136; optimal culture types 133, 162
virtual workspace 135; technology-mediated communication 137
volatility, uncertainty, complexity, and ambiguity 1, 125
VUCA *see* volatility, uncertainty, complexity, and ambiguity
VUCA reality 147